FREE Study Skills DVD Offer

Dear Customer,

Thank you for your purchase from Mometrix! We consider it an honor and a privilege that you have purchased our product and we want to ensure your satisfaction.

As a way of showing our appreciation and to help us better serve you, we have developed a Study Skills DVD that we would like to give you for <u>FREE</u>. This DVD covers our *best practices* for getting ready for your exam, from how to use our study materials to how to best prepare for the day of the test.

All that we ask is that you email us with feedback that would describe your experience so far with our product. Good, bad, or indifferent, we want to know what you think!

To get your FREE Study Skills DVD, email freedvd@mometrix.com with *FREE STUDY SKILLS DVD* in the subject line and the following information in the body of the email:

- The name of the product you purchased.
- Your product rating on a scale of 1-5, with 5 being the highest rating.
- Your feedback. It can be long, short, or anything in between. We just want to know your impressions and experience so far with our product. (Good feedback might include how our study material met your needs and ways we might be able to make it even better. You could highlight features that you found helpful or features that you think we should add.)
- Your full name and shipping address where you would like us to send your free DVD.

If you have any questions or concerns, please don't hesitate to contact me directly.

Thanks again!

Sincerely,

Jay Willis
Vice President
jay.willis@mometrix.com
1-800-673-8175

OGET
(074)
SECRETS

Study Guide
Your Key to Exam Success

Written and edited by the Mometrix Oklahoma Teacher Certification Test Team

Printed in the United States of America

This paper meets the requirements of ANSI/NISO Z39.48-1992 (Permanence of Paper).

Mometrix offers volume discount pricing to institutions. For more information or a price quote, please contact our sales department at sales@mometrix.com or 888-248-1219.

Mometrix Media LLC is not affiliated with or endorsed by any official testing organization. All organizational and test names are trademarks of their respective owners.

ISBN13: 978-1-61072-390-9
ISBN10: 1-61072-390-2

DEAR FUTURE EXAM SUCCESS STORY

First of all, **THANK YOU** for purchasing Mometrix study materials!

Second, congratulations! You are one of the few determined test-takers who are committed to doing whatever it takes to excel on your exam. **You have come to the right place.** We developed these study materials with one goal in mind: to deliver you the information you need in a format that's concise and easy to use.

In addition to optimizing your guide for the content of the test, we've outlined our recommended steps for breaking down the preparation process into small, attainable goals so you can make sure you stay on track.

We've also analyzed the entire test-taking process, identifying the most common pitfalls and showing how you can overcome them and be ready for any curveball the test throws you.

Standardized testing is one of the biggest obstacles on your road to success, which only increases the importance of doing well in the high-pressure, high-stakes environment of test day. Your results on this test could have a significant impact on your future, and this guide provides the information and practical advice to help you achieve your full potential on test day.

Your success is our success

We would love to hear from you! If you would like to share the story of your exam success or if you have any questions or comments in regard to our products, please contact us at **800-673-8175** or **support@mometrix.com**.

Thanks again for your business and we wish you continued success!

Sincerely,
The Mometrix Test Preparation Team

Need more help? Check out our flashcards at:
http://MometrixFlashcards.com/CEOE

TABLE OF CONTENTS

INTRODUCTION _____ 1

SECRET KEY #1 – PLAN BIG, STUDY SMALL _____ 2

SECRET KEY #2 – MAKE YOUR STUDYING COUNT _____ 3

SECRET KEY #3 – PRACTICE THE RIGHT WAY _____ 4

SECRET KEY #4 – PACE YOURSELF _____ 6

SECRET KEY #5 – HAVE A PLAN FOR GUESSING _____ 7

TEST-TAKING STRATEGIES _____ 10

READING AND WRITTEN COMMUNICATION _____ 15

MATHEMATICS _____ 39
    NUMBERS AND OPERATIONS _____ 39
    FRACTIONS, DECIMALS, AND PERCENTAGES _____ 51
    PRE-ALGEBRA _____ 64
    ALGEBRA _____ 68
    MEASUREMENT _____ 100
    GEOMETRY _____ 102
    PROBABILITY _____ 126
    STATISTICS _____ 133

INFORMATION LITERACY AND RESEARCH _____ 148

APPLIED WRITING SKILLS _____ 157

OGET PRACTICE TEST _____ 171
    READING AND WRITTEN COMMUNICATION _____ 171
    MATHEMATICS _____ 179
    INFORMATION LITERACY AND RESEARCH _____ 185
    ESSAY QUESTIONS _____ 188

ANSWER KEY AND EXPLANATIONS _____ 189
    READING AND WRITTEN COMMUNICATION _____ 189
    MATHEMATICS _____ 192
    INFORMATION LITERACY AND RESEARCH _____ 196
    ESSAY SAMPLE RESPONSE #1 _____ 199
    ESSAY SAMPLE RESPONSE #2 _____ 199

HOW TO OVERCOME TEST ANXIETY _____ 201
    CAUSES OF TEST ANXIETY _____ 201
    ELEMENTS OF TEST ANXIETY _____ 202
    EFFECTS OF TEST ANXIETY _____ 202
    PHYSICAL STEPS FOR BEATING TEST ANXIETY _____ 203
    MENTAL STEPS FOR BEATING TEST ANXIETY _____ 204
    STUDY STRATEGY _____ 205
    TEST TIPS _____ 207

IMPORTANT QUALIFICATION _____ 208

HOW TO OVERCOME YOUR FEAR OF MATH _____ 209

FALSE BELIEFS _____ 210
MATH STRATEGIES _____ 212
TEACHING TIPS _____ 214
SELF-CHECK _____ 215

THANK YOU _____ 216

ADDITIONAL BONUS MATERIAL _____ 217

Introduction

Thank you for purchasing this resource! You have made the choice to prepare yourself for a test that could have a huge impact on your future, and this guide is designed to help you be fully ready for test day. Obviously, it's important to have a solid understanding of the test material, but you also need to be prepared for the unique environment and stressors of the test, so that you can perform to the best of your abilities.

For this purpose, the first section that appears in this guide is the **Secret Keys**. We've devoted countless hours to meticulously researching what works and what doesn't, and we've boiled down our findings to the five most impactful steps you can take to improve your performance on the test. We start at the beginning with study planning and move through the preparation process, all the way to the testing strategies that will help you get the most out of what you know when you're finally sitting in front of the test.

We recommend that you start preparing for your test as far in advance as possible. However, if you've bought this guide as a last-minute study resource and only have a few days before your test, we recommend that you skip over the first two Secret Keys since they address a long-term study plan.

If you struggle with **test anxiety**, we strongly encourage you to check out our recommendations for how you can overcome it. Test anxiety is a formidable foe, but it can be beaten, and we want to make sure you have the tools you need to defeat it.

Secret Key #1 – Plan Big, Study Small

There's a lot riding on your performance. If you want to ace this test, you're going to need to keep your skills sharp and the material fresh in your mind. You need a plan that lets you review everything you need to know while still fitting in your schedule. We'll break this strategy down into three categories.

Information Organization

Start with the information you already have: the official test outline. From this, you can make a complete list of all the concepts you need to cover before the test. Organize these concepts into groups that can be studied together, and create a list of any related vocabulary you need to learn so you can brush up on any difficult terms. You'll want to keep this vocabulary list handy once you actually start studying since you may need to add to it along the way.

Time Management

Once you have your set of study concepts, decide how to spread them out over the time you have left before the test. Break your study plan into small, clear goals so you have a manageable task for each day and know exactly what you're doing. Then just focus on one small step at a time. When you manage your time this way, you don't need to spend hours at a time studying. Studying a small block of content for a short period each day helps you retain information better and avoid stressing over how much you have left to do. You can relax knowing that you have a plan to cover everything in time. In order for this strategy to be effective though, you have to start studying early and stick to your schedule. Avoid the exhaustion and futility that comes from last-minute cramming!

Study Environment

The environment you study in has a big impact on your learning. Studying in a coffee shop, while probably more enjoyable, is not likely to be as fruitful as studying in a quiet room. It's important to keep distractions to a minimum. You're only planning to study for a short block of time, so make the most of it. Don't pause to check your phone or get up to find a snack. It's also important to **avoid multitasking**. Research has consistently shown that multitasking will make your studying dramatically less effective. Your study area should also be comfortable and well-lit so you don't have the distraction of straining your eyes or sitting on an uncomfortable chair.

The time of day you study is also important. You want to be rested and alert. Don't wait until just before bedtime. Study when you'll be most likely to comprehend and remember. Even better, if you know what time of day your test will be, set that time aside for study. That way your brain will be used to working on that subject at that specific time and you'll have a better chance of recalling information.

Finally, it can be helpful to team up with others who are studying for the same test. Your actual studying should be done in as isolated an environment as possible, but the work of organizing the information and setting up the study plan can be divided up. In between study sessions, you can discuss with your teammates the concepts that you're all studying and quiz each other on the details. Just be sure that your teammates are as serious about the test as you are. If you find that your study time is being replaced with social time, you might need to find a new team.

Secret Key #2 – Make Your Studying Count

You're devoting a lot of time and effort to preparing for this test, so you want to be absolutely certain it will pay off. This means doing more than just reading the content and hoping you can remember it on test day. It's important to make every minute of study count. There are two main areas you can focus on to make your studying count:

Retention

It doesn't matter how much time you study if you can't remember the material. You need to make sure you are retaining the concepts. To check your retention of the information you're learning, try recalling it at later times with minimal prompting. Try carrying around flashcards and glance at one or two from time to time or ask a friend who's also studying for the test to quiz you.

To enhance your retention, look for ways to put the information into practice so that you can apply it rather than simply recalling it. If you're using the information in practical ways, it will be much easier to remember. Similarly, it helps to solidify a concept in your mind if you're not only reading it to yourself but also explaining it to someone else. Ask a friend to let you teach them about a concept you're a little shaky on (or speak aloud to an imaginary audience if necessary). As you try to summarize, define, give examples, and answer your friend's questions, you'll understand the concepts better and they will stay with you longer. Finally, step back for a big picture view and ask yourself how each piece of information fits with the whole subject. When you link the different concepts together and see them working together as a whole, it's easier to remember the individual components.

Finally, practice showing your work on any multi-step problems, even if you're just studying. Writing out each step you take to solve a problem will help solidify the process in your mind, and you'll be more likely to remember it during the test.

Modality

Modality simply refers to the means or method by which you study. Choosing a study modality that fits your own individual learning style is crucial. No two people learn best in exactly the same way, so it's important to know your strengths and use them to your advantage.

For example, if you learn best by visualization, focus on visualizing a concept in your mind and draw an image or a diagram. Try color-coding your notes, illustrating them, or creating symbols that will trigger your mind to recall a learned concept. If you learn best by hearing or discussing information, find a study partner who learns the same way or read aloud to yourself. Think about how to put the information in your own words. Imagine that you are giving a lecture on the topic and record yourself so you can listen to it later.

For any learning style, flashcards can be helpful. Organize the information so you can take advantage of spare moments to review. Underline key words or phrases. Use different colors for different categories. Mnemonic devices (such as creating a short list in which every item starts with the same letter) can also help with retention. Find what works best for you and use it to store the information in your mind most effectively and easily.

3

Secret Key #3 – Practice the Right Way

Your success on test day depends not only on how many hours you put into preparing, but also on whether you prepared the right way. It's good to check along the way to see if your studying is paying off. One of the most effective ways to do this is by taking practice tests to evaluate your progress. Practice tests are useful because they show exactly where you need to improve. Every time you take a practice test, pay special attention to these three groups of questions:

- The questions you got wrong
- The questions you had to guess on, even if you guessed right
- The questions you found difficult or slow to work through

This will show you exactly what your weak areas are, and where you need to devote more study time. Ask yourself why each of these questions gave you trouble. Was it because you didn't understand the material? Was it because you didn't remember the vocabulary? Do you need more repetitions on this type of question to build speed and confidence? Dig into those questions and figure out how you can strengthen your weak areas as you go back to review the material.

Additionally, many practice tests have a section explaining the answer choices. It can be tempting to read the explanation and think that you now have a good understanding of the concept. However, an explanation likely only covers part of the question's broader context. Even if the explanation makes sense, **go back and investigate** every concept related to the question until you're positive you have a thorough understanding.

As you go along, keep in mind that the practice test is just that: practice. Memorizing these questions and answers will not be very helpful on the actual test because it is unlikely to have any of the same exact questions. If you only know the right answers to the sample questions, you won't be prepared for the real thing. **Study the concepts** until you understand them fully, and then you'll be able to answer any question that shows up on the test.

It's important to wait on the practice tests until you're ready. If you take a test on your first day of study, you may be overwhelmed by the amount of material covered and how much you need to learn. Work up to it gradually.

On test day, you'll need to be prepared for answering questions, managing your time, and using the test-taking strategies you've learned. It's a lot to balance, like a mental marathon that will have a big impact on your future. Like training for a marathon, you'll need to start slowly and work your way up. When test day arrives, you'll be ready.

Start with the strategies you've read in the first two Secret Keys—plan your course and study in the way that works best for you. If you have time, consider using multiple study resources to get different approaches to the same concepts. It can be helpful to see difficult concepts from more than one angle. Then find a good source for practice tests. Many times, the test website will suggest potential study resources or provide sample tests.

4

Practice Test Strategy

When you're ready to start taking practice tests, follow this strategy:

UNTIMED AND OPEN-BOOK PRACTICE

Take the first test with no time constraints and with your notes and study guide handy. Take your time and focus on applying the strategies you've learned.

TIMED AND OPEN-BOOK PRACTICE

Take the second practice test open-book as well, but set a timer and practice pacing yourself to finish in time.

TIMED AND CLOSED-BOOK PRACTICE

Take any other practice tests as if it were test day. Set a timer and put away your study materials. Sit at a table or desk in a quiet room, imagine yourself at the testing center, and answer questions as quickly and accurately as possible.

Keep repeating timed and closed-book tests on a regular basis until you run out of practice tests or it's time for the actual test. Your mind will be ready for the schedule and stress of test day, and you'll be able to focus on recalling the material you've learned.

Secret Key #4 – Pace Yourself

Once you're fully prepared for the material on the test, your biggest challenge on test day will be managing your time. Just knowing that the clock is ticking can make you panic even if you have plenty of time left. Work on pacing yourself so you can build confidence against the time constraints of the exam. Pacing is a difficult skill to master, especially in a high-pressure environment, so **practice is vital**.

Set time expectations for your pace based on how much time is available. For example, if a section has 60 questions and the time limit is 30 minutes, you know you have to average 30 seconds or less per question in order to answer them all. Although 30 seconds is the hard limit, set 25 seconds per question as your goal, so you reserve extra time to spend on harder questions. When you budget extra time for the harder questions, you no longer have any reason to stress when those questions take longer to answer.

Don't let this time expectation distract you from working through the test at a calm, steady pace, but keep it in mind so you don't spend too much time on any one question. Recognize that taking extra time on one question you don't understand may keep you from answering two that you do understand later in the test. If your time limit for a question is up and you're still not sure of the answer, mark it and move on, and come back to it later if the time and the test format allow. If the testing format doesn't allow you to return to earlier questions, just make an educated guess; then put it out of your mind and move on.

On the easier questions, be careful not to rush. It may seem wise to hurry through them so you have more time for the challenging ones, but it's not worth missing one if you know the concept and just didn't take the time to read the question fully. Work efficiently but make sure you understand the question and have looked at all of the answer choices, since more than one may seem right at first.

Even if you're paying attention to the time, you may find yourself a little behind at some point. You should speed up to get back on track, but do so wisely. Don't panic; just take a few seconds less on each question until you're caught up. Don't guess without thinking, but do look through the answer choices and eliminate any you know are wrong. If you can get down to two choices, it is often worthwhile to guess from those. Once you've chosen an answer, move on and don't dwell on any that you skipped or had to hurry through. If a question was taking too long, chances are it was one of the harder ones, so you weren't as likely to get it right anyway.

On the other hand, if you find yourself getting ahead of schedule, it may be beneficial to slow down a little. The more quickly you work, the more likely you are to make a careless mistake that will affect your score. You've budgeted time for each question, so don't be afraid to spend that time. Practice an efficient but careful pace to get the most out of the time you have.

Secret Key #5 – Have a Plan for Guessing

When you're taking the test, you may find yourself stuck on a question. Some of the answer choices seem better than others, but you don't see the one answer choice that is obviously correct. What do you do?

The scenario described above is very common, yet most test takers have not effectively prepared for it. Developing and practicing a plan for guessing may be one of the single most effective uses of your time as you get ready for the exam.

In developing your plan for guessing, there are three questions to address:

- When should you start the guessing process?
- How should you narrow down the choices?
- Which answer should you choose?

When to Start the Guessing Process

Unless your plan for guessing is to select C every time (which, despite its merits, is not what we recommend), you need to leave yourself enough time to apply your answer elimination strategies. Since you have a limited amount of time for each question, that means that if you're going to give yourself the best shot at guessing correctly, you have to decide quickly whether or not you will guess.

Of course, the best-case scenario is that you don't have to guess at all, so first, see if you can answer the question based on your knowledge of the subject and basic reasoning skills. Focus on the key words in the question and try to jog your memory of related topics. Give yourself a chance to bring the knowledge to mind, but once you realize that you don't have (or you can't access) the knowledge you need to answer the question, it's time to start the guessing process.

It's almost always better to start the guessing process too early than too late. It only takes a few seconds to remember something and answer the question from knowledge. Carefully eliminating wrong answer choices takes longer. Plus, going through the process of eliminating answer choices can actually help jog your memory.

Summary: Start the guessing process as soon as you decide that you can't answer the question based on your knowledge.

How to Narrow Down the Choices

The next chapter in this book (**Test-Taking Strategies**) includes a wide range of strategies for how to approach questions and how to look for answer choices to eliminate. You will definitely want to read those carefully, practice them, and figure out which ones work best for you. Here though, we're going to address a mindset rather than a particular strategy.

Your chances of guessing an answer correctly depend on how many options you are choosing from.

How many choices you have	How likely you are to guess correctly
5	20%
4	25%
3	33%
2	50%
1	100%

You can see from this chart just how valuable it is to be able to eliminate incorrect answers and make an educated guess, but there are two things that many test takers do that cause them to miss out on the benefits of guessing:

- Accidentally eliminating the correct answer
- Selecting an answer based on an impression

We'll look at the first one here, and the second one in the next section.

To avoid accidentally eliminating the correct answer, we recommend a thought exercise called **the $5 challenge**. In this challenge, you only eliminate an answer choice from contention if you are willing to bet $5 on it being wrong. Why $5? Five dollars is a small but not insignificant amount of money. It's an amount you could afford to lose but wouldn't want to throw away. And while losing $5 once might not hurt too much, doing it twenty times will set you back $100. In the same way, each small decision you make—eliminating a choice here, guessing on a question there—won't by itself impact your score very much, but when you put them all together, they can make a big difference. By holding each answer choice elimination decision to a higher standard, you can reduce the risk of accidentally eliminating the correct answer.

The $5 challenge can also be applied in a positive sense: If you are willing to bet $5 that an answer choice *is* correct, go ahead and mark it as correct.

Summary: Only eliminate an answer choice if you are willing to bet $5 that it is wrong.

Which Answer to Choose

You're taking the test. You've run into a hard question and decided you'll have to guess. You've eliminated all the answer choices you're willing to bet $5 on. Now you have to pick an answer. Why do we even need to talk about this? Why can't you just pick whichever one you feel like when the time comes?

The answer to these questions is that if you don't come into the test with a plan, you'll rely on your impression to select an answer choice, and if you do that, you risk falling into a trap. The test writers know that everyone who takes their test will be guessing on some of the questions, so they intentionally write wrong answer choices to seem plausible. You still have to pick an answer though, and if the wrong answer choices are designed to look right, how can you ever be sure that you're not falling for their trap? The best solution we've found to this dilemma is to take the decision out of your hands entirely. Here is the process we recommend:

Once you've eliminated any choices that you are confident (willing to bet $5) are wrong, select the first remaining choice as your answer.

Whether you choose to select the first remaining choice, the second, or the last, the important thing is that you use some preselected standard. Using this approach guarantees that you will not be enticed into selecting an answer choice that looks right, because you are not basing your decision on how the answer choices look.

This is not meant to make you question your knowledge. Instead, it is to help you recognize the difference between your knowledge and your impressions. There's a huge difference between thinking an answer is right because of what you know, and thinking an answer is right because it looks or sounds like it should be right.

Summary: To ensure that your selection is appropriately random, make a predetermined selection from among all answer choices you have not eliminated.

Test-Taking Strategies

This section contains a list of test-taking strategies that you may find helpful as you work through the test. By taking what you know and applying logical thought, you can maximize your chances of answering any question correctly!

It is very important to realize that every question is different and every person is different: no single strategy will work on every question, and no single strategy will work for every person. That's why we've included all of them here, so you can try them out and determine which ones work best for different types of questions and which ones work best for you.

Question Strategies

READ CAREFULLY

Read the question and answer choices carefully. Don't miss the question because you misread the terms. You have plenty of time to read each question thoroughly and make sure you understand what is being asked. Yet a happy medium must be attained, so don't waste too much time. You must read carefully, but efficiently.

CONTEXTUAL CLUES

Look for contextual clues. If the question includes a word you are not familiar with, look at the immediate context for some indication of what the word might mean. Contextual clues can often give you all the information you need to decipher the meaning of an unfamiliar word. Even if you can't determine the meaning, you may be able to narrow down the possibilities enough to make a solid guess at the answer to the question.

PREFIXES

If you're having trouble with a word in the question or answer choices, try dissecting it. Take advantage of every clue that the word might include. Prefixes and suffixes can be a huge help. Usually they allow you to determine a basic meaning. Pre- means before, post- means after, pro - is positive, de- is negative. From prefixes and suffixes, you can get an idea of the general meaning of the word and try to put it into context.

HEDGE WORDS

Watch out for critical hedge words, such as *likely, may, can, sometimes, often, almost, mostly, usually, generally, rarely,* and *sometimes.* Question writers insert these hedge phrases to cover every possibility. Often an answer choice will be wrong simply because it leaves no room for exception. Be on guard for answer choices that have definitive words such as *exactly* and *always.*

SWITCHBACK WORDS

Stay alert for *switchbacks.* These are the words and phrases frequently used to alert you to shifts in thought. The most common switchback words are *but, although,* and *however.* Others include *nevertheless, on the other hand, even though, while, in spite of, despite, regardless of.* Switchback words are important to catch because they can change the direction of the question or an answer choice.

FACE VALUE

When in doubt, use common sense. Accept the situation in the problem at face value. Don't read too much into it. These problems will not require you to make wild assumptions. If you have to go beyond creativity and warp time or space in order to have an answer choice fit the question, then you should move on and consider the other answer choices. These are normal problems rooted in reality. The applicable relationship or explanation may not be readily apparent, but it is there for you to figure out. Use your common sense to interpret anything that isn't clear.

Answer Choice Strategies

ANSWER SELECTION

The most thorough way to pick an answer choice is to identify and eliminate wrong answers until only one is left, then confirm it is the correct answer. Sometimes an answer choice may immediately seem right, but be careful. The test writers will usually put more than one reasonable answer choice on each question, so take a second to read all of them and make sure that the other choices are not equally obvious. As long as you have time left, it is better to read every answer choice than to pick the first one that looks right without checking the others.

ANSWER CHOICE FAMILIES

An answer choice family consists of two (in rare cases, three) answer choices that are very similar in construction and cannot all be true at the same time. If you see two answer choices that are direct opposites or parallels, one of them is usually the correct answer. For instance, if one answer choice says that quantity x increases and another either says that quantity x decreases (opposite) or says that quantity y increases (parallel), then those answer choices would fall into the same family. An answer choice that doesn't match the construction of the answer choice family is more likely to be incorrect. Most questions will not have answer choice families, but when they do appear, you should be prepared to recognize them.

ELIMINATE ANSWERS

Eliminate answer choices as soon as you realize they are wrong, but make sure you consider all possibilities. If you are eliminating answer choices and realize that the last one you are left with is also wrong, don't panic. Start over and consider each choice again. There may be something you missed the first time that you will realize on the second pass.

AVOID FACT TRAPS

Don't be distracted by an answer choice that is factually true but doesn't answer the question. You are looking for the choice that answers the question. Stay focused on what the question is asking for so you don't accidentally pick an answer that is true but incorrect. Always go back to the question and make sure the answer choice you've selected actually answers the question and is not merely a true statement.

EXTREME STATEMENTS

In general, you should avoid answers that put forth extreme actions as standard practice or proclaim controversial ideas as established fact. An answer choice that states the "process should be used in certain situations, if..." is much more likely to be correct than one that states the "process should be discontinued completely." The first is a calm rational statement and doesn't even make a definitive, uncompromising stance, using a hedge word *if* to provide wiggle room, whereas the second choice is a radical idea and far more extreme.

BENCHMARK

As you read through the answer choices and you come across one that seems to answer the question well, mentally select that answer choice. This is not your final answer, but it's the one that will help you evaluate the other answer choices. The one that you selected is your benchmark or standard for judging each of the other answer choices. Every other answer choice must be compared to your benchmark. That choice is correct until proven otherwise by another answer choice beating it. If you find a better answer, then that one becomes your new benchmark. Once you've decided that no other choice answers the question as well as your benchmark, you have your final answer.

PREDICT THE ANSWER

Before you even start looking at the answer choices, it is often best to try to predict the answer. When you come up with the answer on your own, it is easier to avoid distractions and traps because you will know exactly what to look for. The right answer choice is unlikely to be word-for-word what you came up with, but it should be a close match. Even if you are confident that you have the right answer, you should still take the time to read each option before moving on.

General Strategies

TOUGH QUESTIONS

If you are stumped on a problem or it appears too hard or too difficult, don't waste time. Move on! Remember though, if you can quickly check for obviously incorrect answer choices, your chances of guessing correctly are greatly improved. Before you completely give up, at least try to knock out a couple of possible answers. Eliminate what you can and then guess at the remaining answer choices before moving on.

CHECK YOUR WORK

Since you will probably not know every term listed and the answer to every question, it is important that you get credit for the ones that you do know. Don't miss any questions through careless mistakes. If at all possible, try to take a second to look back over your answer selection and make sure you've selected the correct answer choice and haven't made a costly careless mistake (such as marking an answer choice that you didn't mean to mark). This quick double check should more than pay for itself in caught mistakes for the time it costs.

PACE YOURSELF

It's easy to be overwhelmed when you're looking at a page full of questions; your mind is confused and full of random thoughts, and the clock is ticking down faster than you would like. Calm down and maintain the pace that you have set for yourself. Especially as you get down to the last few minutes of the test, don't let the small numbers on the clock make you panic. As long as you are on track by monitoring your pace, you are guaranteed to have time for each question.

DON'T RUSH

It is very easy to make errors when you are in a hurry. Maintaining a fast pace in answering questions is pointless if it makes you miss questions that you would have gotten right otherwise. Test writers like to include distracting information and wrong answers that seem right. Taking a little extra time to avoid careless mistakes can make all the difference in your test score. Find a pace that allows you to be confident in the answers that you select.

KEEP MOVING

Panicking will not help you pass the test, so do your best to stay calm and keep moving. Taking deep breaths and going through the answer elimination steps you practiced can help to break through a stress barrier and keep your pace.

Final Notes

The combination of a solid foundation of content knowledge and the confidence that comes from practicing your plan for applying that knowledge is the key to maximizing your performance on test day. As your foundation of content knowledge is built up and strengthened, you'll find that the strategies included in this chapter become more and more effective in helping you quickly sift through the distractions and traps of the test to isolate the correct answer.

Now it's time to move on to the test content chapters of this book, but be sure to keep your goal in mind. As you read, think about how you will be able to apply this information on the test. If you've already seen sample questions for the test and you have an idea of the question format and style, try to come up with questions of your own that you can answer based on what you're reading. This will give you valuable practice applying your knowledge in the same ways you can expect to on test day.

Good luck and good studying!

Reading and Written Communication

IMPACT OF READING SKILLS ON STUDENT SUCCESS

The ability to read is not simply one academic area; it is a basic skill set underlying all academic activity and determines whether students fail or succeed in school. Research shows that of first-graders with poor **reading skills**, 88% still read poorly in fourth grade. By this time, most information that students require is provided in text form. For this reason, the focus shifts from *learning to read* in the earlier grades, to *reading to learn* by fourth grade. Consequently, students with poor reading skills can find it harder to access and interact with the content in their schools' curricula. Moreover, reading abilities that are delayed or disordered usually are identified in higher elementary grades. Yet research finds remediation attempts then could be too late, because children acquire language and have literacy experiences from birth. Phonemic awareness, the alphabetic principle, and print awareness normally develop in early childhood. Children missing such early experiences will fall behind peers without extra instruction. This means elementary school teachers must give these children **literacy-rich environments**.

READING COMPREHENSION

The whole point of reading is to **comprehend** what someone else is trying to say through writing. Without comprehension, a student is just reading the words without understanding them or increasing knowledge of a topic. Comprehension results when the student has the vocabulary and reading skills necessary to make sense of the **whole picture**, not just individual words. Students can self-monitor because they know when they are comprehending the material and when they are not. Teachers can help students solve problems with comprehension by teaching them strategies such as pre-reading titles, sidebars, and follow-up questions; looking at illustrations; predicting what's going to happen in the story; asking questions to check understanding while reading; connecting to background knowledge; and relating to the experiences or feelings of the characters.

> **Review Video: Predicting What Will Happen in a Story**
> Visit mometrix.com/academy and enter code: 288778
>
> **Review Video: Predictions**
> Visit mometrix.com/academy and enter code: 437248
>
> **Review Video: Reading Comprehension Tips**
> Visit mometrix.com/academy and enter code: 280215

SKILLS NEEDED TO DEVELOP LITERACY

According to studies by the National Reading Panel, for children to develop **literacy**, they must have developed skills in phonemic awareness, phonics, vocabulary, comprehension, and fluency. A prerequisite to developing these five skill areas is having an understanding of how literacy works, what it does, and how it is used. While young children exposed to spoken and printed language interactions from birth often develop this understanding of the functions and applications of literacy in a natural way, children with language and learning disabilities may not. A **literacy-rich environment** is defined as one that provides students having disabilities with stimulation to take part in activities involving language and literacy during their everyday life routines. Stimulating such participation in and integration of language and literacy into daily living is an effective way to help disabled students begin to develop understanding of how spoken and printed language

15

function and are used. Teaching strategies to establish literacy-rich environments can not only remediate language and literacy deficits, but also benefit all elementary-level students.

LITERACY-RICH ENVIRONMENT IN ELEMENTARY SCHOOL CLASSROOMS

An elementary classroom constituting a **literacy-rich setting** would engage all students in various literacy activities, some working individually and others in groups. Students would explore different *genres* of books, not only during reading periods or in the library, but during math, social studies, and science periods or lessons. The teacher might read aloud to students from a book about math during math period, and lead class discussions of the book's content, and have students explore eyewitness science books during science time to learn about scientific concepts. These activities help students experience literacy across all curriculum subject content areas. Students also use books on tapes and CD-ROMs. The classroom includes adapted materials to motivate disabled students to read and help them interact with text. Students write in notebooks and journals, write reports in all subjects, and compose books. A literacy-rich classroom environment features *information resources* for students including dictionaries, encyclopedias, books in varied genres, word walls, and computers, as well as teachers and peers.

VOCABULARY INSTRUCTION

There are a number of factors to consider when developing **vocabulary**, academic language, and background knowledge. To begin with, not all words should be given equal emphasis. Some words occur much more frequently and should therefore be of greater importance in instruction. This is yet another reason why the context of vocabulary and academic language is so important. It is a bad idea to find a list of difficult words and proceed through it alphabetically, because the students will have very little context for the words they are learning. Instead, teachers should approach vocabulary *thematically*. For instance, a teacher might spend one week teaching vocabulary words related to government, and the next teaching words related to legislation. It is a good idea to link new vocabulary to the lesson being covered in other content areas. The most important thing is to ensure that students have a context for new words, so that they will be able to incorporate them in their speaking and writing as soon as possible.

WORD ANALYSIS

SEMANTIC AND SYNTACTIC APPROACHES

Word analysis instruction should be balanced and comprehensive. It is a good idea to let students approach unfamiliar words from both the semantic and syntactic perspectives. A **semantic approach** emphasizes the meaning of words. A child is using the semantic approach when he thinks about context and about what type of word would make sense in a given sentence. A teacher can guide the student towards an appreciation of semantics by asking questions about the meaning of the sentence and the likely meaning of an unfamiliar word. The **syntactic approach**, on the other hand, emphasizes the order of the words in a sentence. English has fairly regular syntax, so the reader can often predict what type of word (e.g., noun, verb) will appear next in a sentence. A teacher can stimulate students to think about syntax by asking the student to read a sentence and determine whether it makes sense. A teacher can ask the student whether the words in a sentence appear to be in the right order.

DIFFERENTIATION OF WORD ANALYSIS INSTRUCTION

Word analysis can be a challenge for many students, and so there is likely to be a great range of performance in the same class. Teachers must be able to address the strong and weak students in the class. In particular, teachers need to provide differentiated instruction for students who are struggling or have reading difficulties or disabilities. For instance, a teacher needs to be able to go back and focus on key skills and knowledge, like syllable patterns and morphemes that occur frequently. Some students need to have the same material approached from different perspectives before they fully master it. The teacher should be able to outline a number of real-world examples for an abstract concept. The use of songs and poems to illustrate syllabification is one helpful way to bring struggling students up to speed. Finally, a teacher should be able to provide differentiated practice situations for the skills that have been taught.

> **Review Video: Defining a Word**
> Visit mometrix.com/academy and enter code: 648080
>
> **Review Video: Denotation and Connotation**
> Visit mometrix.com/academy and enter code: 310092

LITERAL AND CRITICAL COMPREHENSION

Literal comprehension refers to the skills a reader uses to deal with the actual words in a text. It involves skills such as identifying the topic sentence, main idea, important facts, and supporting details; using context clues to determine the meaning of a word; and sequencing events.

Critical comprehension involves prior knowledge and an understanding that written material, especially in nonfiction, is the author's version of the subject and not necessarily anybody else's. Critical comprehension involves analysis of meaning, evaluation, validation, questioning, and the reasoning skills a reader uses to recognize:

- Inferences and conclusions
- Purpose, tone, point of view, and themes
- The organizational pattern of a work
- Explicit and implicit relationships among words, phrases, and sentences
- Biased language, persuasive tactics, valid arguments, and the difference between fact and opinion

> **Review Video: Author's Main Point or Purpose**
> Visit mometrix.com/academy and enter code: 734339
>
> **Review Video: Author's Position**
> Visit mometrix.com/academy and enter code: 827954
>
> **Review Video: Inference**
> Visit mometrix.com/academy and enter code: 379203

METACOGNITION

Metacognition is thinking about thinking. For the student, this involves taking control of their own learning process, self-monitoring progress, evaluating the effectiveness of strategies, and making adjustments to strategies and learning behaviors as needed. Students who develop good metacognitive skills become more independent and confident about learning. They develop a sense of ownership about their education and realize that information is readily available to them.

Metacognitive skills can be grouped into three categories:

- **Awareness** – This involves identifying prior knowledge; defining learning goals; inventorying resources such as textbooks, libraries, computers, and study time; identifying task requirements and evaluation standards; and recognizing motivation and anxiety levels.

- **Planning** – This involves doing time estimates for tasks, prioritizing, scheduling study time, making checklists of tasks, gathering needed materials, and choosing strategies for problem solving or task comprehension.
- **Self-monitoring and reflection** – This involves identifying which strategies or techniques work best, questioning throughout the process, considering feedback, and maintaining focus and motivation.

ROLE OF METACOGNITIVE SKILLS IN LITERACY DEVELOPMENT

In terms of literacy development, **metacognitive skills** include taking an active role in reading, recognizing reading behaviors and changing them to employ the behaviors that are most effective, relating information to prior knowledge, and being aware of text structures. For example, if there is a problem with comprehension, the student can try to form a mental image of what is described, read the text again, adjust the rate of reading, or employ other reading strategies such as identifying unknown vocabulary and predicting meaning. Being aware of **text structures** is critical to being able to follow the author's ideas and relationships among ideas. Being aware of difficulties with text structure allows the student to employ strategies such as hierarchical summaries, thematic organizers, or concept maps to remedy the problem.

CRITICAL THINKING TOOLS

It is important to teach students to use critical thinking skills when reading. Three of the **critical thinking tools** that engage the reader are:

- **Summarization** – The student reviews the main point(s) of the reading selection and identifies important details. For nonfiction, a good summary will briefly describe the main arguments and the examples that support those arguments. For fiction, a good summary will identify the main characters and events of the story.
- **Question generation** – A good reader will constantly ask questions while reading about comprehension, vocabulary, connections to personal knowledge or experience, predictions, etc.
- **Textual marking** – This skill engages the reader by having him or her interact with the text. The student should mark the text with questions or comments that are generated by the text using underlining, highlighting, or shorthand marks such as "?," "!," and "*" that indicate lack of understanding, importance, or key points, for example.

CONTEXT CLUES

Context clues are words or phrases that help the reader figure out the meaning of an unknown word. They are built into a sentence or paragraph by the writer to help the reader develop a clear understanding of the writer's message. Context clues can be used to make **intelligent guesses** about the meaning of a word instead of relying on a dictionary. Context clues are the reason most vocabulary is learned through reading. There are four types of commonly used context clues:

- **Synonyms** – A word with the same meaning as the unknown word is placed close by for comparison.
- **Antonyms** – A word with the opposite meaning as the unknown word is placed close by for contrast.
- **Explanations** – An obvious explanation is given close to the unknown word.
- **Examples** – Examples of what the word means are given to help the reader define the term.

TOPIC SENTENCE

The **topic sentence** of a paragraph states the paragraph's subject. It presents the **main idea**. The rest of the paragraph should be related to the topic sentence, which should be explained and supported with facts, details, proofs, and examples. The topic sentence is more general than the **body sentences**, and should cover all the ideas in the body of the paragraph. It may contain words such as "many," "most," or "several." The topic sentence is usually the first sentence in a paragraph, but it can appear after an introductory or background sentence, can be the last sentence in a paragraph, or may simply be implied, meaning a topic sentence is not present. **Supporting sentences** can often be identified by their use of transition terms such as "for example" or "that is." Supporting sentences may also be presented in numbered sequence. The topic sentence provides **unity** to a paragraph because it ties together the supporting details into a coherent whole.

THEME

Theme is the central idea of a work. It is the thread that ties all the elements of a story together and gives them purpose. The theme is not the subject of a work, but what a work says about a subject. A theme must be **universal**, which means it must apply to everyone, not just the characters in a story. Therefore, a theme is a comment about the nature of humanity, society, the relationship of humankind to the world, or moral responsibility. There may be more than one theme in a work, and the determination of the theme is affected by the viewpoint of the reader. Therefore, there is not always necessarily a definite, irrefutable theme. The theme can be implied or stated directly.

TYPES OF DEFINITION PARAGRAPHS OR ESSAYS

A **definition paragraph** or essay describes what a word or term means. There are three ways the explanation can be presented:

- **Definition by synonym** – The term is defined by comparing it to a more familiar term that the reader can more easily understand (A phantom is a ghost or spirit that appears and disappears mysteriously and creates dread).
- **Definition by class** – Most commonly used in exams, papers, and reports, the class definition first puts the term in a larger category or class (The Hereford is a breed of cattle), and then describes the distinguishing characteristics or details of the term that differentiate it from other members of the class (The Hereford is a breed of cattle distinguished by a white face, reddish-brown hide, and short horns).

- **Definition by negation** – The term is defined by stating what it is not and then saying what it is (Courage is not the absence of fear, but the willingness to act in spite of fear).

TYPES OF PARAGRAPHS AND ESSAYS

Illustrative — An illustrative paragraph or essay explains a general statement through the use of specific examples. The writer starts with a topic sentence that is followed by one or more examples that clearly relate to and support the topic.

Narrative — A narrative tells a story. Like a news report, it tells the who, what, when, where, why, and how of an event. A narrative is usually presented in chronological order.

Descriptive — This type of writing appeals to the five senses to describe a person, place, or thing so that the readers can see the subject in their imaginations. Space order is most often used in descriptive writing to indicate place or position.

Process — There are two kinds of process papers: the "how-to" that gives step-by-step directions on how to do something and the explanation paper that tells how an event occurred or how something works.

> **Review Video: Reading Essays**
> Visit mometrix.com/academy and enter code: 169166

CAUSE AND EFFECT

Causes are reasons for actions or events. **Effects** are the results of a cause or causes. There may be multiple causes for one effect (evolutionary extinction, climate changes, and a massive comet caused the demise of the dinosaurs, for example) or multiple effects from one cause (the break-up of the Soviet Union has had multiple effects on the world stage, for instance). Sometimes, one thing leads to another and the effect of one action becomes the cause for another (breaking an arm leads to not driving, which leads to reading more while staying home, for example). The ability to identify causes and effects is part of critical thinking, and enables the reader to follow the course of events, make connections among events, and identify the instigators and receivers of actions. This ability improves comprehension.

> **Review Video: Cause and Effect**
> Visit mometrix.com/academy and enter code: 428037
>
> **Review Video: Rhetorical Strategy of Cause-and-Effect Analysis**
> Visit mometrix.com/academy and enter code: 725944

DISTINGUISHING BETWEEN FACTS AND OPINIONS

Facts are statements that can be verified through research. Facts answer the questions of who, what, when, and where, and evidence can be provided to prove factual statements. For example, it is a fact that water turns into ice when the temperature drops below 32 degrees Fahrenheit. This fact has been proven repeatedly. Water never becomes ice at a higher temperature. **Opinions** are personal views, but facts may be used to support opinions. For example, it may be one person's opinion that Jack is a great athlete, but the fact that he has made many achievements related to sports supports that opinion. It is important for a reader to be able to distinguish between fact and opinion to determine the validity of an argument. Readers need to understand that some unethical

writers will try to pass off an opinion as a fact. Readers with good critical thinking skills will not be deceived by this tactic.

INDUCTIVE AND DEDUCTIVE REASONING

Inductive reasoning is using particulars to draw a general conclusion. The inductive reasoning process starts with **data**. For example, if every apple taken out of the top of a barrel is rotten, it can be inferred without investigating further that all the apples are probably rotten. Unless all data is examined, conclusions are based on probabilities. Inductive reasoning is also used to make inferences about the universe. The entire universe cannot be examined, but inferences can be made based on observations about what can be seen. These inferences may be proven false when more data is available, but they are valid at the time they are made if observable data is used. **Deductive reasoning** is the opposite of inductive reasoning. It involves using general facts or premises to come to a specific conclusion. For example, if Susan is a sophomore in high school, and all sophomores take geometry, it can be inferred that Susan takes geometry. The word "all" does not allow for exceptions. If all sophomores take geometry, assuming Susan does too is a logical conclusion. It is important for a reader to recognize inductive and deductive reasoning so he or she can follow the line of an argument and determine if the inference or conclusion is **valid**.

STYLE, TONE, AND POINT OF VIEW

Style is the manner in which a writer uses language in prose or poetry. Style is affected by:

- Diction or word choices
- Sentence structure and syntax
- Types and extent of use of figurative language
- Patterns of rhythm or sound
- Conventional or creative use of punctuation

Tone is the attitude of the writer or narrator towards the theme of, subject of, or characters in a work. Sometimes the attitude is stated, but it is most often implied through word choices. Examples of tone are serious, humorous, satiric, stoic, cynical, flippant, and surprised.

Point of view is the angle from which a story is told. It is the perspective of the narrator, established by the author. Common points of view are:

- *Third person* – Third person points of view include omniscient (knows everything) and limited (confined to what is known by a single character or a limited number of characters). When the third person is used, characters are referred to as he, she, or they.
- *First person* – When this point of view is used, the narrator refers to himself or herself as "I."

TYPES OF FIGURATIVE LANGUAGE

A **simile** is a comparison between two unlike things using the words "like" or "as." Examples are Robert Burn's sentence "O my love's like a red, red, rose" or the common expression "as pretty as a picture."

A **metaphor** is a direct comparison between two unlike things without the use of "like" or "as." One thing is identified as the other instead of simply compared to it. An example is D. H. Lawrence's sentence "My soul is a dark forest."

Personification is the giving of human characteristics to a non-human thing or idea. An example is "The hurricane howled its frightful rage."

Synecdoche is the use of a part of something to signify the whole. For example, "boots on the ground" could be used to describe soldiers in a field.

Metonymy is the use of one term that is closely associated with another to mean the other. An example is referring to the "crown" to refer to the monarchy.

ALLITERATION, ASSONANCE, AND ONOMATOPOEIA

Alliteration is the repetition of the first sounds or stressed syllables (usually consonants) in words in close proximity. An example is: "Chirp, chirp," said the chickadee.

Assonance is the repetition of identical or similar vowel sounds, particularly in stressed syllables, in words in close proximity. Assonance is considered to be a form of near rhyme. An example is: the quiet bride cried.

Onomatopoeia refers to words that imitate sounds. It is sometimes called echoism. Examples are hiss, buzz, burp, rattle, and pop. It may also refer to words that correspond symbolically to what they describe, with high tones suggesting light and low tones suggesting darkness. An example is the *gloom* of night versus the *gleam* of the stars.

PARALLELISM, EUPHEMISM, HYPERBOLE, AND CLIMAX

Parallelism — Subjects, objects, verbs, modifiers, phrases, and clauses can be structured in sentences to balance one with another through a similar grammatical pattern. Parallelism helps to highlight ideas while showing their relationship and giving style to writing.

Examples are:

- **Parallel words** – The killer behaved coldly, cruelly, and inexplicably.
- **Parallel phrases** – Praised by comrades, honored by commanders, the soldier came home a hero.
- **Parallel clauses** – "We shall fight on the beaches, we shall fight on the landing grounds, we shall fight in the hills." (Winston Churchill)

Euphemism — This is a "cover-up" word that avoids the explicit meaning of an offensive or unpleasant term by substituting a vaguer image. An example is using "expired" instead of "dead."

Hyperbole — This is an example or phrase that exaggerates for effect. An example is the extravagant overstatement "I thought I would die!" Hyperbole is also used in tall tales, such as those describing Paul Bunyan's feats.

Climax — This refers to the process of building up to a dramatic highpoint through a series of phrases or sentences. It can also refer to the highpoint or most intense event in a story.

BATHOS, OXYMORON, IRONY, AND MALAPROPISM

Bathos — This is an attempt to evoke pity, sorrow, or nobility that goes overboard and becomes ridiculous. It is an insincere pathos and a letdown. It is also sometimes called an anticlimax, although an anticlimax might be intentionally included for comic or satiric effect.

Oxymoron — This refers to two terms that are used together for contradictory effect, usually in the form of an adjective that doesn't fit the noun. An example is: a "new classic."

Irony — This refers to a difference between what is and what ought to be, or between what is said and what is meant. Irony can be an unexpected result in literature, such as a twist of fate. For example, it is ironic that the tortoise beat the hare.

Malapropism — This is confusing one word with another, similar-sounding word. For example, saying a movie was a cliff dweller instead of a cliffhanger is a malapropism.

INVALID ARGUMENTS

There are a number of **invalid or false arguments** that are used unethically to gain an advantage, such as:

- The "**ad hominem**" or "against the person" argument – This type attacks the character or behavior of a person taking a stand on an issue rather than the issue itself. The statement "That fat slob wants higher taxes" is an example of this type of argument.
- **Hasty generalizations** – These are condemnations of a group based on the behavior of one person or part. An example of this type of argument is someone saying that all McDonald's restaurants are lousy because he or she had a bad experience at one location.
- **Faulty causation** – This is assigning the wrong cause to an event. An example is blaming a flat tire on losing a lucky penny rather than on driving over a bunch of nails.
- **Bandwagon effect** – This is the argument that if everybody else is doing something, it must be a good thing to do. The absurdity of this type of argument is highlighted by the question: "If everybody else is jumping off a cliff, should you jump, too?"

It is important for a reader to be able to identify various types of invalid arguments to prevent being deceived and making faulty conclusions.

FICTION AND NONFICTION

Fiction is a literary work usually presented in prose form that is not true. It is the product of the writer's imagination. Examples of fiction are novels, short stories, television scripts, and screenplays. **Nonfiction** is a literary work that is based on facts. In other words, the material is true. The purposeful inclusion of false information is considered dishonest, but the expression of opinions or suppositions is acceptable. Libraries divide their collections into works of fiction and nonfiction. Examples of nonfiction include historical materials, scientific reports, memoirs, biographies, most essays, journals, textbooks, documentaries, user manuals, and news reports.

Review Video: <u>Reading Fiction</u>
Visit mometrix.com/academy and enter code: 391411

Review Video: <u>Historical Context</u>
Visit mometrix.com/academy and enter code: 169770

Review Video: <u>Interpretation of Expository or Literary Text</u>
Visit mometrix.com/academy and enter code: 860442

PROSE AND POETRY

Prose is language as it is ordinarily spoken as opposed to verse or language with metric patterns. Prose is used for everyday communication, and is found in textbooks, memos, reports, articles, short stories, and novels. Distinguishing characteristics of prose include:

- It may have some sort of rhythm, but there is **no formal arrangement**.
- The common unit of organization is the **sentence**.
- It may include literary devices of repetition and balance.
- It must have more coherent relationships among sentences than a list would.

Poetry, or verse, is the manipulation of language with respect to meaning, meter, sound, and rhythm. A line of poetry can be any length and may or may not rhyme. Related groups of lines are called **stanzas**, and may also be any length. Some poems are as short as a few lines, and some are as long as a book. Poetry is a more ancient form of literature than prose.

ROLE OF EMOTIONS IN POETRY

Poetry is designed to appeal to the physical and emotional senses. Using appeals to the **physical senses** through words that evoke sight, sound, taste, smell, and touch also causes the imagination to respond **emotionally**. Poetry appeals to the soul and memories with language that can be intriguingly novel and profoundly emotional in connotation. Poetry can focus on any topic, but the feelings associated with the topic are magnified by the ordered presentation found in poetry. Verse, however, is merely a matter of structure. The thing that turns words into poetry is the feeling packed into those words. People write poetry to express their feelings and people read poetry to try to experience those same feelings. Poetry interprets the human condition with understanding and insight. Children respond well to poetry because it has an inviting, entertaining sound that they are eager to mimic.

SHORT STORY

A **short story** is prose fiction that has the same elements as a novel, such as plot, characters, and point of view. Edgar Allan Poe defined the short story as a **narrative** that can be read in **one sitting** (one-half to two hours), and is limited to a **single effect**. In a short story, there is no time for extensive character development, large numbers of characters, in-depth analysis, complicated plot lines, or detailed backgrounds. Historically, the short story is related to the fable, the exemplum, and the folktale. Short stories have become mainly an American art form. Famous short story writers include William Faulkner, Katherine Anne Porter, Eudora Welty, Flannery O'Connor, O. Henry, and J. D. Salinger.

CHARACTER TYPES

Readers need to be able to differentiate between **major and minor characters**. The difference can usually be determined based on whether the characters are round, flat, dynamic, or static. **Round characters** have complex personalities, just like real people. They are more commonly found in longer works such as novels or full-length plays. **Flat characters** display only a few personality traits and are based on stereotypes. Examples include the bigoted redneck, the lazy bum, or the absent-minded professor. **Dynamic characters** are those that change or grow during the course of the narrative. They may learn important lessons, fall in love, or take new paths. **Static characters** remain the same throughout a story. Usually, round characters are dynamic and flat characters are static, but this is not always the case. Falstaff, the loyal and comical character in Shakespeare's plays about Henry IV, is a round character in terms of his complexity. However, he never changes, which makes him a reliable figure in the story.

LINE STRUCTURE IN POEMS

A **line of poetry** can be any length and can have any metrical pattern. A line is determined by the physical position of words on a page. A line is simply a group of words on a single line. Consider the following example:

> When I consider how my light is spent,

> E're half my days, in this dark world and wide,

These are two lines of poetry written by John Milton. Lines may or may not have punctuation at the end, depending, of course, on the need for punctuation. If these two lines were written out in a paragraph, they would be written with a **slash line** and a **space** in between the lines: "When I consider how my light is spent, / E're half my days, in this dark world and wide."

BLANK VERSE AND FREE VERSE

Blank verse is unrhymed verse that consists of lines of iambic pentameter, which is five feet (sets) of unstressed and stressed syllables. The rhythm that results is the closest to natural human speech. It is the most commonly used type of verse because of its versatility. Well-known examples of blank verse are Shakespearean plays, Milton's epic poems, and T. S. Eliot's *The Waste Land*. **Free verse** lacks regular patterns of poetic feet, but has more controlled rhythm than prose in terms of pace and pauses. Free verse has no rhyme and is usually written in short lines of irregular length. Well-known examples of free verse are the King James translation of the Psalms, Walt Whitman's *Leaves of Grass*, and the poetry of Ezra Pound and William Carlos Williams.

> **Review Video: Forms of Poetry**
> Visit mometrix.com/academy and enter code: 451705

STANZA STRUCTURE IN POEMS

A **stanza** is a group of lines. The grouping denotes a relationship among the lines. A stanza can be any length, but the separation of lines into different stanzas indicates an intentional *pattern* created by the poet. The breaks between stanzas indicate a change of subject or thought. As a group of lines, the stanza is a melodic unit that can be analyzed for *metrical and rhyme patterns*. Various common rhyme patterns have been named. The Spenserian stanza, which has a rhyme pattern of a b a b b c b c c, is an example. Stanzas of a certain length also have names. Examples include the **couplet**, which has two lines; the **tercet**, which has three lines; and the **quatrain**, which has four lines.

METER

A recurring pattern of stressed and unstressed syllables in language creates a rhythm when spoken. When the pattern is regular, it is called **meter**. When meter is used in a composition, it is called **verse**. The most common types of meter are:

- **Iambic** – An unstressed syllable followed by a stressed syllable
- **Anapestic** – Two unstressed syllables followed by a stressed syllable
- **Trochaic** – One stressed syllable followed by an unstressed syllable
- **Dactylic** – A stressed syllable followed by two unstressed syllables
- **Spondaic** – Two consecutive syllables that are stressed almost equally
- **Pyrrhic** – Two consecutive syllables that are equally unstressed

TYPES OF CHILDREN'S LITERATURE

A **fairy tale** is a fictional story involving humans, magical events, and usually animals. Characters such as fairies, elves, giants, and talking animals are taken from folklore. The plot often involves impossible events (as in "Jack and the Beanstalk") and/or an enchantment (as in "Sleeping Beauty"). Other examples of fairy tales include "Cinderella," "Little Red Riding Hood," and "Rumpelstiltskin." A **fable** is a tale in which animals, plants, and forces of nature act like humans. A fable also teaches a moral lesson. Examples are "The Tortoise and the Hare," *The Lion King*, and *Animal Farm*. A **tall tale** exaggerates human abilities or describes unbelievable events as if the story were true. Often, the narrator seems to have witnessed the event described. Examples are fish stories, Paul Bunyan and Pecos Bill stories, and hyperboles about real people such as Davy Crockett, Mike Fink, and Calamity Jane.

PREADOLESCENT AND ADOLESCENT LITERATURE

Preadolescent literature is mostly concerned with the "tween" issues of changing lives, relationships, and bodies. **Adolescents** seeking escape from their sometimes difficult lives enjoy fantasy and science fiction. For both groups, books about modern, real people are more interesting than those about historical figures or legends. Boys especially enjoy nonfiction. Reading interests as well as reading levels for this group vary. Reading levels will usually range from 6.0 to 8.9. Examples of popular literature for this age group and reading level include:

- Series – Sweet Valley High, Bluford High, Nancy Drew, Hardy Boys, and Little House on the Prairie
- Juvenile fiction authors – Judy Blume and S. E. Hinton
- Fantasy and horror authors – Ursula LeGuin and Stephen King
- Science fiction authors – Isaac Asimov, Ray Bradbury, and H. G. Wells
- Classic books: Lilies of the Field, Charlie and the Chocolate Factory, Pippi Longstocking, National Velvet, Call of the Wild, Anne of Green Gables, The Hobbit, The Member of the Wedding, and Tom Sawyer

GRAMMATICAL TERMS

The definitions for grammatical terms are as follows:

Adjective – This is a word that modifies or describes a noun or pronoun. Examples are a *green* apple or *every* computer.

Adverb – This is a word that modifies a verb (*instantly* reviewed), an adjective (*relatively* odd), or another adverb (*rather* suspiciously).

Conjunctions: There are three types of conjunctions:

- **Coordinating conjunctions** are used to link words, phrases, and clauses. Examples are and, or, nor, for, but, yet, and so.
- **Correlative conjunctions** are paired terms used to link clauses. Examples are either/or, neither/nor, and if/then.
- **Subordinating conjunctions** relate subordinate or dependent clauses to independent ones. Examples are although, because, if, since, before, after, when, even though, in order that, and while.

Gerund – This is a verb form used as a noun. Most end in "ing." An example is: *Walking* is good exercise.

Infinitive – This is a verbal form comprised of the word "to" followed by the root form of a verb. An infinitive may be used as a noun, adjective, adverb, or absolute. Examples include:

- *To hold* a baby is a joy. (noun)
- Jenna had many files *to reorganize*. (adjective)
- Andrew tried *to remember* the dates. (adverb)
- *To be honest*, your hair looks awful. (absolute)

Noun – This is a word that names a person, place, thing, idea, or quality. A noun can be used as a subject, object, complement, appositive, or modifier.

Object – This is a word or phrase that receives the action of a verb.

- A direct object states *to* whom/what an action was committed. It answers the question "to what?" An example is: Joan served *the meal*.
- An indirect object states *for* whom/what an action was committed. An example is: Joan served *us* the meal.

Preposition – This is a word that links a noun or pronoun to other parts of a sentence. Examples include above, by, for, in, out, through, and to.

Prepositional phrase – This is a combination of a preposition and a noun or pronoun. Examples include across the bridge, against the grain, below the horizon, and toward the sunset.

Pronoun – This is a word that represents a specific noun in a generic way. A pronoun functions like a noun in a sentence. Examples include I, she, he, it, myself, they, these, what, all, and anybody.

Sentence – This is a group of words that expresses a thought or conveys information as an independent unit of speech. A **complete sentence** must contain a noun and a verb (I ran). However, all the other parts of speech can also be represented in a sentence.

Verb – This is a word or phrase in a sentence that expresses action (Mary played) or a state of being (Mary is).

Review Video: Parts of Speech
Visit mometrix.com/academy and enter code: 899611

CAPITALIZATION AND PUNCTUATION

Capitalization refers to the use of capital letters. Capital letters should be placed at the beginning of:

- **Proper names** (Ralph Waldo Emerson, Australia)
- **Places** (Mount Rushmore, Chicago)
- Historical periods and holidays (Renaissance, Christmas)
- **Religious terms** (Bible, Koran)
- **Titles** (Empress Victoria, General Smith)
- All main words in **literary, art, or music titles** (Grapes of Wrath, Sonata in C Major)

Punctuation consists of:

Periods – A period is placed at the end of a sentence.

Commas – A comma is used to separate:

- Two adjectives modifying the same word (long, hot summer)
- Three or more words or phrases in a list (Winken, Blinken, and Nod; life, liberty, and the pursuit of happiness)
- Phrases that are not needed to complete a sentence (The teacher, not the students, will distribute the supplies.)

COLONS AND SEMICOLONS

Colons – A colon is used to:

- Set up a **list** (We will need these items: a pencil, paper, and an eraser.)
- Direct readers to **examples or explanations** (We have one chore left: clean out the garage.)
- Introduce **quotations or dialogue** (The Labor Department reported on unemployment: "There was a 3.67% increase in unemployment in 2010."; Scarlett exclaimed: "What shall I do?")

> **Review Video: Colons**
> Visit mometrix.com/academy and enter code: 868673

Semicolons – A semicolon is used to:

- Join **related independent clauses** (There were five major hurricanes this year; two of them hit Florida.)
- Join **independent clauses connected by conjunctive adverbs** (Popular books are often made into movies; however, it is a rare screenplay that is as good as the book.)
- Separate items in a **series** if commas would be confusing (The characters include: Robin Hood, who robs from the rich to give to the poor; Maid Marian, his true love; and Little John, Robin Hood's comrade-in-arms.)

> **Review Video: Semicolon Usage**
> Visit mometrix.com/academy and enter code: 370605

SUBJECT-VERB AGREEMENT

A verb must **agree** in number with its subject. Therefore, a verb changes form depending on whether the subject is singular or plural. Examples include "I do," "he does," "the ball is," and "the balls are." If two subjects are joined by "and," the **plural** form of a verb is usually used. For example: *Jack and Jill want* to get some water (Jack wants, Jill wants, but together they want). If the compound subjects are preceded by each or every, they take the **singular** form of a verb. For example: *Each man and each woman brings* a special talent to the world (each brings, not bring). If one noun in a compound subject is plural and the other is singular, the verb takes the form of the subject **nearest** to it. For example: Neither the *students* nor their *teacher was* ready for the fire drill. **Collective nouns** that name a group are considered singular if they refer to the group acting as a unit. For example: The *choir is going* on a concert tour.

> **Review Video: <u>Subject Verb Agreement</u>**
> Visit mometrix.com/academy and enter code: 479190

SYNTAX

Syntax refers to the rules related to how to properly **structure** sentences and phrases. Syntax is not the same as grammar. For example, "I does" is syntactically correct because the subject and verb are in proper order, but it is grammatically incorrect because the subject and verb don't agree.

There are three types of sentence structures:

- **Simple** – This type is composed of a single independent clause with one subject and one predicate (verb or verb form).
- **Compound** – This type is composed of two independent clauses joined by a conjunction (Amy flew, but Brenda took the train), a correlative conjunction (Either Tom goes with me or I stay here), or a semicolon (My grandfather stays in shape; he plays tennis nearly every day).
- **Complex** – This type is composed of one independent clause and one or more dependent clauses joined by a subordinating conjunction (Before we set the table, we should replace the tablecloth).

TYPES OF PARAGRAPHS OR ESSAYS

A **comparison and contrast essay** examines the similarities and differences between two things. In a paragraph, the writer presents all the points about subject A and then all the points about subject B. In an essay, the writer might present one point at a time, comparing subject A and subject B side by side.

A **classification paper** sorts information. It opens with a topic sentence that identifies the group to be classified, and then breaks that group into categories. For example, a group might be baseball players, while a category might be positions they play.

A **cause and effect paper** discusses the causes or reasons for an event or the effects of a cause or causes. Topics discussed in this type of essay might include the causes of a war or the effects of global warming.

A **persuasive essay** is one in which the writer tries to convince the audience to agree with a certain opinion or point of view. The argument must be supported with facts, examples, anecdotes, expert testimony, or statistics, and must anticipate and answer the questions of those who hold an opposing view. It may also predict consequences.

ROLE OF PURPOSE AND AUDIENCE IN WRITING A PAPER

Early in the writing process, the writer needs to definitively determine the **purpose** of the paper and then keep that purpose in mind throughout the writing process. The writer needs to ask: "Is the purpose to explain something, to tell a story, to entertain, to inform, to argue a point, or some combination of these purposes?" Also at the beginning of the writing process, the writer needs to determine the **audience** of the paper by asking questions such as: "Who will read this paper?" "For whom is this paper intended?" "What does the audience already know about this topic?" "How much does the audience need to know?" and "Is the audience likely to agree or disagree with my point of view?" The answers to these questions will determine the content of the paper, the tone, and the style.

WRITING PROCESSES

Drafting is creating an early version of a paper. A draft is a prototype or sketch of the finished product. A draft is a rough version of the final paper, and it is expected that there will be multiple drafts.

Revising is the process of making major changes to a draft in regards to clarity of purpose, focus (thesis), audience, organization, and content.

Editing is the process of making changes in style, word choice, tone, examples, and arrangement. These are more minor than the changes made during revision. Editing can be thought of as fine tuning. The writer makes the language more precise, checks for varying paragraph lengths, and makes sure that the title, introduction, and conclusion fit well with the body of the paper.

Proofreading is performing a final check and correcting errors in punctuation, spelling, grammar, and usage. It also involves looking for parts of the paper that may be omitted.

> **Review Video: Recursive Writing Process**
> Visit mometrix.com/academy and enter code: 951611

TITLE AND CONCLUSION OF AN ESSAY

The **title** is centered on the page and the main words are capitalized. The title is not surrounded by quotation marks, nor is it underlined or italicized. The title is rarely more than four or five words, and is very rarely a whole sentence. A good title suggests the subject of the paper and catches the reader's interest. The **conclusion** should flow logically from the body of the essay, should tie back to the introduction, and may provide a summary or a final thought on the subject. New material should never be introduced in the conclusion. The conclusion is a wrap-up that may contain a call to action, something the writer wants the audience to do in response to the paper. The conclusion might end with a question to give the reader something to think about.

> **Review Video: Drafting Conclusions**
> Visit mometrix.com/academy and enter code: 209408

INTRODUCTION OF AN ESSAY

The **introduction** contains the **thesis statement**, which is usually the first or last sentence of the opening paragraph. It needs to be interesting enough to make the reader want to continue reading.

- Possible openings for an introduction include:
- The thesis statement
- A general idea that gives background or sets the scene

- An illustration that will make the thesis more concrete and easy to picture
- A surprising fact or idea to arouse curiosity
- A contradiction to popular belief that attracts interest
- A quotation that leads into the thesis

> **Review Video: Introduction**
> Visit mometrix.com/academy and enter code: 961328
>
> **Review Video: Introduction II**
> Visit mometrix.com/academy and enter code: 254411

SENTENCE TYPES

A **declarative sentence** makes a statement and is punctuated by a period at the end. An example is: The new school will be built at the south end of Main Street.

An **interrogative sentence** asks a question and is punctuated by a question mark at the end. An example is: Why will the new school be built so far out?

An **exclamatory sentence** shows strong emotion and is punctuated by an exclamation mark at the end. An example is: The new school has the most amazing state-of-the-art technology!

An **imperative sentence** gives a direction or command and may be punctuated by an exclamation mark or a period. Sometimes, the subject of an imperative sentence is you, which is understood instead of directly stated. An example is: Come to the open house at the new school next Sunday.

TRANSITIONAL WORDS AND PHRASES

Transitional words are used to signal a relationship. They are used to link thoughts and sentences. Some types of transitional words and phrases are:

- **Addition** – Also, in addition, furthermore, moreover, and then, another
- **Admitting a point** – Granted, although, while it is true that
- **Cause and effect** – Since, so, consequently, as a result, therefore, thus
- **Comparison** – Similarly, just as, in like manner, likewise
- **Contrast** – On the other hand, yet, nevertheless, despite, but, still
- **Emphasis** – Indeed, in fact, without a doubt, certainly, to be sure
- **Illustration** – For example, for instance, in particular, specifically
- **Purpose** – In order to, for this purpose, for this to occur
- **Spatial arrangement** – Beside, above, below, around, across, inside, near, far, to the left
- **Summary or clarification** – In summary, in conclusion, that is, in other words
- **Time sequence** – Before, after, later, soon, next, meanwhile, suddenly, finally

PRE-WRITING TECHNIQUES

Pre-writing techniques that help a writer find, explore, and organize a topic include:

- **Brainstorming** – This involves letting thoughts make every connection to the topic possible, and then spinning off ideas and making notes of them as they are generated. This is a process of using imagination, uninhibited creativity, and instincts to discover a variety of possibilities.

- **Freewriting** – This involves choosing items from the brainstorming list and writing about them nonstop for a short period. This unedited, uncensored process allows one thing to lead to another and permits the writer to think of additional concepts and themes.
- **Clustering/mapping** – This involves writing a general word or phrase related to the topic in the middle of a paper and circling it, and then quickly jotting down related words or phrases. These are circled and lines are drawn to link words and phrases to others on the page. Clustering is a visual representation of brainstorming that reveals patterns and connections.
- **Listing** – Similar to brainstorming, listing is writing down as many descriptive words and phrases (not whole sentences) as possible that relate to the subject. Correct spelling and grouping of these descriptive terms can come later if needed. This list is merely intended to stimulate creativity and provide a vibrant vocabulary for the description of the subject once the actual writing process begins.
- **Charting** – This prewriting technique works well for comparison/contrast purposes or for the examination of advantages and disadvantages (pros and cons). Any kind of chart will work, even a simple two-column list. The purpose is to draw out points and examples that can be used in the paper.

PURPOSE OF WRITING

Writing always has a purpose. The five reasons to write are:

- **To tell a story** – The story does not necessarily need to be fictional. The purposes are to explain what happened, to narrate events, and to explain how things were accomplished. The story will need to make a point, and plenty of details will need to be provided to help the reader imagine the event or process.
- **To express oneself** – This type of writing is commonly found in journals, diaries, or blogs. This kind of writing is an exercise in reflection that allows writers to learn something about themselves and what they have observed, and to work out their thoughts and feelings on paper.
- **To convey information** – Reports are written for this purpose. Information needs to be as clearly organized and accurate as possible. Charts, graphs, tables, and other illustrations can help make the information more understandable.
- **To make an argument** – This type of writing also makes a point, but adds opinion to the facts presented. Argumentative, or persuasive, writing is one of the most common and important types of writing. It should follow rules of logic and ethics.
- **To explore ideas** – This is speculative writing that is quite similar to reflective writing. This type of writing explores possibilities and asks questions without necessarily expecting an answer. The purpose is to stimulate readers to further consider and reflect on the topic.

Review Video: Author's Main Point or Purpose
Visit mometrix.com/academy and enter code: 734339

ARRANGING INFORMATION STRATEGICALLY

The order of the elements in a writing project can be organized in the following ways:

- **Logical order** – There is a coherent pattern in the presentation of information, such as inductive or deductive reasoning or a division of a topic into its parts.
- **Hierarchical order** – There is a ranking of material from most to least important or least to most important, depending on whether the writer needs a strong start or a sweeping finish. It can also involve breaking down a topic from a general form into specifics.
- **Chronological order** – This is an order that follows a sequence. In a narrative, the sequence will follow the time order of beginning to middle to end. In a "how to," the sequence will be step 1, step 2, step 3, and so on.
- **Order defined by genre** – This is a pre-determined order structured according to precedent or professional guidelines, such as the order required for a specific type of research or lab report, a resume, or an application form.
- **Order of importance** – This method of organization relies on a ranking determined by priorities. For example, in a persuasive paper, the writer usually puts the strongest argument in the last body paragraph so that readers will remember it. In a news report, the most important information comes first.
- **Order of interest** – This order is dependent on the level of interest the audience has in the subject. If the writer anticipates that reader knowledge and interest in the subject will be low, normal order choices need to be changed. The piece should begin with something very appealing. This will hook the reader and make for a strong opening.

BEGINNING STAGES OF LEARNING TO WRITE

The following are the beginning stages of learning to write:

- **Drawing pictures** is the first written attempt to express thoughts and feelings. Even when the picture is unrecognizable to the adult, it means something to the child.
- The **scribble stage** begins when the child attempts to draw shapes. He or she may also try to imitate writing. The child may have a story or explanation to go with the shapes.
- Children have the most interest in learning to **write their own names**, so writing lessons usually start with that. Children will soon recognize that there are other letters too.
- Children are learning the **alphabet** and how to associate a **sound with each letter**. Reversing letters is still common, but instruction begins with teaching children to write from left to right.
- Written words may not be complete, but will likely have the correct **beginning and end sounds/letters**.
- Children will make some attempt to use **vowels** in writing.
- Children will write with more ease, although spelling will still be phonetic and only some punctuation will be used.

JOURNAL WRITING

Writing in a **journal** gives students practice in writing, which makes them more comfortable with the writing process. Journal writing also gives students the opportunity to sort out their thoughts, solve problems, examine relationships and values, and see their personal and academic growth when they revisit old entries. The advantages for the teacher are that the students become more experienced with and accustomed to writing. Through reading student journals, the teacher can also gain **insight** into the students' problems and attitudes, which can help the teacher tailor his or her lesson plans. A journal can be kept in a **notebook** or in a **computer file**. It shouldn't be just a record of daily events, but an expression of thoughts and feelings about everything and anything. Grammar and punctuation don't matter since journaling is a form of private communication. Teachers who review journals need to keep in mind that they should not grade journals and that comments should be encouraging and polite.

REVISING A PAPER

Revising a paper involves rethinking the choices that were made while constructing the paper and then rewriting it, making any necessary changes or additions to word choices or arrangement of points. Questions to keep in mind include:

- Is the thesis clear?
- Do the body paragraphs logically flow and provide details to support the thesis?
- Is anything unnecessarily repeated?
- Is there anything not related to the topic?
- Is the language understandable?
- Does anything need to be defined?
- Is the material interesting?

Another consideration when revising is **peer feedback**. It is helpful during the revision process to have someone who is knowledgeable enough to be helpful and will be willing to give an honest critique read the paper.

> **Review Video: <u>General Revision and Proofreading</u>**
> Visit mometrix.com/academy and enter code: 385882

PARAGRAPH COHERENCE

Paragraph coherence can be achieved by linking sentences by using the following strategies:

- **Repetition of key words** – It helps the reader follow the progression of thought from one sentence to another if key words (which should be defined) are repeated to assure the reader that the writer is still on topic and the discussion still relates to the key word.
- **Substitution of pronouns** – This doesn't just refer to using single word pronouns such as I, they, us, etc., but also alternate descriptions of the subject. For example, if someone was writing about Benjamin Franklin, it gets boring to keep saying Franklin or he. Other terms that describe him, such as that notable American statesman, this printer, the inventor, and so forth can also be used.
- **Substitution of synonyms** – This is similar to substitution of pronouns, but refers to using similar terms for any repeated noun or adjective, not just the subject. For example, instead of constantly using the word great, adjectives such as terrific, really cool, awesome, and so on can also be used.

Verbs

In order to understand the role of a verb and be able to identify the verb that is necessary to make a sentence, it helps to know the different types of verbs. These are:

- **Action verbs** – These are verbs that express an action being performed by the subject. An example is: The outfielder caught the ball (outfielder = subject and caught = action).
- **Linking verbs** – These are verbs that link the subject to words that describe or identify the subject. An example is: Mary is an excellent teacher (Mary = subject and "is" links Mary to her description as an excellent teacher). Common linking verbs are all forms of the verb "to be," appear, feel, look, become, and seem.
- **Helping verbs** – When a single verb cannot do the job by itself because of tense issues, a second, helping verb is added. Examples include: should have gone ("gone" is the main verb, while "should" and "have" are helping verbs), and was playing ("playing" is the main verb, while "was" is the helping verb).

Coordinating Conjunctions and Subordinating Conjunctions

There are different ways to connect two clauses and show their relationship:

- A **coordinating conjunction** is one that can join two independent clauses by placing a comma and a coordinating conjunction between them. The most common coordinating conjunctions are and, but, or, nor, yet, for, and so. Examples include: "It was warm, so I left my jacket at home" and "It was warm, and I left my jacket at home."
- A **subordinating conjunction** is one that joins a subordinate clause and an independent clause and establishes the relationship between them. An example is: "We can play a game after Steve finishes his homework." The dependent clause is "after Steve finishes his homework" because the reader immediately asks, "After Steve finishes, then what?" The independent clause is "We can play a game." The concern is not the ability to play a game, but "when?" The answer to this question is dependent on when Steve finishes his homework.

> **Review Video: Conjunctions**
> Visit mometrix.com/academy and enter code: 904603

Run-On Sentences and Comma Splices

A **run-on sentence** is one that tries to connect two independent clauses without the needed conjunction or punctuation and makes it hard for the reader to figure out where one sentence ends and the other starts. An example is: "Meagan is three years old she goes to pre-school." Two possible ways to fix the run-on would be: "Meagan is three years old, and she goes to pre-school" or "Meagan is three years old; however, she goes to pre-school." A **comma splice** occurs when a comma is used to join two independent clauses without a proper conjunction. The comma should be replaced by a period or one of the methods for coordination or subordination should be used. An example of a comma splice is: "Meagan is three years old, she goes to pre-school."

FRAGMENTS

A **fragment** is an incomplete sentence, which is one that does not have a subject to go with the verb, or vice versa. The following are types of fragments:

- **Dependent clause fragments** – These usually start with a subordinating conjunction. An example is: "Before you can graduate." "You can graduate" is a sentence, but the subordinating conjunction "before" makes the clause dependent, which means it needs an independent clause to go with it. An example is: "Before you can graduate, you have to meet all the course requirements."
- **Relative clause fragments** – These often start with who, whose, which, or that. An example is: "Who is always available to the students." This is a fragment because the "who" is not identified. A complete sentence would be: "Mr. Jones is a principal who is always available to the students."
- **The "-ing" fragment** lacks a subject. The "-ing" form of a verb has to have a helping verb. An example is: "Walking only three blocks to his job." A corrected sentence would be: "Walking only three blocks to his job, Taylor has no need for a car."
- **Prepositional phrase fragments** are ones that begin with a preposition and are only a phrase, not a complete thought. An example is: "By the time we arrived." "We arrived" by itself would be a complete sentence, but the "by" makes the clause dependent and the reader asks, "By the time you arrived, what happened?" A corrected sentence would be: "By the time we arrived, all the food was gone."
- **Infinitive phrase fragments** have the same problem as prepositional phrase ones. An example is: "To plant the seed." A corrected sentence would be: "To plant the seed, Isaac used a trowel."

> **Review Video: Fragments and Run-on Sentences**
> Visit mometrix.com/academy and enter code: 541989

PRIMARY AND SECONDARY RESEARCH INFORMATION

Primary research material is material that comes from the "horse's mouth." It is a document or object that was created by the person under study or during the time period under study. Examples of primary sources are original documents such as manuscripts, diaries, interviews, autobiographies, government records, letters, news videos, and artifacts (such as Native American pottery or wall writings in Egyptian tombs). **Secondary research material** is anything that is not primary. Secondary sources are those things that are written or otherwise recorded about the main subject. Examples include a critical analysis of a literary work (a poem by William Blake is primary, but the analysis of the poem by T. S. Eliot is secondary), a magazine article about a person (a direct quote would be primary, but the report is secondary), histories, commentaries, and encyclopedias.

Primary sources are the raw material of research. This can include results of experiments, notes, and surveys or interviews done by the researcher. Other primary sources are books, letters, diaries, eyewitness accounts, and performances attended by the researcher. **Secondary sources** consist of oral and written accounts prepared by others. This includes reports, summaries, critical reviews, and other sources not developed by the researcher. Most research writing uses both primary and secondary sources: primary sources from first-hand accounts and secondary sources for background and supporting documentation. The research process calls for active reading and writing throughout. As research yields information, it often calls for more reading and research, and the cycle continues.

DRAFTING RESEARCH ESSAYS

INTRODUCTION

The **introduction** to a research essay is particularly important, as it sets the *context* for the essay. It needs to draw the reader into the subject and provide necessary background to understand the subject. It is sometimes helpful to open with the research question and explain how the question will be answered. The major points of the essay may be forecast or previewed to prepare readers for the coming arguments. In a research essay, it is a good idea to establish the writer's credibility by reviewing credentials and experience with the subject. Another useful opening involves quoting several sources that support the points of the essay, again to establish credibility. The tone should be appropriate to the audience and subject, maintaining a sense of careful authority while building the arguments. *Jargon* should be kept to a minimum, and language should be carefully chosen to reflect the appropriate tone.

CONCLUSION

The **conclusion** to a research essay helps readers summarize what they have learned. Conclusions are not meant to convince, as this has been done in the body of the essay. It can be useful to leave the reader with a memorable phrase or example that supports the argument. Conclusions should be both memorable and logical restatements of the arguments in the body of the essay. A *specific-to-general pattern* can be helpful, opening with the thesis statement and expanding to more general observations. A good idea is to restate the main points in the body of the essay, leading to the conclusion. An ending that evokes a vivid image or asks a provocative question makes the essay memorable. The same effect can be achieved by a call for action, or a warning. Conclusions may be tailored to the audience's background, in terms of language, tone, and style.

REVIEWING THE DRAFT

Checklist for Reviewing a Draft of a Research Essay

1. **Introduction**: Is the reader's attention gained and held by the introduction?
2. **Thesis**: Does the essay fulfill the promise of the thesis? Is it strong enough?
3. **Main points**: Are the main points listed and ranked in order of importance?
4. **Organization**: What is the organizing principle of the essay? Does it work?
5. **Supporting information**: Is the thesis adequately supported? Is the thesis convincing?
6. **Source material**: Are there adequate sources and are they smoothly integrated into the essay?
7. **Conclusion**: Does the conclusion have sufficient power? Does it summarize the essay well?
8. **Paragraphs, sentences, words**: Are these elements effective in promoting the thesis?
9. **Overall review**: Evaluate the essay's strengths and weaknesses. What revisions are needed?

MODERN LANGUAGE ASSOCIATION STYLE

The **Modern Language Association style** is widely used in literature and languages as well as other fields. The MLA style calls for noting brief references to sources in parentheses in the text of an essay and adding an alphabetical list of sources, called "Works Cited," at the end. Specific recommendations of the MLA include the following:

1. **"Works Cited"**: Include in this section only works actually cited. List on a separate page the author's name, title, and publication information, which must include the location of the publisher, the publisher's name, and the date of publication.

2. **Parenthetical citations**: MLA style uses parenthetical citations following each quotation, reference, paraphrase, or summary to a source. Each citation is made up of the author's last name and page reference, keyed to a reference in Works Cited.

3. **Explanatory notes**: Explanatory notes are numbered consecutively and identified by superscript numbers in the text. The full notes may appear as endnotes or as footnotes at the bottom of the page.

Mathematics

Numbers and Operations

CLASSIFICATIONS OF NUMBERS

Numbers are the basic building blocks of mathematics. Specific features of numbers are identified by the following terms:

Integer – any positive or negative whole number, including zero. Integers do not include fractions $\left(\frac{1}{3}\right)$, decimals (0.56), or mixed numbers $\left(7\frac{3}{4}\right)$.

Prime number – any whole number greater than 1 that has only two factors, itself and 1; that is, a number that can be divided evenly only by 1 and itself.

Composite number – any whole number greater than 1 that has more than two different factors; in other words, any whole number that is not a prime number. For example: The composite number 8 has the factors of 1, 2, 4, and 8.

Even number – any integer that can be divided by 2 without leaving a remainder. For example: 2, 4, 6, 8, and so on.

Odd number – any integer that cannot be divided evenly by 2. For example: 3, 5, 7, 9, and so on.

Decimal number – any number that uses a decimal point to show the part of the number that is less than one. Example: 1.234.

Decimal point – a symbol used to separate the ones place from the tenths place in decimals or dollars from cents in currency.

Decimal place – the position of a number to the right of the decimal point. In the decimal 0.123, the 1 is in the first place to the right of the decimal point, indicating tenths; the 2 is in the second place, indicating hundredths; and the 3 is in the third place, indicating thousandths.

The **decimal**, or base 10, system is a number system that uses ten different digits (0, 1, 2, 3, 4, 5, 6, 7, 8, 9). An example of a number system that uses something other than ten digits is the **binary**, or base 2, number system, used by computers, which uses only the numbers 0 and 1. It is thought that the decimal system originated because people had only their 10 fingers for counting.

Rational numbers include all integers, decimals, and fractions. Any terminating or repeating decimal number is a rational number.

Irrational numbers cannot be written as fractions or decimals because the number of decimal places is infinite and there is no recurring pattern of digits within the number. For example, pi (π) begins with 3.141592 and continues without terminating or repeating, so pi is an irrational number.

Real numbers are the set of all rational and irrational numbers.

> **Review Video: <u>Numbers and Their Classifications</u>**
> Visit mometrix.com/academy and enter code: 461071

39

PLACE VALUE

WRITE THE PLACE VALUE OF EACH DIGIT IN THE FOLLOWING NUMBER: <u>14,059.826</u>

1: ten-thousands
4: thousands
0: hundreds
5: tens
9: ones
8: tenths
2: hundredths
6: thousandths

> **Review Video: <u>Number Place Value</u>**
> Visit mometrix.com/academy and enter code: 205433

WRITING NUMBERS IN WORD FORM

EXAMPLE 1

Write each number in words.

29: twenty-nine
478: four hundred seventy-eight
9,435: nine thousand four hundred thirty-five
98,542: ninety-eight thousand five hundred forty-two
302, 876: three hundred two thousand eight hundred seventy-six

EXAMPLE 2

Write each decimal in words.

0.06: six hundredths
0.6: six tenths
6.0: six
0.009: nine thousandths
0.113: one hundred thirteen thousandths
0.901: nine hundred one thousandths

ROUNDING AND ESTIMATION

Rounding is reducing the digits in a number while still trying to keep the value similar. The result will be less accurate, but will be in a simpler form, and will be easier to use. Whole numbers can be rounded to the nearest ten, hundred or thousand.

EXAMPLE 1

Round each number:

1. Round each number to the nearest ten: 11, 47, 118
2. Round each number to the nearest hundred: 78, 980, 248
3. Round each number to the nearest thousand: 302, 1274, 3756

ANSWER

1. Remember, when rounding to the nearest ten, anything ending in 5 or greater rounds up. So, 11 rounds to 10, 47 rounds to 50, and 118 rounds to 120.
2. Remember, when rounding to the nearest hundred, anything ending in 50 or greater rounds up. So, 78 rounds to 100, 980 rounds to 1000, and 248 rounds to 200.
3. Remember, when rounding to the nearest thousand, anything ending in 500 or greater rounds up. So, 302 rounds to 0, 1274 rounds to 1000, and 3756 rounds to 4000.

When you are asked to estimate the solution a problem, you will need to provide only an approximate figure or **estimation** for your answer. In this situation, you will need to round each number in the calculation to the level indicated (nearest hundred, nearest thousand, etc.) or to a level that makes sense for the numbers involved. When estimating a sum **all numbers must be rounded to the same level**. You cannot round one number to the nearest thousand while rounding another to the nearest hundred.

EXAMPLE 2

Estimate the solution to 345,932 + 96,369 by rounding each number to the nearest ten thousand.

Start by rounding each number to the nearest ten thousand: 345,932 becomes 350,000, and 96,369 becomes 100,000.

Then, add the rounded numbers: 350,000 + 100,000 = 450,000. So, the answer is approximately 450,000.

The exact answer would be 345,932 + 96,369 = 442,301. So, the estimate of 450,000 is a similar value to the exact answer.

EXAMPLE 3

A runner's heart beats 422 times over the course of six minutes. About how many times did the runner's heart beat during each minute?

"About how many" indicates that you need to estimate the solution. In this case, look at the numbers you are given. 422 can be rounded down to 420, which is easily divisible by 6. A good estimate is $420 \div 6 = 70$ beats per minute. More accurately, the patient's heart rate was just over 70 beats per minute since his heart actually beat a little more than 420 times in six minutes.

> **Review Video: Rounding and Estimation**
> Visit mometrix.com/academy and enter code: 126243

MEASUREMENT CONVERSION

When going from a larger unit to a smaller unit, multiply the number of the known amount by the **equivalent amount**. When going from a smaller unit to a larger unit, divide the number of the known amount by the equivalent amount.

Also, you can set up conversion fractions. In these fractions, one fraction is the **conversion factor**. The other fraction has the unknown amount in the numerator. So, the known value is placed in the denominator. Sometimes the second fraction has the known value from the problem in the numerator, and the unknown in the denominator. Multiply the two fractions to get the converted measurement.

ꞮN UNITS

ꞱNVERSIONS

ᴊ0 mcg (microgram)	1 mg
ᴔ00 mg (milligram)	1 g
ᴊ000 g (gram)	1 kg
1000 kg (kilogram)	1 metric ton
1000 mL (milliliter)	1 L
1000 um (micrometer)	1 mm
1000 mm (millimeter)	1 m
100 cm (centimeter)	1 m
1000 m (meter)	1 km

U.S. AND METRIC EQUIVALENTS

Unit	U.S. equivalent	Metric equivalent
Inch	1 inch	2.54 centimeters
Foot	12 inches	0.305 meters
Yard	3 feet	0.914 meters
Mile	5280 feet	1.609 kilometers

CAPACITY MEASUREMENTS

Unit	U.S. equivalent	Metric equivalent
Ounce	8 drams	29.573 milliliters
Cup	8 ounces	0.237 liter
Pint	16 ounces	0.473 liter
Quart	2 pints	0.946 liter
Gallon	4 quarts	3.785 liters

WEIGHT MEASUREMENTS

Unit	U.S. equivalent	Metric equivalent
Ounce	16 drams	28.35 grams
Pound	16 ounces	453.6 grams
Ton	2,000 pounds	907.2 kilograms

FLUID MEASUREMENTS

Unit	English equivalent	Metric equivalent
1 tsp	1 fluid dram	5 milliliters
3 tsp	4 fluid drams	15 or 16 milliliters
2 tbsp	1 fluid ounce	30 milliliters
1 glass	8 fluid ounces	240 milliliters

MEASUREMENT CONVERSION PRACTICE PROBLEMS

EXAMPLE 1

a. Convert 1.4 meters to centimeters.
b. Convert 218 centimeters to meters.

EXAMPLE 2

a. Convert 42 inches to feet.
b. Convert 15 feet to yards.

EXAMPLE 3

a. How many pounds are in 15 kilograms?
b. How many pounds are in 80 ounces?

EXAMPLE 4

a. How many kilometers are in 2 miles?
b. How many centimeters are in 5 feet?

EXAMPLE 5

a. How many gallons are in 15.14 liters?
b. How many liters are in 8 quarts?

EXAMPLE 6

a. How many grams are in 13.2 pounds?
b. How many pints are in 9 gallons?

MEASUREMENT CONVERSION PRACTICE SOLUTIONS

EXAMPLE 1

Write ratios with the conversion factor $\frac{100 \text{ cm}}{1 \text{ m}}$. Use proportions to convert the given units.

a. $\frac{100 \text{ cm}}{1 \text{ m}} = \frac{x \text{ cm}}{1.4 \text{ m}}$. Cross multiply to get $x = 140$. So, 1.4 m is the same as 140 cm.

b. $\frac{100 \text{ cm}}{1 \text{ m}} = \frac{218 \text{ cm}}{x \text{ m}}$. Cross multiply to get $100x = 218$, or $x = 2.18$. So, 218 cm is the same as 2.18 m.

EXAMPLE 2

Write ratios with the conversion factors $\frac{12 \text{ in}}{1 \text{ ft}}$ and $\frac{3 \text{ ft}}{1 \text{ yd}}$. Use proportions to convert the given units.

a. $\frac{12 \text{ in}}{1 \text{ ft}} = \frac{42 \text{ in}}{x \text{ ft}}$. Cross multiply to get $12x = 42$, or $x = 3.5$. So, 42 inches is the same as 3.5 feet.

b. $\frac{3 \text{ ft}}{1 \text{ yd}} = \frac{15 \text{ ft}}{x \text{ yd}}$. Cross multiply to get $3x = 15$, or $x = 5$. So, 15 feet is the same as 5 yards.

EXAMPLE 3

a. 15 kilograms $\times \frac{2.2 \text{ pounds}}{1 \text{ kilogram}} = 33$ pounds

b. 80 ounces $\times \frac{1 \text{ pound}}{16 \text{ ounces}} = 5$ pounds

EXAMPLE 4

a. 2 miles $\times \frac{1.609 \text{ kilometers}}{1 \text{ mile}} = 3.218$ kilometers

b. 5 feet $\times \frac{12 \text{ inches}}{1 \text{ foot}} \times \frac{2.54 \text{ centimeters}}{1 \text{ inch}} = 152.4$ centimeters

43

EXAMPLE 5

a. 15.14 liters $\times \frac{1 \text{ gallon}}{3.785 \text{ liters}} = 4$ gallons

b. 8 quarts $\times \frac{1 \text{ gallon}}{4 \text{ quarts}} \times \frac{3.785 \text{ liters}}{1 \text{ gallon}} = 7.57$ liters

EXAMPLE 6

a. 13.2 pounds $\times \frac{1 \text{ kilogram}}{2.2 \text{ pounds}} \times \frac{1000 \text{ grams}}{1 \text{ kilogram}} = 6000$ grams

b. 9 gallons $\times \frac{4 \text{ quarts}}{1 \text{ gallon}} \times \frac{2 \text{ pints}}{1 \text{ quarts}} = 72$ pints

OPERATIONS

There are four basic mathematical operations:

ADDITION AND SUBTRACTION

Addition increases the value of one quantity by the value of another quantity. Example: $2 + 4 = 6$; $8 + 9 = 17$. The result is called the **sum**. With addition, the order does not matter. $4 + 2 = 2 + 4$.

Subtraction is the opposite operation to addition; it decreases the value of one quantity by the value of another quantity. Example: $6 - 4 = 2$; $17 - 8 = 9$. The result is called the **difference**. Note that with subtraction, the order does matter. $6 - 4 \neq 4 - 6$.

> **Review Video: Addition and Subtraction**
> Visit mometrix.com/academy and enter code: 521157

MULTIPLICATION AND DIVISION

Multiplication can be thought of as repeated addition. One number tells how many times to add the other number to itself. Example: 3×2 (three times two) $= 2 + 2 + 2 = 6$. With multiplication, the order does not matter. $2 \times 3 = 3 \times 2$ or $3 + 3 = 2 + 2 + 2$.

Division is the opposite operation to multiplication; one number tells us how many parts to divide the other number into. Example: $20 \div 4 = 5$; if 20 is split into 4 equal parts, each part is 5. With division, the order of the numbers does matter. $20 \div 4 \neq 4 \div 20$.

> **Review Video: Multiplication and Division**
> Visit mometrix.com/academy and enter code: 643326

ORDER OF OPERATIONS

Order of operations is a set of rules that dictates the order in which we must perform each operation in an expression so that we will evaluate it accurately. If we have an expression that includes multiple different operations, order of operations tells us which operations to do first. The most common mnemonic for order of operations is **PEMDAS**, or "Please Excuse My Dear Aunt Sally." PEMDAS stands for parentheses, exponents, multiplication, division, addition, and subtraction. It is important to understand that multiplication and division have equal precedence, as do addition and subtraction, so those pairs of operations are simply worked from left to right in order.

44

Example: Evaluate the expression $5 + 20 \div 4 \times (2 + 3) - 6$ using the correct order of operations.

- **P:** Perform the operations inside the parentheses: $(2 + 3) = 5$
- **E:** Simplify the exponents.
  - The equation now looks like this: $5 + 20 \div 4 \times 5 - 6$
- **MD:** Perform multiplication and division from left to right: $20 \div 4 = 5$; then $5 \times 5 = 25$
  - The equation now looks like this: $5 + 25 - 6$
- **AS:** Perform addition and subtraction from left to right: $5 + 25 = 30$; then $30 - 6 = 24$

Review Video: <u>Order of Operations</u>
Visit mometrix.com/academy and enter code: 259675

SUBTRACTION WITH REGROUPING

EXAMPLE 1

Demonstrate how to subtract 189 from 525 using regrouping.

First, set up the subtraction problem:

$$
\begin{array}{r}
525 \\
-\ 189 \\
\end{array}
$$

Notice that the numbers in the ones and tens columns of 525 are smaller than the numbers in the ones and tens columns of 189. This means you will need to use regrouping to perform subtraction:

$$
\begin{array}{rccc}
 & 5 & 2 & 5 \\
- & 1 & 8 & 9 \\
\hline
\end{array}
$$

To subtract 9 from 5 in the ones column you will need to borrow from the 2 in the tens columns:

$$
\begin{array}{rccc}
 & 5 & 1 & 15 \\
- & 1 & 8 & 9 \\
\hline
 & & & 6 \\
\end{array}
$$

Next, to subtract 8 from 1 in the tens column you will need to borrow from the 5 in the hundreds column:

$$
\begin{array}{rccc}
 & 4 & 11 & 15 \\
- & 1 & 8 & 9 \\
\hline
 & & 3 & 6 \\
\end{array}
$$

Last, subtract the 1 from the 4 in the hundreds column:

$$
\begin{array}{rccc}
 & 4 & 11 & 15 \\
- & 1 & 8 & 9 \\
\hline
 & 3 & 3 & 6 \\
\end{array}
$$

EXAMPLE 2

Demonstrate how to subtract 477 from 620 using regrouping.

First, set up the subtraction problem:

$$
\begin{array}{r}
620 \\
-\ 477 \\
\hline
\end{array}
$$

Notice that the numbers in the ones and tens columns of 620 are smaller than the numbers in the ones and tens columns of 477. This means you will need to use regrouping to perform subtraction:

$$
\begin{array}{ccc}
6 & 2 & 0 \\
-\ 4 & 7 & 7 \\
\hline
\end{array}
$$

To subtract 7 from 0 in the ones column you will need to borrow from the 2 in the tens column:

$$
\begin{array}{ccc}
6 & 1 & 10 \\
-\ 4 & 7 & 7 \\
\hline
 & & 3 \\
\end{array}
$$

Next, to subtract 7 from the 1 that's still in the tens column you will need to borrow from the 6 in the hundreds column:

$$
\begin{array}{ccc}
5 & 11 & 10 \\
-\ 4 & 7 & 7 \\
\hline
 & 4 & 3 \\
\end{array}
$$

Lastly, subtract 4 from the 5 remaining in the hundreds column:

$$
\begin{array}{ccc}
5 & 11 & 10 \\
-\ 4 & 7 & 7 \\
\hline
1 & 4 & 3 \\
\end{array}
$$

REAL WORLD ONE OR MULTI-STEP PROBLEMS WITH RATIONAL NUMBERS

EXAMPLE 1

A woman's age is thirteen more than half of 60. How old is the woman?

"More than" indicates addition, and "of" indicates multiplication. The expression can be written as $\frac{1}{2}(60) + 13$. So, the woman's age is equal to $\frac{1}{2}(60) + 13 = 30 + 13 = 43$. The woman is 43 years old.

EXAMPLE 2

A patient was given pain medicine at a dosage of 0.22 grams. The patient's dosage was then increased to 0.80 grams. By how much was the patient's dosage increased?

The first step is to determine what operation (addition, subtraction, multiplication, or division) the problem requires. Notice the keywords and phrases "by how much" and "increased." "Increased" means that you go from a smaller amount to a larger amount. This change can be found by subtracting the smaller amount from the larger amount: 0.80 grams– 0.22 grams = 0.58 grams.

Remember to line up the decimal when subtracting:

$$
\begin{array}{r}
0.80 \\
- \ 0.22 \\
\hline
0.58
\end{array}
$$

EXAMPLE 3

At a hotel, $\frac{3}{4}$ of the 100 rooms are occupied today. Yesterday, $\frac{4}{5}$ of the 100 rooms were occupied. On which day were more of the rooms occupied and by how much more?

First, find the number of rooms occupied each day. To do so, multiply the fraction of rooms occupied by the number of rooms available:

$$\text{Number occupied} = \text{Fraction occupied} \times \text{Total number}$$

Today:

$$\text{Number of rooms occupied today} = \frac{3}{4} \times 100 = 75$$

Today, 75 rooms are occupied.

Yesterday:

$$\text{Number of rooms occupied} = \frac{4}{5} \times 100 = 80$$

Yesterday, 80 rooms were occupied.

The difference in the number of rooms occupied is

$$80 - 75 = 5 \text{ rooms}$$

Therefore, five more rooms were occupied yesterday than today.

> **Review Video: Rational Numbers**
> Visit mometrix.com/academy and enter code: 280645

EXAMPLE 4

At a school, 40% of the teachers teach English. If 20 teachers teach English, how many teachers work at the school?

To answer this problem, first think about the number of teachers that work at the school. Will it be more or less than the number of teachers who work in a specific department such as English? More teachers work at the school, so the number you find to answer this question will be greater than 20.

40% of the teachers are English teachers. "Of" indicates multiplication, and words like "is" and "are" indicate equivalence. Translating the problem into a mathematical sentence gives $40\% \times t = 20$, where t represents the total number of teachers. Solving for t gives $t = \frac{20}{40\%} = \frac{20}{0.40} = 50$. Fifty teachers work at the school.

EXAMPLE 5

A patient was given blood pressure medicine at a dosage of 2 grams. The patient's dosage was then decreased to 0.45 grams. By how much was the patient's dosage decreased?

The decrease is represented by the difference between the two amounts:

$$2 \text{ grams} - 0.45 \text{ grams} = 1.55 \text{ grams}.$$

Remember to line up the decimal point before subtracting.

$$
\begin{array}{r}
2.00 \\
- \quad 0.45 \\
\hline
1.55
\end{array}
$$

EXAMPLE 6

Two weeks ago, $\frac{2}{3}$ of the 60 customers at a skate shop were male. Last week, $\frac{3}{6}$ of the 80 customers were male. During which week were there more male customers?

First, you need to find the number of male customers that were in the skate shop each week. You are given this amount in terms of fractions. To find the actual number of male customers, multiply the fraction of male customers by the number of customers in the store.

Actual number of male customers = fraction of male customers × total number of customers.

Number of male customers two weeks ago $= \frac{2}{3} \times 60 = \frac{120}{3} = 40$.

Number of male customers last week $= \frac{3}{6} \times 80 = \frac{1}{2} \times 80 = \frac{80}{2} = 40$.

The number of male customers was the same both weeks.

EXAMPLE 7

Jane ate lunch at a local restaurant. She ordered a $4.99 appetizer, a $12.50 entrée, and a $1.25 soda. If she wants to tip her server 20%, how much money will she spend in all?

To find total amount, first find the sum of the items she ordered from the menu and then add 20% of this sum to the total.

$$\$4.99 + \$12.50 + \$1.25 = \$18.74$$
$$\$18.74 \times 20\% = (0.20)(\$18.74) = \$3.748 \approx \$3.75$$
$$\text{Total} = \$18.74 + \$3.75 = \$22.49.$$

Another way to find this sum is to multiply 120% by the cost of the meal.

$$\$18.74(120\%) = \$18.74(1.20) = \$22.49.$$

PARENTHESES

Parentheses are used to designate which operations should be done first when there are multiple operations. Example: $4 - (2 + 1) = 1$; the parentheses tell us that we must add 2 and 1, and then subtract the sum from 4, rather than subtracting 2 from 4 and then adding 1 (this would give us an answer of 3).

EXPONENTS

An **exponent** is a superscript number placed next to another number at the top right. It indicates how many times the base number is to be multiplied by itself. Exponents provide a shorthand way to write what would be a longer mathematical expression. Example: $a^2 = a \times a$; $2^4 = 2 \times 2 \times 2 \times 2$. A number with an exponent of 2 is said to be "squared," while a number with an exponent of 3 is said to be "cubed." The value of a number raised to an exponent is called its power. So, 8^4 is read as "8 to the 4th power," or "8 raised to the power of 4." A negative exponent is the same as the **reciprocal** of a positive exponent. Example: $a^{-2} = \frac{1}{a^2}$.

ROOTS

A **root**, such as a square root, is another way of writing a fractional exponent. Instead of using a superscript, roots use the radical symbol ($\sqrt{}$) to indicate the operation. A radical will have a number underneath the bar, and may sometimes have a number in the upper left: $\sqrt[n]{a}$, read as "the nth root of a." The relationship between radical notation and exponent notation can be described by this equation: $\sqrt[n]{a} = a^{\frac{1}{n}}$. The two special cases of $n = 2$ and $n = 3$ are called square roots and cube roots. If there is no number to the upper left, it is understood to be a square root ($n = 2$). Nearly all of the roots you encounter will be square roots. A square root is the same as a number raised to the one-half power. When we say that a is the square root of b ($a = \sqrt{b}$), we mean that a multiplied by itself equals b: ($a \times a = b$).

A **perfect square** is a number that has an integer for its square root. There are 10 perfect squares from 1 to 100: 1, 4, 9, 16, 25, 36, 49, 64, 81, 100 (the squares of integers 1 through 10).

ABSOLUTE VALUE

A precursor to working with negative numbers is understanding what **absolute values** are. A number's absolute value is simply the distance away from zero a number is on the number line. The absolute value of a number is always positive and is written $|x|$.

EXAMPLE

Show that $|3| = |-3|$.

The absolute value of 3, written as $|3|$, is 3 because the distance between 0 and 3 on a number line is three units. Likewise, the absolute value of –3, written as $|-3|$, is 3 because the distance between 0 and –3 on a number line is three units. So, $|3| = |-3|$.

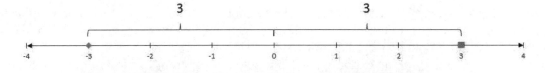

Review Video: Absolute Value
Visit mometrix.com/academy and enter code: 314669

OPERATIONS WITH POSITIVE AND NEGATIVE NUMBERS

ADDITION

When adding signed numbers, if the signs are the same simply add the absolute values of the addends and apply the original sign to the sum. For example, $(+4) + (+8) = +12$ and $(-4) + (-8) = -12$. When the original signs are different, take the absolute values of the addends and subtract the smaller value from the larger value, then apply the original sign of the larger value to the difference. For instance, $(+4) + (-8) = -4$ and $(-4) + (+8) = +4$.

SUBTRACTION

For subtracting signed numbers, change the sign of the number after the minus symbol and then follow the same rules used for addition. For example, $(+4) - (+8) = (+4) + (-8) = -4$.

MULTIPLICATION

If the signs are the same the product is positive when multiplying signed numbers. For example, $(+4) \times (+8) = +32$ and $(-4) \times (-8) = +32$. If the signs are opposite, the product is negative. For example, $(+4) \times (-8) = -32$ and $(-4) \times (+8) = -32$. When more than two factors are multiplied together, the sign of the product is determined by how many negative factors are present. If there are an odd number of negative factors then the product is negative, whereas an even number of negative factors indicates a positive product. For instance, $(+4) \times (-8) \times (-2) = +64$ and $(-4) \times (-8) \times (-2) = -64$.

DIVISION

The rules for dividing signed numbers are similar to multiplying signed numbers. If the dividend and divisor have the same sign, the quotient is positive. If the dividend and divisor have opposite signs, the quotient is negative. For example, $(-4) \div (+8) = -0.5$.

THE NUMBER LINE

A number line is a graph to see the distance between numbers. Basically, this graph shows the relationship between numbers. So, a number line may have a point for zero and may show negative numbers on the left side of the line. Also, any positive numbers are placed on the right side of the line.

EXAMPLE

Name each point on the number line below:

Use the dashed lines on the number line to identify each point. Each dashed line between two whole numbers is $\frac{1}{4}$. The line halfway between two numbers is $\frac{1}{2}$.

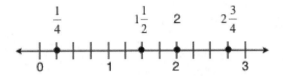

Fractions, Decimals, and Percentages

FRACTIONS

A **fraction** is a number that is expressed as one integer written above another integer, with a dividing line between them $\left(\frac{x}{y}\right)$. It represents the **quotient** of the two numbers "x divided by y." It can also be thought of as x out of y equal parts.

The top number of a fraction is called the **numerator**, and it represents the number of parts under consideration. The 1 in $\frac{1}{4}$ means that 1 part out of the whole is being considered in the calculation. The bottom number of a fraction is called the **denominator**, and it represents the total number of equal parts. The 4 in $\frac{1}{4}$ means that the whole consists of 4 equal parts. A fraction cannot have a denominator of zero; this is referred to as "*undefined*."

Fractions can be manipulated, without changing the value of the fraction, by multiplying or dividing (but not adding or subtracting) both the numerator and denominator by the same number. If you divide both numbers by a common factor, you are **reducing** or simplifying the fraction. Two fractions that have the same value but are expressed differently are known as **equivalent fractions**. For example, $\frac{2}{10}, \frac{3}{15}, \frac{4}{20}$, and $\frac{5}{25}$ are all equivalent fractions. They can also all be reduced or simplified to $\frac{1}{5}$.

When two fractions are manipulated so that they have the same denominator, this is known as finding a **common denominator**. The number chosen to be that common denominator should be the least common multiple of the two original denominators. Example: $\frac{3}{4}$ and $\frac{5}{6}$; the least common multiple of 4 and 6 is 12. Manipulating to achieve the common denominator: $\frac{3}{4} = \frac{9}{12}; \frac{5}{6} = \frac{10}{12}$.

PROPER FRACTIONS AND MIXED NUMBERS

A fraction whose denominator is greater than its numerator is known as a **proper fraction**, while a fraction whose numerator is greater than its denominator is known as an **improper fraction**. Proper fractions have values *less than one* and improper fractions have values *greater than one*.

A **mixed number** is a number that contains both an integer and a fraction. Any improper fraction can be rewritten as a mixed number. Example: $\frac{8}{3} = \frac{6}{3} + \frac{2}{3} = 2 + \frac{2}{3} = 2\frac{2}{3}$. Similarly, any mixed number can be rewritten as an improper fraction. Example: $1\frac{3}{5} = 1 + \frac{3}{5} = \frac{5}{5} + \frac{3}{5} = \frac{8}{5}$.

> **Review Video: Proper and Improper Fractions and Mixed Numbers**
> Visit mometrix.com/academy and enter code: 211077
>
> **Review Video: Fractions**
> Visit mometrix.com/academy and enter code: 262335

DECIMALS

DECIMAL ILLUSTRATION

<u>USE A MODEL TO REPRESENT THE DECIMAL: 0.24. WRITE 0.24 AS A FRACTION.</u>

The decimal 0.24 is twenty-four hundredths. One possible model to represent this fraction is to draw 100 pennies, since each penny is worth one-hundredth of a dollar. Draw one hundred circles to represent one hundred pennies. Shade 24 of the pennies to represent the decimal twenty-four hundredths.

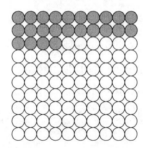

To write the decimal as a fraction, write a fraction: $\frac{\text{\# shaded spaces}}{\text{\# total spaces}}$. The number of shaded spaces is 24, and the total number of spaces is 100, so as a fraction 0.24 equals $\frac{24}{100}$. This fraction can then be reduced to $\frac{6}{25}$.

> **Review Video: Decimals**
> Visit mometrix.com/academy and enter code: 837268

PERCENTAGES

Percentages can be thought of as fractions that are based on a whole of 100; that is, one whole is equal to 100%. The word **percent** means "per hundred." Fractions can be expressed as a percentage by finding equivalent fractions with a denomination of 100. Example: $\frac{7}{10} = \frac{70}{100} = 70\%$; $\frac{1}{4} = \frac{25}{100} = 25\%$.

To express a *percentage as a fraction*, divide the percentage number by 100 and reduce the fraction to its simplest possible terms. Example: $60\% = \frac{60}{100} = \frac{3}{5}$; $96\% = \frac{96}{100} = \frac{24}{25}$.

REAL WORLD PROBLEMS WITH PERCENTAGES

A percentage problem can be presented three main ways: (1) Find what percentage of some number another number is. Example: What percentage of 40 is 8? (2) Find what number is some percentage of a given number. Example: What number is 20% of 40? (3) Find what number another number is a given percentage of. Example: What number is 8 20% of?

The three components in all of these cases are the same: a **whole** (W), a **part** (P), and a **percentage** (%). These are related by the equation: $P = W \times \%$. This is the form of the equation you would use to solve problems of type (2). To solve types (1) and (3), you would use these two forms:

$$\% = \frac{P}{W} \text{ and } W = \frac{P}{\%}$$

The thing that frequently makes percentage problems difficult is that they are most often also word problems, so a large part of solving them is figuring out which quantities are what. Example: In a school cafeteria, 7 students choose pizza, 9 choose hamburgers, and 4 choose tacos. Find the percentage that chooses tacos. To find the whole, you must first add all of the parts: $7 + 9 + 4 = 20$. The percentage can then be found by dividing the part by the whole ($\% = \frac{P}{W}$): $\frac{4}{20} = \frac{20}{100} = 20\%$.

EXAMPLE 1

What is 30% of 120?

The word *of* indicates multiplication, so 30% of 120 is found by multiplying 120 by 30%. Change 30% to a fraction or decimal, then multiply:

$$30\% = \frac{30}{100} = 0.3$$

$$120 \times 0.3 = 36$$

EXAMPLE 2

What is 150% of 20?

The word *of* indicates multiplication, so 150% of 20 is found by multiplying 20 by 150%. Change 150% to a fraction or decimal, then multiply:

$$150\% = \frac{150}{100} = 1.5$$

$$20 \times 1.5 = 30$$

Notice that 30 is greater than the original number of 20. This makes sense because you are finding a number that is more than 100% of the original number.

EXAMPLE 3

What is 14.5% of 96?

Change 14.5% to a decimal before multiplying. $0.145 \times 96 = 13.92$. Notice that 13.92 is much smaller than the original number of 96. This makes sense because you are finding a small percentage of the original number.

EXAMPLE 4

According to a survey, about 82% of engineers were highly satisfied with their job. If 145 engineers were surveyed, how many reported that they were highly satisfied?

$$82\% \text{ of } 145 = 0.82 \times 145 = 118.9$$

Because you can't have 0.9 of a person, we must round up to say that 119 engineers reported that they were highly satisfied with their jobs.

EXAMPLE 5

On Monday, Lucy spent 5 hours observing sales, 3 hours working on advertising, and 4 hours doing paperwork. On Tuesday, she spent 4 hours observing sales, 6 hours working on advertising, and 2 hours doing paperwork. What was the percent change for time spent on each task between the two days?

The three tasks are observing sales, working on advertising, and doing paperwork. To find the amount of change, compare the first amount with the second amount for each task. Then, write this difference as a percentage compared to the initial amount.

Amount of change for observing sales:

$$5 \text{ hours} - 4 \text{ hours} = 1 \text{ hour}$$

The percent of change is

$$\frac{\text{amount of change}}{\text{original amount}} \times 100\%. \frac{1 \text{ hour}}{5 \text{ hours}} \times 100\% = 20\%.$$

Lucy spent 20% less time observing sales on Tuesday than she did on Monday.

Amount of change for working on advertising:

$$6 \text{ hours} - 3 \text{ hours} = 3 \text{ hours}$$

The percent of change is

$$\frac{\text{amount of change}}{\text{original amount}} \times 100\%. \frac{3 \text{ hours}}{3 \text{ hours}} \times 100\% = 100\%.$$

Lucy spent 100% more time (or twice as much time) working on advertising on Tuesday than she did on Monday.

Amount of change for doing paperwork:

$$4 \text{ hours} - 2 \text{ hours} = 2 \text{ hours}$$

The percent of change is

$$\frac{\text{amount of change}}{\text{original amount}} \times 100\%. \frac{2 \text{ hours}}{4 \text{ hours}} \times 100\% = 50\%.$$

Lucy spent 50% less time (or half as much time) working on paperwork on Tuesday than she did on Monday.

EXAMPLE 6

A patient was given 40 mg of a certain medicine. Later, the patient's dosage was increased to 45 mg. What was the percent increase in his medication?

To find the percent increase, first compare the original and increased amounts. The original amount was 40 mg, and the increased amount is 45 mg, so the dosage of medication was increased by 5 mg (45– 40 = 5). Note, however, that the question asks not by how much the dosage increased but by what percentage it increased. Percent increase $= \frac{\text{new amount} - \text{original amount}}{\text{original amount}} \times 100\%$.

$$\frac{45 \text{ mg} - 40 \text{ mg}}{40 \text{ mg}} \times 100\% = \frac{5}{40} \times 100\% = 0.125 \times 100\% = 12.5\%$$

The percent increase is 12.5%.

EXAMPLE 7

A patient was given 100 mg of a certain medicine. The patient's dosage was later decreased to 88 mg. What was the percent decrease?

The medication was decreased by 12 mg:

$$(100 \text{ mg} - 88 \text{ mg} = 12 \text{ mg})$$

To find by what percent the medication was decreased, this change must be written as a percentage when compared to the original amount.

In other words, $\frac{\text{new amount} - \text{original amount}}{\text{original amount}} \times 100\% = \text{percent change}$

So $\frac{12 \text{ mg}}{100 \text{ mg}} \times 100\% = 0.12 \times 100\% = 12\%$.

The percent decrease is 12%.

EXAMPLE 8

A barista used 125 units of coffee grounds to make a liter of coffee. The barista later reduced the amount of coffee to 100 units. By what percentage was the amount of coffee grounds reduced?

In this problem you must determine which information is necessary to answer the question. The question asks by what percentage the coffee grounds were reduced. Find the two amounts and perform subtraction to find their difference. The first pot of coffee used 125 units. The second time, the barista used 100 units. Therefore, the difference is 125 units − 100 units = 25 units. The percentage reduction can then be calculated as:

$$\frac{\text{change}}{\text{original}} = \frac{25}{125} = \frac{1}{5} = 20\%$$

EXAMPLE 9

In a performance review, an employee received a score of 70 for efficiency and 90 for meeting project deadlines. Six months later, the employee received a score of 65 for efficiency and 96 for meeting project deadlines. What was the percent change for each score on the performance review?

To find the percent change, compare the first amount with the second amount for each score; then, write this difference as a percentage of the initial amount.

Percent change for efficiency score:

$$70 - 65 = 5; \quad \frac{5}{70} \approx 7.1\%$$

The employee's efficiency decreased by about 7.1%.

Percent change for meeting project deadlines score:

$$96 - 90 = 6; \quad \frac{6}{90} \approx 6.7\%$$

The employee increased his ability to meet project deadlines by about 6.7%.

SIMPLIFY

EXAMPLE 1

Simplify the following expression:

$$\frac{\frac{2}{5}}{\frac{4}{7}}$$

Dividing a fraction by a fraction may appear tricky, but it's not if you write out your steps carefully. Follow these steps to divide a fraction by a fraction.

Step 1: Rewrite the problem as a multiplication problem. Dividing by a fraction is the same as multiplying by its **reciprocal**, also known as its **multiplicative inverse**. The product of a number and its reciprocal is 1. Because $\frac{4}{7}$ times $\frac{7}{4}$ is 1, these numbers are reciprocals. Note that reciprocals can be found by simply interchanging the numerators and denominators. So, rewriting the problem as a multiplication problem gives $\frac{2}{5} \times \frac{7}{4}$.

Step 2: Perform multiplication of the fractions by multiplying the numerators by each other and the denominators by each other. In other words, multiply across the top and then multiply across the bottom.

$$\frac{2}{5} \times \frac{7}{4} = \frac{2 \times 7}{5 \times 4} = \frac{14}{20}$$

Step 3: Make sure the fraction is reduced to lowest terms. Both 14 and 20 can be divided by 2.

$$\frac{14}{20} = \frac{14 \div 2}{20 \div 2} = \frac{7}{10}$$

The answer is $\frac{7}{10}$.

EXAMPLE 2

Simplify the following expression:

$$\frac{1}{4} + \frac{3}{6}$$

Fractions with common denominators can be easily added or subtracted. Recall that the denominator is the bottom number in the fraction and that the numerator is the top number in the fraction.

The denominators of $\frac{1}{4}$ and $\frac{3}{6}$ are 4 and 6, respectively. The lowest common denominator of 4 and 6 is 12 because 12 is the least common multiple of 4 (multiples 4, 8, 12, 16, …) and 6 (multiples 6, 12, 18, 24, …). Convert each fraction to its equivalent with the newly found common denominator of 12.

$$\frac{1 \times 3}{4 \times 3} = \frac{3}{12}; \frac{3 \times 2}{6 \times 2} = \frac{6}{12}$$

Now that the fractions have the same denominator, you can add them.

$$\frac{3}{12} + \frac{6}{12} = \frac{9}{12}$$

Be sure to write your answer in lowest terms. Both 9 and 12 can be divided by 3, so the answer is $\frac{3}{4}$.

EXAMPLE 3

Simplify the following expression:

$$\frac{7}{8} - \frac{8}{16}$$

The denominators of $\frac{7}{8}$ and $\frac{8}{16}$ are 8 and 16, respectively. The lowest common denominator of 8 and 16 is 16 because 16 is the least common multiple of 8 (multiples 8, 16, 24 …) and 16 (multiples 16, 32, 48, …). Convert each fraction to its equivalent with the newly found common denominator of 16.

$$\frac{7 \times 2}{8 \times 2} = \frac{14}{16}; \frac{8 \times 1}{16 \times 1} = \frac{8}{16}$$

Now that the fractions have the same denominator, you can subtract them.

$$\frac{14}{16} - \frac{8}{16} = \frac{6}{16}$$

Be sure to write your answer in lowest terms. Both 6 and 16 can be divided by 2, so the answer is $\frac{3}{8}$.

EXAMPLE 4

Simplify the following expression:

$$\frac{1}{2} + \left(3\left(\frac{3}{4}\right) - 2\right) + 4$$

When simplifying expressions, first perform operations within groups. Within the set of parentheses are multiplication and subtraction operations. Perform the multiplication first to get $\frac{1}{2} + \left(\frac{9}{4} - 2\right) + 4$. Then, subtract two to obtain $\frac{1}{2} + \frac{1}{4} + 4$. Finally, perform addition from left to right:

$$\frac{1}{2} + \frac{1}{4} + 4 = \frac{2}{4} + \frac{1}{4} + \frac{16}{4} = \frac{19}{4}$$

EXAMPLE 5

Simplify the following expression:

$$0.22 + 0.5 - (5.5 + 3.3 \div 3)$$

First, evaluate the terms in the parentheses $(5.5 + 3.3 \div 3)$ using order of operations. $3.3 \div 3 = 1.1$, and $5.5 + 1.1 = 6.6$.

Next, rewrite the problem: $0.22 + 0.5 - 6.6$.

Finally, add and subtract from left to right: $0.22 + 0.5 = 0.72$; $0.72 - 6.6 = -5.88$. The answer is -5.88.

EXAMPLE 6

Simplify the following expression:

$$\frac{3}{2} + (4(0.5) - 0.75) + 2$$

First, simplify within the parentheses:

$$\frac{3}{2} + (2 - 0.75) + 2 =$$
$$\frac{3}{2} + 1.25 + 2$$

Finally, change the fraction to a decimal and perform addition from left to right:

$$1.5 + 1.25 + 2 = 4.75$$

EXAMPLE 7

Simplify the following expression:

$$1.45 + 1.5 + (6 - 9 \div 2) + 45$$

First, evaluate the terms in the parentheses using proper order of operations.

$$1.45 + 1.5 + (6 - 4.5) + 45$$
$$1.45 + 1.5 + 1.5 + 45$$

Finally, add from left to right.

$$1.45 + 1.5 + 1.5 + 45 = 49.45$$

CONVERTING PERCENTAGES, FRACTIONS, AND DECIMALS

Converting decimals to percentages and percentages to decimals is as simple as moving the decimal point. To *convert from a decimal to a percentage*, move the decimal point **two places to the right**. To *convert from a percentage to a decimal*, move it **two places to the left**. Example: 0.23 = 23%; 5.34 = 534%; 0.007 = 0.7%; 700% 7.00; 86% = 0.86; 0.15% = 0.0015.

It may be helpful to remember that the percentage number will always be larger than the equivalent decimal number.

> **Review Video: Converting Decimals to Fractions and Percentages**
> Visit mometrix.com/academy and enter code: 986765

EXAMPLE 1

Convert 15% to both a fraction and a decimal.

First, write the percentage over 100 because percent means "per one hundred." So, 15% can be written as $\frac{15}{100}$. Fractions should be written in the simplest form, which means that the numbers in the numerator and denominator should be reduced if possible. Both 15 and 100 can be divided by 5:

$$\frac{15 \div 5}{100 \div 5} = \frac{3}{20}$$

As before, write the percentage over 100 because percent means "per one hundred." So, 15% can be written as $\frac{15}{100}$. Dividing a number by a power of ten (10, 100, 1000, etc.) is the same as moving the decimal point to the left by the same number of spaces that there are zeros in the divisor. Since 100 has 2 zeros, move the decimal point two places to the left:

$$15\% = 0.15$$

In other words, when converting from a percentage to a decimal, drop the percent sign and move the decimal point two places to the left.

EXAMPLE 2

Write 24.36% as a fraction and then as a decimal. Explain how you made these conversions.

24.36% written as a fraction is $\frac{24.36}{100}$, or $\frac{2436}{10,000}$, which reduces to $\frac{609}{2500}$. 24.36% written as a decimal is 0.2436. Recall that dividing by 100 moves the decimal two places to the left.

> **Review Video: Converting Percentages to Decimals and Fractions**
> Visit mometrix.com/academy and enter code: 287297

EXAMPLE 3

Convert $\frac{4}{5}$ to a decimal and to a percentage.

To convert a fraction to a decimal, simply divide the numerator by the denominator in the fraction. The numerator is the top number in the fraction and the denominator is the bottom number in a fraction.

$$\frac{4}{5} = 4 \div 5 = 0.80 = 0.8$$

Percent means "per hundred."

$$\frac{4 \times 20}{5 \times 20} = \frac{80}{100} = 80\%$$

EXAMPLE 4

Convert $3\frac{2}{5}$ to a decimal and to a percentage.

The mixed number $3\frac{2}{5}$ has a whole number and a fractional part. The fractional part $\frac{2}{5}$ can be written as a decimal by dividing 5 into 2, which gives 0.4. Adding the whole to the part gives 3.4. Alternatively, note that $3\frac{2}{5} = 3\frac{4}{10} = 3.4$

To change a decimal to a percentage, multiply it by 100.

$$3.4(100) = 340\%$$

Notice that this percentage is greater than 100%. This makes sense because the original mixed number $3\frac{2}{5}$ is greater than 1.

> **Review Video: <u>Converting Fractions to Percentages and Decimals</u>**
> Visit mometrix.com/academy and enter code: 306233

SCIENTIFIC NOTATION

Scientific notation is a way of writing large numbers in a shorter form. The form $a \times 10^n$ is used in scientific notation, where a is greater than or equal to 1, but less than 10, and n is the number of places the decimal must move to get from the original number to a. Example: The number 230,400,000 is cumbersome to write. To write the value in scientific notation, place a decimal point between the first and second numbers, and include all digits through the last non-zero digit ($a = 2.304$). To find the appropriate power of 10, count the number of places the decimal point had to move ($n = 8$). The number is positive if the decimal moved to the left, and negative if it moved to the right. We can then write 230,400,000 as 2.304×10^8. If we look instead at the number 0.00002304, we have the same value for a, but this time the decimal moved 5 places to the right ($n = -5$). Thus, 0.00002304 can be written as 2.304×10^{-5}. Using this notation makes it simple to compare very large or very small numbers. By comparing exponents, it is easy to see that 3.28×10^4 is smaller than 1.51×10^5, because 4 is less than 5.

> **Review Video: <u>Scientific Notation</u>**
> Visit mometrix.com/academy and enter code: 976454

OPERATIONS WITH DECIMALS

ADDING AND SUBTRACTING DECIMALS

When adding and subtracting decimals, the decimal points must always be aligned. Adding decimals is just like adding regular whole numbers. Example: $4.5 + 2 = 6.5$.

If the problem-solver does not properly align the decimal points, an incorrect answer of 4.7 may result. An easy way to add decimals is to align all of the decimal points in a vertical column visually. This will allow one to see exactly where the decimal should be placed in the final answer. Begin adding from right to left. Add each column in turn, making sure to carry the number to the left if a column adds up to more than 9. The same rules apply to the subtraction of decimals.

> **Review Video: Adding and Subtracting Decimals**
> Visit mometrix.com/academy and enter code: 381101

MULTIPLYING DECIMALS

A simple multiplication problem has two components: a **multiplicand** and a **multiplier**. When multiplying decimals, work as though the numbers were whole rather than decimals. Once the final product is calculated, count the number of places to the right of the decimal in both the multiplicand and the multiplier. Then, count that number of places from the right of the product and place the decimal in that position.

For example, 12.3×2.56 has three places to the right of the respective decimals. Multiply 123×256 to get 31488. Now, beginning on the right, count three places to the left and insert the decimal. The final product will be 31.488.

> **Review Video: Multiplying Decimals**
> Visit mometrix.com/academy and enter code: 731574

DIVIDING DECIMALS

Every division problem has a **divisor** and a **dividend**. The dividend is the number that is being divided. In the problem $14 \div 7$, 14 is the dividend and 7 is the divisor. In a division problem with decimals, the divisor must be converted into a whole number. Begin by moving the decimal in the divisor to the right until a whole number is created. Next, move the decimal in the dividend the same number of spaces to the right. For example, 4.9 into 24.5 would become 49 into 245. The decimal was moved one space to the right to create a whole number in the divisor, and then the same was done for the dividend. Once the whole numbers are created, the problem is carried out normally: $245 \div 49 = 5$.

> **Review Video: Dividing Decimals**
> Visit mometrix.com/academy and enter code: 560690

OPERATIONS WITH FRACTIONS

ADDING AND SUBTRACTING FRACTIONS

If two fractions have a common denominator, they can be added or subtracted simply by adding or subtracting the two numerators and retaining the same denominator. Example: $\frac{1}{2} + \frac{1}{4} = \frac{2}{4} + \frac{1}{4} = \frac{3}{4}$. If the two fractions do not already have the same denominator, one or both of them must be manipulated to achieve a common denominator before they can be added or subtracted.

MULTIPLYING FRACTIONS

Two fractions can be multiplied by multiplying the two numerators to find the new numerator and the two denominators to find the new denominator. Example: $\frac{1}{3} \times \frac{2}{3} = \frac{1 \times 2}{3 \times 3} = \frac{2}{9}$.

DIVIDING FRACTIONS

Two fractions can be divided by flipping the numerator and denominator of the second fraction and then proceeding as though it were a multiplication. Example: $\frac{2}{3} \div \frac{3}{4} = \frac{2}{3} \times \frac{4}{3} = \frac{8}{9}$.

RATIONAL NUMBERS FROM LEAST TO GREATEST

EXAMPLE

Order the following rational numbers from least to greatest: 0.55, 17%, $\sqrt{25}$, $\frac{64}{4}$, $\frac{25}{50}$, 3.

Recall that the term **rational** simply means that the number can be expressed as a ratio or fraction. The set of rational numbers includes integers and decimals. Notice that each of the numbers in the problem can be written as a decimal or integer:

$$17\% = 0.1717$$
$$\sqrt{25} = 5$$
$$\frac{64}{4} = 16$$
$$\frac{25}{50} = \frac{1}{2} = 0.5$$

So, the answer is 17%, $\frac{25}{50}$, 0.55, 3, $\sqrt{25}$, $\frac{64}{4}$.

RATIONAL NUMBERS FROM GREATEST TO LEAST

EXAMPLE

Order the following rational numbers from greatest to least: $0.3, 27\%, \sqrt{100}, \frac{72}{9}, \frac{1}{9}. 4.5$

$$27\% = 0.27$$
$$\sqrt{100} = 10$$
$$\frac{72}{9} = 8$$
$$\frac{1}{9} \approx 0.11$$

So, the answer is $\sqrt{100}, \frac{72}{9}, 4.5, 0.3, 27\%, \frac{1}{9}$.

> **Review Video: Ordering Rational Numbers**
> Visit mometrix.com/academy and enter code: 419578

FACTORS AND GREATEST COMMON FACTOR

Factors are numbers that are multiplied together to obtain a **product**. For example, in the equation $2 \times 3 = 6$, the numbers 2 and 3 are factors. A **prime number** has only two factors (1 and itself), but other numbers can have many factors.

A **common factor** is a number that divides exactly into two or more other numbers. For example, the factors of 12 are 1, 2, 3, 4, 6, and 12, while the factors of 15 are 1, 3, 5, and 15. The common factors of 12 and 15 are 1 and 3.

A **prime factor** is also a prime number. Therefore, the prime factors of 12 are 2 and 3. For 15, the prime factors are 3 and 5.

> **Review Video: Factors**
> Visit mometrix.com/academy and enter code: 920086

The **greatest common factor** (GCF) is the largest number that is a factor of two or more numbers. For example, the factors of 15 are 1, 3, 5, and 15; the factors of 35 are 1, 5, 7, and 35. Therefore, the greatest common factor of 15 and 35 is 5.

> **Review Video: Greatest Common Factor (GCF)**
> Visit mometrix.com/academy and enter code: 838699

MULTIPLES AND LEAST COMMON MULTIPLE

The least common multiple (**LCM**) is the smallest number that is a multiple of two or more numbers. For example, the multiples of 3 include 3, 6, 9, 12, 15, etc.; the multiples of 5 include 5, 10, 15, 20, etc. Therefore, the least common multiple of 3 and 5 is 15.

> **Review Video: Multiples**
> Visit mometrix.com/academy and enter code: 626738
>
> **Review Video: Multiples and Least Common Multiple (LCM)**
> Visit mometrix.com/academy and enter code: 520269

Pre-Algebra

PROPORTIONS AND RATIOS

PROPORTIONS

A proportion is a relationship between two quantities that dictates how one changes when the other changes. A **direct proportion** describes a relationship in which a quantity increases by a set amount for every increase in the other quantity, or decreases by that same amount for every decrease in the other quantity. Example: Assuming a constant driving speed, the time required for a car trip increases as the distance of the trip increases. The distance to be traveled and the time required to travel are directly proportional.

Inverse proportion is a relationship in which an increase in one quantity is accompanied by a decrease in the other, or vice versa. Example: the time required for a car trip decreases as the speed increases, and increases as the speed decreases, so the time required is inversely proportional to the speed of the car.

> **Review Video: Proportions**
> Visit mometrix.com/academy and enter code: 505355

RATIOS

A **ratio** is a comparison of two quantities in a particular order. Example: If there are 14 computers in a lab, and the class has 20 students, there is a student to computer ratio of 20 to 14, commonly written as 20:14. Ratios are normally reduced to their smallest whole number representation, so 20:14 would be reduced to 10:7 by dividing both sides by 2.

> **Review Video: Ratios**
> Visit mometrix.com/academy and enter code: 996914

REAL WORLD PROBLEMS WITH PROPORTIONS AND RATIOS

EXAMPLE 1

A child was given 100 mg of chocolate every two hours. How much chocolate will the child receive in five hours?

Using proportional reasoning, since five hours is two and a half times as long as two hours, the child will receive two and a half times as much chocolate, 2.5×100 mg $= 250$ mg, in five hours.

To compute the answer methodically, first write the amount of chocolate per 2 hours as a ratio.

$$\frac{100 \text{ mg}}{2 \text{ hours}}$$

Next create a proportion to relate the different time increments of 2 hours and 5 hours.

$\frac{100 \text{ mg}}{2 \text{ hours}} = \frac{x \text{ mg}}{5 \text{ hours}}$, where x is the amount of chocolate the child receives in five hours. Make sure to keep the same units in either the numerator or denominator. In this case the numerator units must be mg for both ratios and the denominator units must be hours for both ratios.

Use cross multiplication and division to solve for x:

$$\frac{100 \text{ mg}}{2 \text{ hours}} = \frac{x \text{ mg}}{5 \text{ hours}}$$
$$100(5) = 2(x)$$
$$500 = 2x$$
$$500 \div 2 = 2x \div 2$$
$$250 = x$$

Therefore, the child receives 250 mg every five hours.

Review Video: <u>Proportions in the Real World</u>
Visit mometrix.com/academy and enter code: 221143

EXAMPLE 2

At a school, for every 20 female students there are 15 male students. This same student ratio happens to exist at another school. If there are 100 female students at the second school, how many male students are there?

One way to find the number of male students is to set up and solve a proportion.

$$\frac{\text{number of female students}}{\text{number of male students}} = \frac{20}{15} = \frac{100}{\text{number of male students}}$$

Represent the unknown number of male students as the variable x.

$$\frac{20}{15} = \frac{100}{x}$$

Cross multiply and then solve for x:

$$20x = 15 \times 100 = 1500$$
$$x = \frac{1500}{20} = 75$$

Alternatively, notice that: $\frac{20 \times 5}{15 \times 5} = \frac{100}{75}$, so $x = 75$.

EXAMPLE 3

In a hospital emergency room, there are 4 nurses for every 12 patients. What is the ratio of nurses to patients? If the nurse-to-patient ratio remains constant, how many nurses must be present to care for 24 patients?

The ratio of nurses to patients can be written as 4 to 12, 4:12, or $\frac{4}{12}$. Because four and twelve have a common factor of four, the ratio should be reduced to 1:3, which means that there is one nurse present for every three patients. If this ratio remains constant, there must be eight nurses present to care for 24 patients.

EXAMPLE 4

In a bank, the banker-to-customer ratio is 1:2. If seven bankers are on duty, how many customers are currently in the bank?

Use proportional reasoning or set up a proportion to solve. Because there are twice as many customers as bankers, there must be fourteen customers when seven bankers are on duty. Setting up and solving a proportion gives the same result:

$$\frac{\text{number of bankers}}{\text{number of customers}} = \frac{1}{2} = \frac{7}{\text{number of customers}}$$

Represent the unknown number of patients as the variable x.

$$\frac{1}{2} = \frac{7}{x}$$

To solve for x, cross multiply:

$1 \times x = 7 \times 2$, so $x = 14$.

CONSTANT OF PROPORTIONALITY

When two quantities have a proportional relationship, there exists a **constant of proportionality** between the quantities; the product of this constant and one of the quantities is equal to the other quantity. For example, if one lemon costs $0.25, two lemons cost $0.50, and three lemons cost $0.75, there is a proportional relationship between the total cost of lemons and the number of lemons purchased. The constant of proportionality is the **unit price**, namely $0.25/lemon. Notice that the total price of lemons, t, can be found by multiplying the unit price of lemons, p, and the number of lemons, n: $t = pn$.

SLOPE

On a graph with two points, (x_1, y_1) and (x_2, y_2), the **slope** is found with the formula $m = \frac{y_2 - y_1}{x_2 - x_1}$; where $x_1 \neq x_2$ and m stands for slope. If the value of the slope is **positive**, the line has an *upward direction* from left to right. If the value of the slope is **negative**, the line has a *downward direction* from left to right.

UNIT RATE AS THE SLOPE

A new book goes on sale in bookstores and online stores. In the first month, 5,000 copies of the book are sold. Over time, the book continues to grow in popularity. The data for the number of copies sold is in the table below.

# of Months on Sale	1	2	3	4	5
# of Copies Sold (In Thousands)	5	10	15	20	25

So, the number of copies that are sold and the time that the book is on sale is a proportional relationship. In this example, an equation can be used to show the data: $y = 5x$, where x is the number of months that the book is on sale. Also, y is the number of copies sold. So, the slope is $\frac{\text{rise}}{\text{run}} = \frac{5}{1}$. This can be reduced to 5.

WORK/UNIT RATE

Unit rate expresses a quantity of one thing in terms of one unit of another. For example, if you travel 30 miles every two hours, a unit rate expresses this comparison in terms of one hour: in one hour you travel 15 miles, so your unit rate is 15 miles per hour. Other examples are how much one ounce of food costs (price per ounce) or figuring out how much one egg costs out of the dozen (price per 1 egg, instead of price per 12 eggs). The denominator of a unit rate is always 1. Unit rates are used to compare different situations to solve problems. For example, to make sure you get the best deal when deciding which kind of soda to buy, you can find the unit rate of each. If Soda #1 costs $1.50 for a 1-liter bottle, and soda #2 costs $2.75 for a 2-liter bottle, it would be a better deal to buy Soda #2, because its unit rate is only $1.375 per 1-liter, which is cheaper than Soda #1. Unit rates can also help determine the length of time a given event will take. For example, if you can paint 2 rooms in 4.5 hours, you can determine how long it will take you to paint 5 rooms by solving for the unit rate per room and then multiplying that by 5.

> **Review Video: Rates and Unit Rates**
> Visit mometrix.com/academy and enter code: 185363

EXAMPLE 1

Janice made $40 during the first 5 hours she spent babysitting. She will continue to earn money at this rate until she finishes babysitting in 3 more hours. Find how much money Janice earned babysitting and how much she earns per hour.

Janice will earn $64 babysitting in her 8 total hours (adding the first 5 hours to the remaining 3 gives the 8 hour total). This can be found by setting up a proportion comparing money earned to babysitting hours. Since she earns $40 for 5 hours and since the rate is constant, she will earn a proportional amount in 8 hours: $\frac{40}{5} = \frac{x}{8}$. Cross multiplying will yield $5x = 320$, and division by 5 shows that $x = 64$.

Janice earns $8 per hour. This can be found by taking her total amount earned, $64, and dividing it by the total number of hours worked, 8. Since $\frac{64}{8} = 8$, Janice makes $8 in one hour. This can also be found by finding the unit rate, money earned per hour: $\frac{64}{8} = \frac{x}{1}$. Since cross multiplying yields $8x = 64$, and division by 8 shows that $x = 8$, Janice earns $8 per hour.

EXAMPLE 2

The McDonalds are taking a family road trip, driving 300 miles to their cabin. It took them 2 hours to drive the first 120 miles. They will drive at the same speed all the way to their cabin. Find the speed at which the McDonalds are driving and how much longer it will take them to get to their cabin.

The McDonalds are driving 60 miles per hour. This can be found by setting up a proportion to find the unit rate, the number of miles they drive per one hour: $\frac{120}{2} = \frac{x}{1}$. Cross multiplying yields $2x = 120$ and division by 2 shows that $x = 60$.

Since the McDonalds will drive this same speed, it will take them another 3 hours to get to their cabin. This can be found by first finding how many miles the McDonalds have left to drive, which is $300 - 120 = 180$. The McDonalds are driving at 60 miles per hour, so a proportion can be set up to determine how many hours it will take them to drive 180 miles: $\frac{180}{x} = \frac{60}{1}$. Cross multiplying yields $60x = 180$, and division by 60 shows that $x = 3$. This can also be found by using the formula $D = r \times t$ (or Distance = rate × time), where $180 = 60 \times t$, and division by 60 shows that $t = 3$.

EXAMPLE 3

It takes Andy 10 minutes to read 6 pages of his book. He has already read 150 pages in his book that is 210 pages long. Find how long it takes Andy to read 1 page and also find how long it will take him to finish his book if he continues to read at the same speed.

It takes Andy 1 minute and 40 seconds to read one page in his book. This can be found by finding the unit rate per one page, by dividing the total time it takes him to read 6 pages by 6. Since it takes him 10 minutes to read 6 pages, $\frac{10}{6} = 1\frac{2}{3}$ minutes, which is 1 minute and 40 seconds.

It will take Andy another 100 minutes, or 1 hour and 40 minutes to finish his book. This can be found by first figuring out how many pages Andy has left to read, which is $210 - 150 = 60$. Since it is now known that it takes him $1\frac{2}{3}$ minutes to read each page, then that rate must be multiplied by however many pages he has left to read (60) to find the time he'll need: $60 \times 1\frac{2}{3} = 100$, so it will take him 100 minutes, or 1 hour and 40 minutes, to read the rest of his book.

Algebra

FUNCTION AND RELATION

When expressing functional relationships, the **variables** x and y are typically used. These values are often written as the **coordinates** (x, y). The x-value is the independent variable and the y-value is the dependent variable. A **relation** is a set of data in which there is not a unique y-value for each x-value in the dataset. This means that there can be two of the same x-values assigned to different y-values. A relation is simply a relationship between the x and y-values in each coordinate but does not apply to the relationship between the values of x and y in the data set. A **function** is a relation where one quantity depends on the other. For example, the amount of money that you make depends on the number of hours that you work. In a function, each x-value in the data set has one unique y-value because the y-value depends on the x-value.

> **Review Video: <u>Definition of a Function</u>**
> Visit mometrix.com/academy and enter code: 784611

FUNCTIONS

A **function** is an equation that has exactly one value of **output variable** (dependent variable) for each value of the **input variable** (independent variable). The set of all values for the input variable (here assumed to be x) is the domain of the function, and the set of all corresponding values of output variable (here assumed to be y) is the range of the function. When looking at a graph of an equation, the easiest way to determine if the equation is a function or not is to conduct the vertical line test. If a vertical line drawn through any value of x crosses the graph in more than one place, the equation is not a function.

DETERMINING A FUNCTION

You can determine whether an equation is a **function** by substituting different values into the equation for x. These values are called input values. All possible input values are referred to as the **domain**. The result of substituting these values into the equation is called the output, or **range**. You can display and organize these numbers in a data table. A **data table** contains the values for x and y, which you can also list as coordinates. In order for a function to exist, the table cannot contain any repeating x-values that correspond with different y-values. If each x-coordinate has a unique y-coordinate, the table contains a function. However, there can be repeating y-values that correspond with different *x*-values. An example of this is when the function contains an exponent. For example, if $x^2 = y$, $2^2 = 4$, and $(-2)^2 = 4$.

PROPERTIES OF FUNCTIONS

In functions with the notation f(x), the value substituted for x in the equation is called the argument. The domain is the set of all values for x in a function. Unless otherwise given, assume the domain is the set of real numbers that will yield real numbers for the range. This is the domain of definition.

The graph of a function is the set of all ordered pairs (x, y) that satisfy the equation of the function. The points that have zero as the value for y are called the zeros of the function. These are also the x-intercepts, because that is the point at which the graph crosses, or intercepts, the x-axis. The points that have zero as the value for x are the y-intercepts because that is where the graph crosses the y-axis.

WRITING A FUNCTION RULE USING A TABLE

If given a set of data, place the corresponding *x* and *y*-values into a table and analyze the relationship between them. Consider what you can do to each *x*-value to obtain the corresponding *y*-value. Try adding or subtracting different numbers to and from *x* and then try multiplying or dividing different numbers to and from *x*. If none of these **operations** give you the *y*-value, try combining the operations. Once you find a rule that works for one pair, make sure to try it with each additional set of ordered pairs in the table. If the same operation or combination of operations satisfies each set of coordinates, then the table contains a function. The rule is then used to write the equation of the function in "*y* =" form.

EQUATIONS AND GRAPHING

When algebraic functions and equations are shown graphically, they are usually shown on a *Cartesian coordinate plane*. The Cartesian coordinate plane consists of two number lines placed perpendicular to each other, and intersecting at the zero point, also known as the origin. The horizontal number line is known as the *x*-axis, with positive values to the right of the origin, and negative values to the left of the origin. The vertical number line is known as the *y*-axis, with positive values above the origin, and negative values below the origin. Any point on the plane can be identified by an ordered pair in the form (*x*,*y*), called coordinates. The *x*-value of the coordinate is called the abscissa, and the *y*-value of the coordinate is called the ordinate. The two number lines divide the plane into *four quadrants*: I, II, III, and IV.

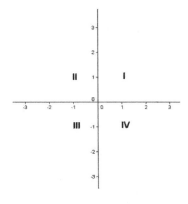

Before learning the different forms in which equations can be written, it is important to understand some terminology. A ratio of the change in the vertical distance to the change in horizontal distance is called the *slope*. On a graph with two points, (x_1, y_1) and (x_2, y_2), the slope is represented by the formula $s = \frac{y_2 - y_1}{x_2 - x_1}$; $x_1 \neq x_2$. If the value of the slope is positive, the line slopes upward from left to right. If the value of the slope is negative, the line slopes downward from left to right. If the *y*-coordinates are the same for both points, the slope is 0 and the line is a *horizontal line*. If the *x*-coordinates are the same for both points, there is no slope and the line is a *vertical line*. Two or more lines that have equal slopes are *parallel lines*. *Perpendicular lines* have slopes that are negative reciprocals of each other, such as $\frac{a}{b}$ and $\frac{-b}{a}$.

Review Video: Graphs of Functions
Visit mometrix.com/academy and enter code: 492785

Equations are made up of monomials and polynomials. A *monomial* is a single variable or product of constants and variables, such as x, $2x$, or $\frac{2}{x}$. There will never be addition or subtraction symbols in a monomial. Like monomials have like variables, but they may have different coefficients. *Polynomials* are algebraic expressions which use addition and subtraction to combine two or more monomials. Two terms make a binomial; three terms make a trinomial; etc.. The *degree of a monomial* is the sum of the exponents of the variables. The *degree of a polynomial* is the highest degree of any individual term.

As mentioned previously, equations can be written many ways. Below is a list of the many forms equations can take.

- Standard Form: $Ax + By = C$; the slope is $\frac{-A}{B}$ and the y-intercept is $\frac{C}{B}$
- *Slope Intercept Form*: $y = mx + b$, where m is the slope and b is the *y*-intercept
- Point-Slope Form: $y - y_1 = m(x - x_1)$, where m is the slope and (x_1, y_1) is a point on the line
- Two-Point Form: $\frac{y - y_1}{x - x_1} = \frac{y_2 - y_1}{x_2 - x_1}$, where (x_1, y_1) and (x_2, y_2) are two points on the given line
- *Intercept Form*: $\frac{x}{x_1} + \frac{y}{y_1} = 1$, where $(x_1, 0)$ is the point at which a line intersects the *x*-axis, and $(0, y_1)$ is the point at which the same line intersects the *y*-axis

Review Video: Slope-Intercept and Point-Slope Forms
Visit mometrix.com/academy and enter code: 113216

Equations can also be written as $ax + b = 0$, where $a \neq 0$. These are referred to as **one variable linear equations**. A solution to such an equation is called a **root**. In the case where we have the equation $5x + 10 = 0$, if we solve for x we get a solution of $x = -2$. In other words, the root of the equation is -2. This is found by first subtracting 10 from both sides, which gives $5x = -10$. Next, simply divide both sides by the coefficient of the variable, in this case 5, to get $x = -2$. This can be checked by plugging -2 back into the original equation $(5)(-2) + 10 = -10 + 10 = 0$.

The **solution set** is the set of all solutions of an equation. In our example, the solution set would simply be -2. If there were more solutions (there usually are in multivariable equations) then they would also be included in the solution set. When an equation has no true solutions, this is referred to as an **empty set**. Equations with identical solution sets are *equivalent equations*. An **identity** is a term whose value or determinant is equal to 1.

SOLVING ONE-VARIABLE LINEAR EQUATIONS

Multiply all terms by the lowest common denominator to eliminate any fractions. Look for addition or subtraction to undo so you can isolate the variable on one side of the equal sign. Divide both sides by the coefficient of the variable. When you have a value for the variable, substitute this value into the original equation to make sure you have a true equation.

MANIPULATION OF FUNCTIONS

Horizontal and vertical shift occur when values are added to or subtracted from the x or y values, respectively.

If a constant is added to the y portion of each point, the graph shifts up. If a constant is subtracted from the y portion of each point, the graph shifts down. This is represented by the expression $f(x) \pm k$, where k is a constant.

If a constant is added to the x portion of each point, the graph shifts left. If a constant is subtracted from the x portion of each point, the graph shifts right. This is represented by the expression $f(x \pm k)$, where k is a constant.

Stretch, compression, and reflection occur when different parts of a function are multiplied by different groups of constants. If the function as a whole is multiplied by a real number constant greater than 1, $(k \times f(x))$, the graph is stretched vertically. If k in the previous equation is greater than zero but less than 1, the graph is compressed vertically. If k is less than zero, the graph is reflected about the x-axis, in addition to being either stretched or compressed vertically if k is less than or greater than -1, respectively. If instead, just the x-term is multiplied by a constant greater than 1 $(f(k \times x))$, the graph is compressed horizontally. If k in the previous equation is greater than zero but less than 1, the graph is stretched horizontally. If k is less than zero, the graph is reflected about the y-axis, in addition to being either stretched or compressed horizontally if k is greater than or less than -1, respectively.

CLASSIFICATION OF FUNCTIONS

There are many different ways to classify functions based on their structure or behavior. Listed here are a few common classifications.

Constant functions are given by the equation y=b or $f(x) = b$, where b is a real number. There is no independent variable present in the equation, so the function has a constant value for all x. The graph of a constant function is a horizontal line of slope 0 that is positioned b units from the x-axis. If b is positive, the line is above the x-axis; if b is negative, the line is below the x-axis.

Identity functions are identified by the equation y=x or $f(x) = x$, where every value of y is equal to its corresponding value of x. The only zero is the point (0, 0). The graph is a diagonal line with slope 1.

In **linear functions**, the value of the function changes in direct proportion to x. The rate of change,represented by the slope on its graph, is constant throughout. The standard form of a linear equation is $ax + by = c$, where a, b, and c are real numbers. As a function, this equation is commonly written as $y = mx + b$ or $f(x) = mx + b$. This is known as the slope-intercept form, because the coefficients give the slope of the graphed function (m) and its y-intercept (b). Solve the equation $mx + b = 0$ for x to get $x = -\frac{b}{m}$, which is the only zero of the function. The domain and range are both the set of all real numbers.

A **polynomial function** is a function with multiple terms and multiple powers of x, such as:

$$f(x) = a_n x^n + a_{n-1} x^{n-1} + a_{n-2} x^{n-2} + \cdots + a_1 x + a_0$$

where n is a non-negative integer that is the highest exponent in the polynomial, and $a_n \neq 0$. The domain of a polynomial function is the set of all real numbers. If the greatest exponent in the polynomial is even, the polynomial is said to be of even degree and the range is the set of real numbers that satisfy the function. If the greatest exponent in the polynomial is odd, the polynomial is said to be odd and the range, like the domain, is the set of all real numbers.

A **quadratic function** is a polynomial function that follows the equation pattern $y = ax^2 + bx + c$, or $f(x) = ax^2 + bx + c$, where a, b, and c are real numbers and $a \neq 0$. The domain of a quadratic function is the set of all real numbers. The range is also real numbers, but only those in the subset of the domain that satisfy the equation. The root(s) of any quadratic function can be found by plugging the values of a, b, and c into the **quadratic formula**:

$$x = \frac{-b \pm \sqrt{b^2 - 4ac}}{2a}$$

If the expression $b^2 - 4ac$ is negative, you will instead find complex roots.

A quadratic function has a parabola for its graph. In the equation $f(x) = ax^2 + bx + c$, if a is positive, the parabola will open upward. If a is negative, the parabola will open downward. The axis of symmetry is a vertical line that passes through the vertex. To determine whether or not the parabola will intersect the x-axis, check the number of real roots. An equation with two real roots will cross the x-axis twice. An equation with one real root will have its vertex on the x-axis. An equation with no real roots will not contact the x-axis.

A **rational function** is a function that can be constructed as a ratio of two polynomial expressions: $f(x) = \frac{p(x)}{q(x)}$, where $p(x)$ and $q(x)$ are both polynomial expressions and $q(x) \neq 0$. The domain is the set of all real numbers, except any values for which $q(x) = 0$. The range is the set of real numbers that satisfies the function when the domain is applied. When you graph a rational function, you will have vertical asymptotes wherever $q(x) = 0$. If the polynomial in the numerator is of lesser degree than the polynomial in the denominator, the x-axis will also be a horizontal asymptote. If the numerator and denominator have equal degrees, there will be a horizontal asymptote not on the x-axis. If the degree of the numerator is exactly one greater than the degree of the denominator, the graph will have an oblique, or diagonal, asymptote. The asymptote will be along the line $y =$

$\frac{p_n}{q_{n-1}}x + \frac{p_{n-1}}{q_{n-1}}$, where p_n and q_{n-1} are the coefficients of the highest degree terms in their respective polynomials.

A **square root function** is a function that contains a radical and is in the format $f(x) = \sqrt{ax + b}$. The domain is the set of all real numbers that yields a positive radicand or a radicand equal to zero. Because square root values are assumed to be positive unless otherwise identified, the range is all real numbers from zero to infinity. To find the zero of a square root function, set the radicand equal to zero and solve for x. The graph of a square root function is always to the right of the zero and always above the x-axis.

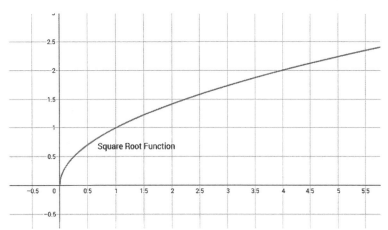

An **absolute value function** is in the format $f(x) = |ax + b|$. Like other functions, the domain is the set of all real numbers. However, because absolute value indicates positive numbers, the range is limited to positive real numbers. To find the zero of an absolute value function, set the portion inside the absolute value sign equal to zero and solve for x.

An absolute value function is also known as a piecewise function because it must be solved in pieces – one for if the value inside the absolute value sign is positive, and one for if the value is negative. The function can be expressed as

$$f(x) = \begin{cases} ax + b \text{ if } ax + b \geq 0 \\ -(ax + b) \text{ if } ax + b < 0 \end{cases}$$

This will allow for an accurate statement of the range.

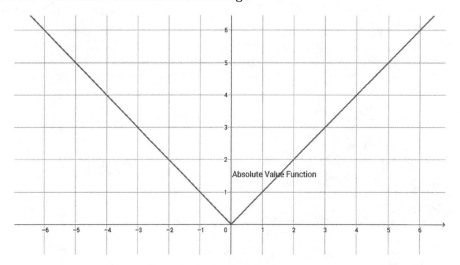

Absolute Value Function

Exponential functions are equations that have the format $y = b^x$, where base $b > 0$ and $b \neq 1$. The exponential function can also be written $f(x) = b^x$.

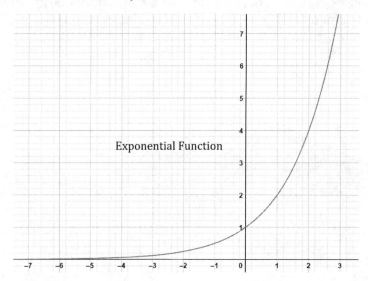

Exponential Function

Logarithmic functions are equations that have the format $y = \log_b x$ or $f(x) = \log_b x$. The base b may be any number except one; however, the most common bases for logarithms are base 10 and base e. The log base e is known the natural logarithm, or ln, expressed by the function $f(x) = \ln x$.

Any logarithm that does not have an assigned value of b is assumed to be base 10: $\log x = \log_{10} x$. Exponential functions and logarithmic functions are related in that one is the inverse of the other. If $f(x) = b^x$, then $f^{-1}(x) = \log_b x$. This can perhaps be expressed more clearly by the two equations: $y = b^x$ and $x = \log_b y$.

The following properties apply to logarithmic expressions:

$$\log_b 1 = 0$$
$$\log_b b = 1$$
$$\log_b b^p = p$$
$$\log_b MN = \log_b M + \log_b N$$
$$\log_b \frac{M}{N} = \log_b M - \log_b N$$
$$\log_b M^p = p \log_b M$$

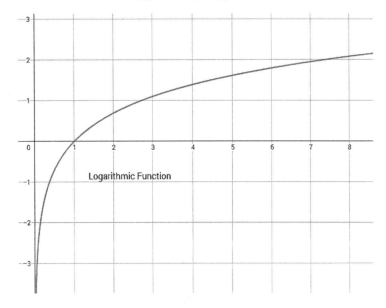

Logarithmic Function

In a **one-to-one function**, each value of x has exactly one value for y (this is the definition of a function) *and* each value of y has exactly one value for x. While the vertical line test will determine if a graph is that of a function, the horizontal line test will determine if a function is a one-to-one function. If a horizontal line drawn at any value of y intersects the graph in more than one place, the graph is not that of a one-to-one function. Do not make the mistake of using the horizontal line test exclusively in determining if a graph is that of a one-to-one function. A one-to-one function must pass both the vertical line test and the horizontal line test. One-to-one functions are also **invertible functions**.

A **monotone function** is a function whose graph either constantly increases or constantly decreases. Examples include the functions $f(x) = x$, $f(x) = -x$, or $f(x) = x^3$.

An **even function** has a graph that is symmetric with respect to the y-axis and satisfies the equation $f(x) = f(-x)$. Examples include the functions $f(x) = x^2$ and $f(x) = ax^n$, where a is any real number and n is a positive even integer.

An **odd function** has a graph that is symmetric with respect to the origin and satisfies the equation $f(x) = -f(-x)$. Examples include the functions $f(x) = x^3$ and $f(x) = ax^n$, where a is any real number and n is a positive odd integer.

Algebraic functions are those that exclusively use polynomials and roots. These would include polynomial functions, rational functions, square root functions, and all combinations of these functions, such as polynomials as the radicand. These combinations may be joined by addition, subtraction, multiplication, or division, but may not include variables as exponents.

Transcendental functions are all functions that are non-algebraic. Any function that includes logarithms, trigonometric functions, variables as exponents, or any combination that includes any of these is not algebraic in nature, even if the function includes polynomials or roots.

RELATED CONCEPTS

According to the **fundamental theorem of algebra**, every non-constant, single variable polynomial has exactly as many roots as the polynomial's highest exponent. For example, if x^4 is the largest exponent of a term, the polynomial will have exactly 4 roots. However, some of these roots may have multiplicity or be non-real numbers. For instance, in the polynomial function $f(x) = x^4 - 4x + 3$, the only real roots are 1 and -1. The root 1 has multiplicity of 2 and there is one non-real root $(-1 - \sqrt{2}i)$.

The **remainder theorem** is useful for determining the remainder when a polynomial is divided by a binomial. The Remainder Theorem states that if a polynomial function $f(x)$ is divided by a binomial $x - a$, where a is a real number, the remainder of the division will be the value of $f(a)$. If $f(a) = 0$, then a is a root of the polynomial.

The **factor theorem** is related to the Remainder Theorem and states that if $f(a) = 0$ then $(x - a)$ is a factor of the function.

According to the **rational root theorem,** any rational root of a polynomial function $f(x) = a_n x^n + a_{n-1}x^{n-1} + \cdots + a_1 x + a_0$ with integer coefficients will, when reduced to its lowest terms, be a positive or negative fraction such that the numerator is a factor of a_0 and the denominator is a factor of a_n. For instance, if the polynomial function $f(x) = x^3 + 3x^2 - 4$ has any rational roots, the numerators of those roots can only be factors of 4 (1, 2, 4), and the denominators can only be factors of 1 (1). The function in this example has roots of 1 $\left(\text{or } \frac{1}{1} \right)$ and -2 $\left(\text{or } -\frac{2}{1} \right)$.

Variables that vary directly are those that either both increase at the same rate or both decrease at the same rate. For example, in the functions $f(x) = kx$ or $f(x) = kx^n$, where k and n are positive, the value of $f(x)$ increases as the value of x increases and decreases as the value of x decreases.

Variables that vary inversely are those where one increases while the other decreases. For example, in the functions $f(x) = \frac{k}{x}$ or $f(x) = \frac{k}{x^n}$ where k is a positive constant, the value of y increases as the value of x decreases, and the value of y decreases as the value of x increases.

In both cases, k is the constant of variation.

APPLYING THE BASIC OPERATIONS TO FUNCTIONS

For each of the basic operations, we will use these functions as examples: $f(x) = x^2$ and $g(x) = x$.

To find the sum of two functions f and g, assuming the domains are compatible, simply add the two functions together: $(f + g)(x) = f(x) + g(x) = x^2 + x$

To find the difference of two functions f and g, assuming the domains are compatible, simply subtract the second function from the first: $(f - g)(x) = f(x) - g(x) = x^2 - x$.

To find the product of two functions f and g, assuming the domains are compatible, multiply the two functions together: $(f \cdot g)(x) = f(x) \cdot g(x) = x^2 \cdot x = x^3$.

To find the quotient of two functions f and g, assuming the domains are compatible, divide the first function by the second: $\frac{f}{g}(x) = \frac{f(x)}{g(x)} = \frac{x^2}{x} = x$; $x \neq 0$.

The example given in each case is fairly simple, but on a given problem, if you are looking only for the value of the sum, difference, product or quotient of two functions at a particular x-value, it may be simpler to solve the functions individually and then perform the given operation using those values.

The composite of two functions f and g, written as $(f \circ g)(x)$ simply means that the output of the second function is used as the input of the first. This can also be written as $f(g(x))$. In general, this can be solved by substituting $g(x)$ for all instances of x in $f(x)$ and simplifying. Using the example functions $f(x) = x^2 - x + 2$ and $g(x) = x + 1$, we can find that $(f \circ g)(x)$ or $f(g(x))$ is equal to $f(x + 1) = (x + 1)^2 - (x + 1) + 2$, which simplifies to $x^2 + x + 2$.

It is important to note that $(f \circ g)(x)$ is not necessarily the same as $(g \circ f)(x)$. The process is not commutative like addition or multiplication expressions. If $(f \circ g)(x)$ does equal $(g \circ f)(x)$, the two functions are inverses of each other.

SOLVE EQUATIONS IN ONE VARIABLE

MANIPULATING EQUATIONS

Sometimes you will have variables missing in equations. So, you need to find the missing variable. To do this, you need to remember one important thing: *whatever you do to one side of an equation, you need to do to the other side*. If you subtract 100 from one side of an equation, you need to subtract 100 from the other side of the equation. This will allow you to change the form of the equation to find missing values.

EXAMPLE

Ray earns \$10 an hour at his job. Write an equation for his earnings as a function of time spent working. Determine how long Ray has to work in order to earn \$360.

The number of dollars that Ray earns is dependent on the number of hours he works, so earnings will be represented by the dependent variable y and hours worked will be represented by the independent variable x. He earns 10 dollars per hour worked, so his earning can be calculated as

$$y = 10x$$

To calculate the number of hours Ray must work in order to earn \$360, plug in 360 for y and solve for x:

$$360 = 10x$$

$$x = \frac{360}{10} = 36$$

So, Ray must work 36 hours in order to earn \$360.

> **Review Video: <u>Dependent and Independent Variables and Inverting Functions</u>**
> Visit mometrix.com/academy and enter code: 704764

SOLVING ONE VARIABLE LINEAR EQUATIONS

Another way to write an equation is $ax + b = 0$ where $a \neq 0$. This is known as a **one-variable linear equation**. A solution to an equation is called a **root**. Consider the following equation:

$$5x + 10 = 0$$

If we solve for x, the solution is $x = -2$. In other words, the root of the equation is –2.

The first step is to subtract 10 from both sides. This gives $5x = -10$.

Next, divide both sides by the **coefficient** of the variable. For this example, that is 5. So, you should have $x = -2$. You can make sure that you have the correct answer by substituting –2 back into the original equation. So, the equation now looks like this: $(5)(-2) + 10 = -10 + 10 = 0$.

EXAMPLE 1

Solve for x.

$$\frac{45\%}{12\%} = \frac{15\%}{x}$$

First, cross multiply; then, solve for x:

$$45x = 12 \times 15 = 180$$
$$x = \frac{180}{45} = 4\%$$

Alternatively, notice that $\frac{45\% \div 3}{12\% \div 3} = \frac{15\%}{4\%}$, so $x = 4\%$.

EXAMPLE 2

Solve for x in the following equation:

$$\frac{0.50}{2} = \frac{1.50}{x}$$

First, cross multiply; then, solve for x:

$$0.5x = 1.5 \times 2 = 3$$
$$x = \frac{3}{0.5} = 3 \times 2 = 6$$

Alternatively, notice that $\frac{0.50 \times 3}{2 \times 3} = \frac{1.50}{6}$, so $x = 6$.

EXAMPLE 3

Solve for x in the following equation:

$$\frac{40}{8} = \frac{x}{24}$$

First, cross multiply; then, solve for x:

$$8x = 40 \times 24 = 960$$
$$x = \frac{960}{8} = 120$$

Alternatively, notice that $\frac{40 \times 3}{8 \times 3} = \frac{120}{24}$, so $x = 120$.

OTHER IMPORTANT CONCEPTS

Commonly in algebra and other upper-level fields of math you find yourself working with mathematical expressions that do not equal each other. The statement comparing such expressions with symbols such as < (less than) or > (greater than) is called an *inequality*. An example of an inequality is $7x > 5$. To solve for x, simply divide both sides by 7 and the solution is shown to be $x > \frac{5}{7}$. Graphs of the solution set of inequalities are represented on a number line. Open circles are used to show that an expression approaches a number but is never quite equal to that number.

Conditional inequalities are those with certain values for the variable that will make the condition true and other values for the variable where the condition will be false. **Absolute inequalities** can have any real number as the value for the variable to make the condition true, while there is no real number value for the variable that will make the condition false. Solving inequalities is done by following the same rules as for solving equations with the exception that when multiplying or dividing by a negative number the direction of the inequality sign must be flipped or reversed. **double inequalities** are situations where two inequality statements apply to the same variable expression. An example of this is $-c < ax + b < c$.

A **weighted mean**, or weighted average, is a mean that uses "weighted" values. The formula is weighted mean $= \frac{w_1 x_1 + w_2 x_2 + w_3 x_3 \ldots + w_n x_n}{w_1 + w_2 + w_3 + \cdots + w_n}$. Weighted values, such as $w_1, w_2, w_3, \ldots w_n$ are assigned to each member of the set $x_1, x_2, x_3, \ldots x_n$. If calculating weighted mean, make sure a weight value for each member of the set is used.

GRAPHING INEQUALITIES

Graph the inequality $10 > -2x + 4$.

In order to **graph the inequality** $10 > -2x + 4$, you must first solve for x. The opposite of addition is subtraction, so subtract 4 from both sides. This results in $6 > -2x$. Next, the opposite of multiplication is division, so divide both sides by -2. Don't forget to flip the inequality symbol since you are dividing by a negative number. This results in $-3 < x$. You can rewrite this as $x > -3$. To graph an inequality, you create a number line and put a circle around the value that is being compared to x. If you are graphing a greater than or less than inequality, as the one shown, the circle remains open. This represents all of the values excluding -3. If the inequality happens to be a greater than or equal to or less than or equal to, you draw a closed circle around the value. This would represent all of the values including the number. Finally, take a look at the values that the solution represents and shade the number line in the appropriate direction. You are graphing all of the values greater than -3 and since this is all of the numbers to the right of -3, shade this region on the number line.

DETERMINING SOLUTIONS TO INEQUALITIES

Determine whether $(-2, 4)$ is a solution of the inequality $y \geq -2x + 3$.

To determine whether a coordinate is a **solution of an inequality**, you can either use the inequality or its graph. Using $(-2, 4)$ as (x, y), substitute the values into the inequality to see if it makes a true statement. This results in $4 \geq -2(-2) + 3$. Using the integer rules, simplify the right side of the inequality by multiplying and then adding. The result is $4 \geq 7$, which is a false statement. Therefore, the coordinate is not a solution of the inequality. You can also use the **graph** of an inequality to see if a coordinate is a part of the solution. The graph of an inequality is shaded over the section of the coordinate grid that is included in the solution. The graph of $y \geq -2x + 3$ includes the solid line $y = -2x + 3$ and is shaded to the right of the line, representing all of the points greater than and including the points on the line. This excludes the point $(-2, 4)$, so it is not a solution of the inequality.

CALCULATIONS USING POINTS

Sometimes you need to perform calculations using only points on a graph as input data. Using points, you can determine what the **midpoint** and **distance** are. If you know the equation for a line you can calculate the distance between the line and the point.

To find the **midpoint** of two points (x_1, y_1) and (x_2, y_2), average the x-coordinates to get the x-coordinate of the midpoint, and average the y-coordinates to get the y-coordinate of the midpoint. The formula is Midpoint $= \left(\frac{x_1 + x_2}{2}, \frac{y_1 + y_2}{2}\right)$.

The **distance** between two points is the same as the length of the hypotenuse of a right triangle with the two given points as endpoints, and the two sides of the right triangle parallel to the x-axis and y-axis, respectively. The length of the segment parallel to the x-axis is the difference between the x-coordinates of the two points. The length of the segment parallel to the y-axis is the difference between the y-coordinates of the two points. Use the Pythagorean theorem $a^2 + b^2 = c^2$ or $c = \sqrt{a^2 + b^2}$ to find the distance. The formula is distance $= \sqrt{(x_2 - x_1)^2 + (y_2 - y_1)^2}$.

When a line is in the format $Ax + By + C = 0$, where A, B, and C are coefficients, you can use a point (x_1, y_1) not on the line and apply the formula $d = \frac{|Ax_1 + By_1 + C|}{\sqrt{A^2 + B^2}}$ to find the distance between the line and the point (x_1, y_1).

EXAMPLE

Find the distance and midpoint between points $(2, 4)$ and $(8, 6)$.

MIDPOINT

$$\text{Midpoint} = \left(\frac{x_1 + x_2}{2}, \frac{y_1 + y_2}{2}\right)$$
$$\text{Midpoint} = \left(\frac{2+8}{2}, \frac{4+6}{2}\right)$$
$$\text{Midpoint} = \left(\frac{10}{2}, \frac{10}{2}\right)$$
$$\text{Midpoint} = (5, 5)$$

DISTANCE

$$\text{Distance} = \sqrt{(x_2 - x_1)^2 + (y_2 - y_1)^2}$$
$$\text{Distance} = \sqrt{(8 - 2)^2 + (6 - 4)^2}$$
$$\text{Distance} = \sqrt{(6)^2 + (2)^2}$$
$$\text{Distance} = \sqrt{36 + 4}$$
$$\text{Distance} = \sqrt{40} \text{ or } 2\sqrt{10}$$

SYSTEMS OF EQUATIONS

Systems of equations are a set of simultaneous equations that all use the same variables. A solution to a system of equations must be true for each equation in the system. *Consistent systems* are those with at least one solution. *Inconsistent systems* are systems of equations that have no solution.

> **Review Video: Systems of Equations**
> Visit mometrix.com/academy and enter code: 658153

SUBSTITUTION

To solve a system of linear equations by *substitution*, start with the easier equation and solve for one of the variables. Express this variable in terms of the other variable. Substitute this expression in the other equation and solve for the other variable. The solution should be expressed in the form (x, y). Substitute the values into both of the original equations to check your answer. Consider the following problem.

Solve the system using substitution:

$$x + 6y = 15$$
$$3x - 12y = 18$$

Solve the first equation for x:

$$x = 15 - 6y$$

Substitute this value in place of x in the second equation, and solve for y:

$$3(15 - 6y) - 12y = 18$$
$$45 - 18y - 12y = 18$$
$$30y = 27$$
$$y = \frac{27}{30} = \frac{9}{10} = 0.9$$

Plug this value for y back into the first equation to solve for x:

$$x = 15 - 6(0.9) = 15 - 5.4 = 9.6$$

Check both equations if you have time:

$$9.6 + 6(0.9) = 9.6 + 5.4 = 15$$
$$3(9.6) - 12(0.9) = 28.8 - 10.8 = 18$$

Therefore, the solution is (9.6, 0.9).

ELIMINATION

To solve a system of equations using *elimination*, begin by rewriting both equations in standard form $Ax + By = C$. Check to see if the coefficients of one pair of like variables add to zero. If not, multiply one or both of the equations by a non-zero number to make one set of like variables add to zero. Add the two equations to solve for one of the variables. Substitute this value into one of the original equations to solve for the other variable. Check your work by substituting into the other equation. Next, we will solve the same problem as above, but using the addition method.

Solve the system using elimination:

$$x + 6y = 15$$
$$3x - 12y = 18$$

If we multiply the first equation by 2, we can eliminate the y terms:

$$2x + 12y = 30$$
$$3x - 12y = 18$$

Add the equations together and solve for x:

$$5x = 48$$
$$x = \frac{48}{5} = 9.6$$

Plug the value for x back into either of the original equations and solve for y:

$$9.6 + 6y = 15$$
$$y = \frac{15 - 9.6}{6} = 0.9$$

Check both equations if you have time:

$$9.6 + 6(0.9) = 9.6 + 5.4 = 15$$
$$3(9.6) - 12(0.9) = 28.8 - 10.8 = 18$$

Therefore, the solution is (9.6, 0.9).

GRAPHICALLY

To solve a system of linear equations **graphically**, plot both equations on the same graph. The solution of the equations is the point where both lines cross. If the lines do not cross (are parallel), then there is **no solution**.

For example, consider the following system of equations:

$$y = 2x + 7$$
$$y = -x + 1$$

Since these equations are given in slope-intercept form, they are easy to graph; the y intercepts of the lines are $(0, 7)$ and $(0, 1)$. The respective slopes are 2 and -1, thus the graphs look like this:

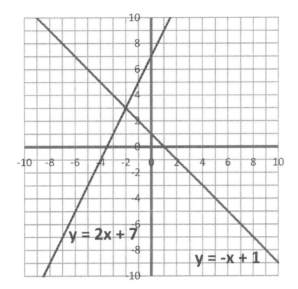

The two lines intersect at the point $(-2, 3)$, thus this is the solution to the system of equations.

Solving a system graphically is generally only practical if both coordinates of the solution are integers; otherwise the intersection will lie between gridlines on the graph and the coordinates will be difficult or impossible to determine exactly. It also helps if, as in this example, the equations are in slope-intercept form or some other form that makes them easy to graph. Otherwise, another method of solution (by substitution or elimination) is likely to be more useful.

SOLVING SYSTEMS OF EQUATIONS USING THE TRACE FEATURE

Using the **trace feature** on a calculator requires that you rewrite each equation, isolating the y-variable on one side of the equal sign. Enter both equations in the graphing calculator and plot the graphs simultaneously. Use the trace cursor to find where the two lines cross. Use the zoom feature if necessary to obtain more accurate results. Always check your answer by substituting into the original equations. The trace method is likely to be less accurate than other methods due to the resolution of graphing calculators, but is a useful tool to provide an approximate answer.

SOLVING A SYSTEM OF EQUATIONS CONSISTING OF A LINEAR EQUATION AND A QUADRATIC EQUATION

ALGEBRAICALLY

Generally, the simplest way to solve a system of equations consisting of a linear equation and a quadratic equation algebraically is through the method of **substitution**. One possible strategy is to solve the linear equation for y and then substitute that expression into the quadratic equation. After expansion and combining like terms, this will result in a new quadratic equation for x which, like all quadratic equations, may have zero, one, or two solutions. Plugging each solution for x back into one of the original equations will then produce the corresponding value of y.

83

For example, consider the following system of equations:

$$x + y = 1$$
$$y = (x + 3)^2 - 2$$

We can solve the linear equation for y to yield $y = -x + 1$.

Substituting this expression into the quadratic equation produces $-x + 1 = (x + 3)^2 - 2$

We can simplify this equation:

$$-x + 1 = (x + 3)^2 - 2$$
$$-x + 1 = x^2 + 6x + 9 - 2$$
$$-x + 1 = x^2 + 6x + 7$$
$$x^2 + 7x + 6 = 0$$

This quadratic equation can be factored as $(x + 1)(x + 6) = 0$. It therefore has two solutions: $x_1 = -1$ and $x_2 = -6$. Plugging each of these back into the original linear equation yields $y_1 = -x_1 + 1 = -(-1) + 1 = 2$ and $y_2 = -x_2 + 1 = -(-6) + 1 = 7$. Thus this system of equations has two solutions, $(-1, 2)$ and $(-6, 7)$.

It may help to check your work by putting each x and y value back into the original equations and verifying that they do provide a solution.

GRAPHICALLY

To solve a system of equations consisting of a linear equation and a quadratic equation **graphically**, plot both equations on the same graph. The linear equation will of course produce a straight line, while the quadratic equation will produce a parabola. These two graphs will intersect at zero, one, or two points; each point of intersection is a solution of the system.

For example, consider the following system of equations:

$$y = -2x + 2$$
$$y = -2x^2 + 4x + 2$$

The linear equation describes a line with a y-intercept of $(0, 2)$ and a slope of -2.

To graph the quadratic equation, we can first find the vertex of the parabola: the x-coordinate of the vertex is $h = -\frac{b}{2a} = -\frac{4}{2(-2)} = 1$, and the y coordinate is $k = -2(1)^2 + 4(1) + 2 = 4$. Thus, the vertex lies at $(1, 4)$. To get a feel for the rest of the parabola, we can plug in a few more values of x to find more points; by putting in $x = 2$ and $x = 3$ in the quadratic equation, we find that the points $(2, 2)$ and $(3, -4)$ lie on the parabola; by symmetry thus do $(0, 2)$ and $(-1, -4)$. We can now plot both equations:

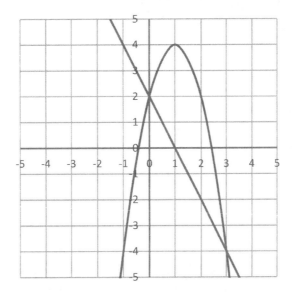

These two curves intersect at the points $(0, 2)$ and $(3, -4)$, thus these are the solutions of the equation.

POLYNOMIAL ALGEBRA

To multiply two binomials, follow the **FOIL** method. FOIL stands for:

- First: Multiply the first term of each binomial
- Outer: Multiply the outer terms of each binomial
- Inner: Multiply the inner terms of each binomial
- Last: Multiply the last term of each binomial

Using FOIL $(Ax + By)(Cx + Dy) = ACx^2 + ADxy + BCxy + BDy^2$.

EXAMPLE

Use the FOIL method on binomials $(x + 2)$ and $(x - 3)$.

$$\text{First: } (x + 2)(x - 3) = (x)(x) = x^2$$
$$\text{Outer: } (x + 2)(x - 3) = (x)(-3) = -3x$$
$$\text{Inner: } (x + 2)(x - 3) = (2)(x) = 2x$$
$$\text{Last: } (x + 2)(x - 3) = (2)(-3) = -6$$

Combine like Terms:

$$(x^2) + (-3x) + (2x) + (-6) = x^2 - x - 6$$

Review Video: <u>Multiplying Terms Using the FOIL Method</u>
Visit mometrix.com/academy and enter code: 854792

To divide polynomials, begin by arranging the terms of each polynomial in order of one variable. You may arrange in ascending or descending order, but make sure to be consistent with both polynomials. To get the first term of the quotient, divide the first term of the dividend by the first term of the divisor. Multiply the first term of the quotient by the entire divisor and subtract that product from the dividend. Repeat for the second and successive terms until you either get a remainder of zero or a remainder whose degree is less than the degree of the divisor. If the quotient has a remainder, write the answer as a mixed expression in the form: $quotient + \frac{remainder}{divisor}$.

Rational expressions are fractions with polynomials in both the numerator and the denominator; the value of the polynomial in the denominator cannot be equal to zero. To add or subtract rational expressions, first find the common denominator, then rewrite each fraction as an equivalent fraction with the common denominator. Finally, add or subtract the numerators to get the numerator of the answer, and keep the common denominator as the denominator of the answer. When multiplying rational expressions factor each polynomial and cancel like factors (a factor which appears in both the numerator and the denominator). Then, multiply all remaining factors in the numerator to get the numerator of the product, and multiply the remaining factors in the denominator to get the denominator of the product. Remember – cancel entire factors, not individual terms. To divide rational expressions, take the reciprocal of the divisor (the rational expression you are dividing by) and multiply by the dividend.

Below are patterns of some special products to remember: *perfect trinomial squares*, the *difference between two squares*, the *sum and difference of two cubes*, and *perfect cubes*.

- Perfect trinomial squares: $x^2 + 2xy + y^2 = (x + y)^2$ or $x^2 - 2xy + y^2 = (x - y)^2$
- Difference between two squares: $x^2 - y^2 = (x + y)(x - y)$
- Sum of two cubes: $x^3 + y^3 = (x + y)(x^2 - xy + y^2)$
- Note: the second factor is *not* the same as a perfect trinomial square, so do not try to factor it further.
- Difference between two cubes: $x^3 - y^3 = (x - y)(x^2 + xy + y^2)$
- Again, the second factor is *not* the same as a perfect trinomial square.
- Perfect cubes: $x^3 + 3x^2y + 3xy^2 + y^3 = (x + y)^3$ and $x^3 - 3x^2y + 3xy^2 - y^3 = (x - y)^3$

In order to **factor a polynomial**, first check for a common monomial factor. When the greatest common monomial factor has been factored out, look for patterns of special products: differences of two squares, the sum or difference of two cubes for binomial factors, or perfect trinomial squares for trinomial factors. If the factor is a trinomial but not a perfect trinomial square, look for a factorable form, such as $x^2 + (a + b)x + ab = (x + a)(x + b)$ or $(ac)x^2 + (ad + bc)x + bd = (ax + b)(cx + d)$. For factors with four terms, look for groups to factor. Once you have found the factors, write the original polynomial as the product of all the factors. Make sure all of the polynomial factors are prime. Monomial factors may be prime or composite. Check your work by multiplying the factors to make sure you get the original polynomial.

SOLVING QUADRATIC EQUATIONS

The **quadratic formula** is used to solve quadratic equations when other methods are more difficult. To use the quadratic formula to solve a quadratic equation, begin by rewriting the equation in standard form $ax^2 + bx + c = 0$, where a, b, and c are coefficients. Once you have identified the values of the coefficients, substitute those values into the quadratic formula $x = \frac{-b \pm \sqrt{b^2 - 4ac}}{2a}$. Evaluate the equation and simplify the expression. Again, check each root by substituting into the original equation. In the quadratic formula, the portion of the formula under the radical ($b^2 - 4ac$) is called the **discriminant**. If the discriminant is zero, there is only one root: $-\frac{b}{2a}$. If the discriminant is positive, there are two different real roots. If the discriminant is negative, there are no real roots.

To solve a quadratic equation by factoring, begin by rewriting the equation in standard form, if necessary. Factor the side with the variable then set each of the factors equal to zero and solve the resulting linear equations. Check your answers by substituting the roots you found into the original equation. If, when writing the equation in standard form, you have an equation in the form $x^2 + c = 0$ or $x^2 - c = 0$, set $x^2 = -c$ or $x^2 = c$ and take the square root of c. If $c = 0$, the only real root is zero. If c is positive, there are two real roots—the positive and negative square root values. If c is negative, there are no real roots because you cannot take the square root of a negative number.

> **Review Video: Factoring Quadratic Equations**
> Visit mometrix.com/academy and enter code: 336566

To solve a quadratic equation by **completing the square**, rewrite the equation so that all terms containing the variable are on the left side of the equal sign, and all the constants are on the right side of the equal sign. Make sure the coefficient of the squared term is 1. If there is a coefficient with the squared term, divide each term on both sides of the equal side by that number. Next, work with the coefficient of the single-variable term. Square half of this coefficient and add that value to both sides. Now you can factor the left side (the side containing the variable) as the square of a binomial. $x^2 + 2ax + a^2 = C \Rightarrow (x + a)^2 = C$, where x is the variable, and a and C are constants. Take the square root of both sides and solve for the variable. Substitute the value of the variable in the original problem to check your work.

QUADRATIC FUNCTION

A *quadratic function* is a function in the form $y = ax^2 + bx + c$, where a does not equal 0. While a linear function forms a line, a quadratic function forms a **parabola**, which is a u-shaped figure that either opens upward or downward. A parabola that opens upward is said to be a **positive quadratic function** and a parabola that opens downward is said to be a **negative quadratic function**. The shape of a parabola can differ, depending on the values of a, b, and c. All parabolas contain a **vertex**, which is the highest possible point, the **maximum**, or the lowest possible point, the **minimum**. This is the point where the graph begins moving in the opposite direction. A quadratic function can have zero, one, or two solutions, and therefore, zero, one, or two x-intercepts. Recall that the x-intercepts are referred to as the zeros, or roots, of a function. A quadratic function will have only one y-intercept. Understanding the basic components of a quadratic function can give you an idea of the shape of its graph.

Example graph of a positive quadratic function:

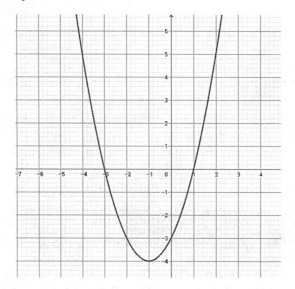

SIMPLIFYING POLYNOMIAL EXPRESSIONS

A polynomial is a group of monomials added or subtracted together. Simplifying polynomials requires combining like terms. The like terms in a polynomial expression are those that have the same variable raised to the same power. It is often helpful to connect the like terms with arrows or lines in order to separate them from the other monomials. Once you have determined the like terms, you can rearrange the polynomial by placing them together. Remember to include the sign that is in front of each term. Once the like terms are placed together, you can apply each operation and simplify. When adding and subtracting polynomials, only add and subtract the **coefficient**, or the number part; the variable and exponent stay the same.

POSITION OF PARABOLA

A **quadratic function** is written in the form $y = ax^2 + bx + c$. Changing the leading coefficient, a, in the equation changes the direction of the parabola. If the value of a is **positive**, the graph opens upward. The vertex of this parabola is the **minimum** value of the graph. If the value of a is **negative**, the graph opens downward. The vertex of this parabola is the **maximum** value of the graph. The leading coefficient, a, also affects the width of the parabola. The closer a is to 0, the wider the parabola will be. The values of b and c both affect the position of the parabola on the graph. The effect from changing b depends on the sign of a. If a is negative, increasing the value of b moves the parabola to the right and decreasing the value of b moves it to the left. If a is positive, changes to b have the opposite effect. The value of c in the quadratic equation represents the y-intercept and therefore, moves the parabola up and down the y-axis. The larger the c-value, the higher the parabola is on the graph.

FINDING ROOTS

Find the roots of $y = x^2 + 6x - 16$ and explain why these values are important.

The **roots** of a quadratic equation are the solutions when $ax^2 + bx + c = 0$. To find the roots of a quadratic equation, first replace y with 0. If $0 = x^2 + 6x - 16$, then to find the values of x, you can factor the equation if possible. When factoring a quadratic equation where $a = 1$, find the factors of c that add up to b. That is the factors of -16 that add up to 6. The factors of -16 include, -4 and 4, -8 and 2 and -2 and 8. The factors that add up to equal 6 are -2 and 8. Write these factors as the product of two binomials, $0 = (x - 2)(x + 8)$. You can verify that these are the correct factors by

88

using FOIL to multiply them together. Finally, since these binomials multiply together to equal zero, set them each equal to zero and solve for x. This results in $x - 2 = 0$, which simplifies to $x = 2$ and $x + 8 = 0$, which simplifies to $x = -8$. Therefore, the roots of the equation are 2 and -8. These values are important because they tell you where the graph of the equation crosses the x-axis. The points of intersection are $(2, 0)$ and $(-8, 0)$.

> **Review Video: Finding the Missing Roots**
> Visit mometrix.com/academy and enter code: 198376

SOLVING QUADRATIC EQUATIONS

METHODS

One way to find the solution or solutions of a quadratic equation is to use its **graph**. The solution(s) of a quadratic equation are the values of x when $y = 0$. On the graph, $y = 0$ is where the parabola crosses the x-axis, or the x-intercepts. This is also referred to as the **roots**, or zeros of a function. Given a graph, you can locate the x-intercepts to find the solutions. If there are no x-intercepts, the function has no solution. If the parabola crosses the x-axis at one point, there is one solution and if it crosses at two points, there are two solutions. Since the solutions exist where $y = 0$, you can also solve the equation by substituting 0 in for y. Then, try factoring the equation by finding the factors of ac that add up to equal b. You can use the guess and check method, the box method, or grouping. Once you find a pair that works, write them as the product of two binomials and set them equal to zero. Finally, solve for x to find the solutions. The last way to solve a quadratic equation is to use the **quadratic formula**. The quadratic formula is $x = \frac{-b \pm \sqrt{b^2 - 4ac}}{2a}$. Substitute the values of a, b, and c into the formula and solve for x. Remember that $\pm$ refers to two different solutions. Always check your solutions with the original equation to make sure they are valid.

EXAMPLE

List the steps used in solving $y = 2x^2 + 8x + 4$.

First, substitute 0 in for y in the quadratic equation:

$$0 = 2x^2 + 8x + 4$$

Next, try to factor the quadratic equation. If $a \neq 1$, list the factors of ac, or 8:

$$(1, 8), (-1, -8), (2, 4), (-2, -4)$$

Look for the factors of ac that add up to b, or 8. Since none do, the equation cannot be factored with whole numbers. Substitute the values of a, b, and c into the quadratic formula, $x = \frac{-b \pm \sqrt{b^2 - 4ac}}{2a}$:

$$x = \frac{-8 \pm \sqrt{8^2 - 4(2)(4)}}{2(2)}$$

Use the order of operations to simplify:

$$x = \frac{-8 \pm \sqrt{64 - 32}}{4}$$
$$x = \frac{-8 \pm \sqrt{32}}{4}$$

89

Reduce and simplify:

$$x = \frac{-8 \pm \sqrt{(16)(2)}}{4}$$
$$x = \frac{-8 \pm 4\sqrt{2}}{4}$$
$$x = -2 \pm \sqrt{2}$$
$$x = -2 + \sqrt{2} \text{ and}$$
$$x = -2 - \sqrt{2}$$

Check both solutions with the original equation to make sure they are valid.

Simplify the square roots and round to two decimal places.

$$x = -3.41 \text{ and } x = -0.586$$

LAWS OF EXPONENTS

Multiply $(2x^4)^2(xy)^4 \cdot 4y^3$ using the **laws of exponents**.

According the order of operations, the first step in simplifying expressions is to evaluate within the parentheses. Moving from left to right, the first set of parentheses contains a power raised to a power. The rules of exponents state that when a power is raised to a power, you *multiply* the exponents. Since $4 \times 2 = 8$, $(2x^4)^2$ can be written as $4x^8$. The second set of parentheses raises a product to a power. The **rules of exponents** state that you raise every value within the parentheses to the given power. Therefore, $(xy)^4$ can be written as x^4y^4. Combining these terms with the last term gives you, $4x^8 \cdot x^4y^4 \cdot 4y^3$. In this expression, there are powers with the same base. The rules of exponents state that you *add* powers with the same base, while multiplying the coefficients. You can group the expression as $(4x^8 \cdot x^4) \cdot (y^4 \cdot 4y^3)$ to organize the values with the same base. Then, using this rule add the exponents. The result is $4x^{12} \cdot 4y^7$, or $16x^{12}y^7$.

> **Review Video: Laws of Exponents**
> Visit mometrix.com/academy and enter code: 532558

USING GIVEN ROOTS TO FIND QUADRATIC EQUATION

EXAMPLE

Find a quadratic equation whose real roots are $x = 2$ and $x = -1$.

One way to find the roots of a quadratic equation is to factor the equation and use the **zero product property**, setting each factor of the equation equal to zero to find the corresponding root. We can use this technique in reverse to find an equation given its roots. Each root corresponds to a linear equation which in turn corresponds to a factor of the quadratic equation.

For example, the root $x=2$ corresponds to the equation $x - 2 = 0$, and the root $x = -1$ corresponds to the equation $x + 1 = 0$.

These two equations correspond to the factors $(x - 2)$ and $(x+1)$, from which we can derive the equation $(x - 2)(x + 1) = 0$, or $x^2 - x - 2 = 0$.

Any integer multiple of this entire equation will also yield the same roots, as the integer will simply cancel out when the equation is factored. For example, $2x^2 - 2x - 4 = 0$ factors as

$2(x - 2)(x + 1) = 0$.

SIMPLIFYING RATIONAL EXPRESSIONS

To *simplify a rational expression*, factor the numerator and denominator completely. Factors that are the same and appear in the numerator and denominator have a ratio of 1. The denominator, $(1 - x^2)$, is a difference of squares. It can be factored as $(1 - x)(1 + x)$. The factor $1 - x$ and the numerator $x - 1$ are opposites and have a ratio of –1. Rewrite the numerator as $-1(1 - x)$. So, the rational expression can be simplified as follows:

$$\frac{x - 1}{1 - x^2} = \frac{-1(1 - x)}{(1 - x)(1 + x)} = \frac{-1}{1 + x}$$

(Note that since the original expression is defined for $x \neq \{-1, 1\}$, the simplified expression has the same restrictions.)

> **Review Video: <u>Reducing Rational Expressions</u>**
> Visit mometrix.com/academy and enter code: 788868

MATRIX BASICS

A **matrix** (plural: matrices) is a rectangular array of numbers or variables, often called **elements**, which are arranged in columns and rows. A matrix is generally represented by a capital letter, with its elements represented by the corresponding lowercase letter with two subscripts indicating the row and column of the element. For example, n_{ab} represents the element in row a column b of matrix N.

$$N = \begin{bmatrix} n_{11} & n_{12} & n_{13} \\ n_{21} & n_{22} & n_{23} \end{bmatrix}$$

A matrix can be described in terms of the number of rows and columns it contains in the format $a \times b$, where a is the number of rows and b is the number of columns. The matrix shown above is a 2×3 matrix. Any $a \times b$ matrix where $a = b$ is a square matrix. A **vector** is a matrix that has exactly one column (**column vector**) or exactly one row (**row vector**).

The **main diagonal** of a matrix is the set of elements on the diagonal from the top left to the bottom right of a matrix. Because of the way it is defined, only square matrices will have a main diagonal. For the matrix shown below, the main diagonal consists of the elements $n_{11}, n_{22}, n_{33}, n_{44}$.

$$\begin{bmatrix} n_{11} & n_{12} & n_{13} & n_{14} \\ n_{21} & n_{22} & n_{23} & n_{24} \\ n_{31} & n_{32} & n_{33} & n_{34} \\ n_{41} & n_{42} & n_{43} & n_{44} \end{bmatrix}$$

A 3×4 matrix such as the one shown below would not have a main diagonal because there is no straight line of elements between the top left corner and the bottom right corner that joins the elements.

$$\begin{bmatrix} n_{11} & n_{12} & n_{13} & n_{14} \\ n_{21} & n_{22} & n_{23} & n_{24} \\ n_{31} & n_{32} & n_{33} & n_{34} \end{bmatrix}$$

A **diagonal matrix** is a square matrix that has a zero for every element in the matrix except the elements on the main diagonal. All the elements on the main diagonal must be nonzero numbers.

$$\begin{bmatrix} n_{11} & 0 & 0 & 0 \\ 0 & n_{22} & 0 & 0 \\ 0 & 0 & n_{33} & 0 \\ 0 & 0 & 0 & n_{44} \end{bmatrix}$$

If every element on the main diagonal of a diagonal matrix is equal to one, the matrix is called an **identity matrix**. The identity matrix is often represented by the letter I.

$$I = \begin{bmatrix} 1 & 0 & 0 & 0 \\ 0 & 1 & 0 & 0 \\ 0 & 0 & 1 & 0 \\ 0 & 0 & 0 & 1 \end{bmatrix}$$

A **zero matrix** is a matrix that has zero as the value for every element in the matrix.

$$\begin{bmatrix} 0 & 0 & 0 & 0 \\ 0 & 0 & 0 & 0 \\ 0 & 0 & 0 & 0 \\ 0 & 0 & 0 & 0 \end{bmatrix}$$

The zero matrix is the *identity for matrix addition*. Do not confuse the zero matrix with the identity matrix.

The **negative of a matrix** is also known as the additive inverse of a matrix. If matrix N is the given matrix, then matrix $-N$ is its negative. This means that every element n_{ab} is equal to $-n_{ab}$ in the negative. To find the negative of a given matrix, change the sign of every element in the matrix and keep all elements in their original corresponding positions in the matrix.

If two matrices have the same order and all corresponding elements in the two matrices are the same, then the two matrices are **equal matrices**.

A matrix N may be **transposed** to matrix N^T by changing all rows into columns and changing all columns into rows. The easiest way to accomplish this is to swap the positions of the row and column notations for each element. For example, suppose the element in the second row of the third column of matrix N is $n_{23} = 6$. In the transposed matrix N^T, the transposed element would be $n_{32} = 6$, and it would be placed in the third row of the second column.

$$N = \begin{bmatrix} 1 & 2 & 3 \\ 4 & 5 & 6 \end{bmatrix}; \ N^T = \begin{bmatrix} 1 & 4 \\ 2 & 5 \\ 3 & 6 \end{bmatrix}$$

To quickly transpose a matrix by hand, begin with the first column and rewrite a new matrix with those same elements in the same order in the first row. Write the elements from the second column of the original matrix in the second row of the transposed matrix. Continue this process until all columns have been completed. If the original matrix is identical to the transposed matrix, the matrices are symmetric.

The **determinant** of a matrix is a scalar value that is calculated by taking into account all the elements of a square matrix. A determinant only exists for square matrices. Finding the determinant of a 2×2 matrix is as simple as remembering a simple equation. For a 2×2 matrix

$M = \begin{bmatrix} m_{11} & m_{12} \\ m_{21} & m_{22} \end{bmatrix}$, the determinant is obtained by the equation $|M| = m_{11}m_{22} - m_{12}m_{21}$. Anything larger than 2×2 requires multiple steps. Take matrix $N = \begin{bmatrix} a & b & c \\ d & e & f \\ g & h & j \end{bmatrix}$. The determinant of N is calculated as $|N| = a\begin{vmatrix} e & f \\ h & j \end{vmatrix} - b\begin{vmatrix} d & f \\ g & j \end{vmatrix} + c\begin{vmatrix} d & e \\ g & h \end{vmatrix}$ or $|N| = a(ej - fh) - b(dj - fg) + c(dh - eg)$.

There is a shortcut for 3×3 matrices: add the products of each unique set of elements diagonally left-to-right and subtract the products of each unique set of elements diagonally right-to-left. In matrix N, the left-to-right diagonal elements are (a, e, j), (b, f, g), and (c, d, h). The right-to-left diagonal elements are (a, f, h), (b, d, j), and (c, e, g). $\det(N) = aej + bfg + cdh - afh - bdj - ceg$.

Calculating the determinants of matrices larger than 3×3 is rarely, if ever, done by hand.

The **inverse** of a matrix M is the matrix that, when multiplied by matrix M, yields a product that is the identity matrix. Multiplication of matrices will be explained in greater detail shortly. Not all matrices have inverses. Only a square matrix whose determinant is not zero has an inverse. If a matrix has an inverse, that inverse is unique to that matrix. For any matrix M that has an inverse, the inverse is represented by the symbol M^{-1}. To calculate the inverse of a 2×2 square matrix, use the following pattern:

$$M = \begin{bmatrix} m_{11} & m_{12} \\ m_{21} & m_{22} \end{bmatrix}; \; M^{-1} = \begin{bmatrix} \dfrac{m_{22}}{|M|} & \dfrac{-m_{12}}{|M|} \\ \dfrac{-m_{21}}{|M|} & \dfrac{m_{11}}{|M|} \end{bmatrix}$$

Another way to find the inverse of a matrix by hand is use an augmented matrix and elementary row operations. An **augmented matrix** is formed by appending the entries from one matrix onto the end of another. For example, given a 2×2 invertible matrix $N = \begin{bmatrix} a & b \\ c & d \end{bmatrix}$, you can find the inverse N^{-1} by creating an augmented matrix by appending a 2×2 identity matrix: $\begin{bmatrix} a & b & 1 & 0 \\ c & d & 0 & 1 \end{bmatrix}$. To find the inverse of the original 2×2 matrix, perform elementary row operations to convert the original matrix on the left to an identity matrix: $\begin{bmatrix} 1 & 0 & e & f \\ 0 & 1 & g & h \end{bmatrix}$.

Elementary row operations include multiplying a row by a non-zero scalar, adding scalar multiples of two rows, or some combination of these. For instance, the first step might be to multiply the second row by $\frac{b}{d}$ and then subtract it from the first row to make its second column a zero. The end result is that the 2×2 section on the right will become the inverse of the original matrix: $N^{-1} = \begin{bmatrix} e & f \\ g & h \end{bmatrix}$.

Calculating the inverse of any matrix larger than 2×2 is cumbersome and using a graphing calculator is recommended.

BASIC OPERATIONS WITH MATRICES

There are two categories of basic operations with regard to matrices: operations between a matrix and a scalar, and operations between two matrices.

SCALAR OPERATIONS

A scalar being added to a matrix is treated as though it were being added to each element of the matrix:

$$M + 4 = \begin{bmatrix} m_{11} + 4 & m_{12} + 4 \\ m_{21} + 4 & m_{22} + 4 \end{bmatrix}$$

The same is true for the other three operations.

SUBTRACTION:

$$M - 4 = \begin{bmatrix} m_{11} - 4 & m_{12} - 4 \\ m_{21} - 4 & m_{22} - 4 \end{bmatrix}$$

MULTIPLICATION:

$$M \times 4 = \begin{bmatrix} m_{11} \times 4 & m_{12} \times 4 \\ m_{21} \times 4 & m_{22} \times 4 \end{bmatrix}$$

DIVISION:

$$M \div 4 = \begin{bmatrix} m_{11} \div 4 & m_{12} \div 4 \\ m_{21} \div 4 & m_{22} \div 4 \end{bmatrix}$$

MATRIX ADDITION AND SUBTRACTION

All four of the basic operations can be used with operations between matrices (although division is usually discarded in favor of multiplication by the inverse), but there are restrictions on the situations in which they can be used. Matrices that meet all the qualifications for a given operation are called **conformable matrices**. However, conformability is specific to the operation; two matrices that are conformable for addition are not necessarily conformable for multiplication.

For two matrices to be conformable for addition or subtraction, they must be of the same dimension; otherwise the operation is not defined. If matrix M is a 3×2 matrix and matrix N is a 2×3 matrix, the operations $M + N$ and $M - N$ are meaningless. If matrices M and N are the same size, the operation is as simple as adding or subtracting all of the corresponding elements:

$$\begin{bmatrix} m_{11} & m_{12} \\ m_{21} & m_{22} \end{bmatrix} + \begin{bmatrix} n_{11} & n_{12} \\ n_{21} & n_{22} \end{bmatrix} = \begin{bmatrix} m_{11} + n_{11} & m_{12} + n_{12} \\ m_{21} + n_{21} & m_{22} + n_{22} \end{bmatrix}$$

$$\begin{bmatrix} m_{11} & m_{12} \\ m_{21} & m_{22} \end{bmatrix} - \begin{bmatrix} n_{11} & n_{12} \\ n_{21} & n_{22} \end{bmatrix} = \begin{bmatrix} m_{11} - n_{11} & m_{12} - n_{12} \\ m_{21} - n_{21} & m_{22} - n_{22} \end{bmatrix}$$

The result of addition or subtraction is a matrix of the same dimension as the two original matrices involved in the operation.

MATRIX MULTIPLICATION

The first thing it is necessary to understand about matrix multiplication is that it is not commutative. In scalar multiplication, the operation is commutative, meaning that $a \times b = b \times a$. For matrix multiplication, this is not the case: $A \times B \neq B \times A$. The terminology must be specific when describing matrix multiplication. The operation $A \times B$ can be described as A multiplied (or **post-multiplied**) by B, or B **pre-multiplied** by A.

For two matrices to be conformable for multiplication, they need not be of the same dimension, but specific dimensions must correspond. Taking the example of two matrices M and N to be multiplied $M \times N$, matrix M must have the same number of columns as matrix N has rows. Put another way, if matrix M has the dimensions $a \times b$ and matrix N has the dimensions $c \times d$, b must equal c if the two matrices are to be conformable for this multiplication. The matrix that results from the multiplication will have the dimensions $a \times d$. If a and d are both equal to 1, the product is simply a scalar. Square matrices of the same dimensions are always conformable for multiplication, and their product is always a matrix of the same size.

The simplest type of matrix multiplication is a 1×2 matrix (a row vector) times a 2×1 matrix (a column vector). These will multiply in the following way:

$$[m_{11} \quad m_{12}] \times \begin{bmatrix} n_{11} \\ n_{21} \end{bmatrix} = m_{11}n_{11} + m_{12}n_{21}$$

The two matrices are conformable for multiplication because matrix M has the same number of columns as matrix N has rows. Because the other dimensions are both 1, the result is a scalar. Expanding our matrices to 1×3 and 3×1, the process is the same:

$$[m_{11} \quad m_{12} \quad m_{13}] \times \begin{bmatrix} n_{11} \\ n_{21} \\ n_{31} \end{bmatrix} = m_{11}n_{11} + m_{12}n_{21} + m_{13}n_{31}$$

Once again, the result is a scalar. This type of basic matrix multiplication is the building block for the multiplication of larger matrices.

To multiply larger matrices, treat each **row from the first matrix** and each **column from the second matrix** as individual vectors and follow the pattern for multiplying vectors. The scalar value found from multiplying the first-row vector by the first column vector is placed in the first row, first column of the new matrix. The scalar value found from multiplying the second-row vector by the first column vector is placed in the second row, first column of the new matrix. Continue this pattern until each row of the first matrix has been multiplied by each column of the second vector.

Below is an example of the multiplication of a 3×2 matrix and a 2×3 matrix.

$$\begin{bmatrix} m_{11} & m_{12} \\ m_{21} & m_{22} \\ m_{31} & m_{32} \end{bmatrix} \times \begin{bmatrix} n_{11} & n_{12} & n_{13} \\ n_{21} & n_{22} & n_{23} \end{bmatrix} = \begin{bmatrix} m_{11}n_{11} + m_{12}n_{21} & m_{11}n_{12} + m_{12}n_{22} & m_{11}n_{13} + m_{12}n_{23} \\ m_{21}n_{11} + m_{22}n_{21} & m_{21}n_{12} + m_{22}n_{22} & m_{21}n_{13} + m_{22}n_{23} \\ m_{31}n_{11} + m_{32}n_{21} & m_{31}n_{12} + m_{32}n_{22} & m_{31}n_{13} + m_{32}n_{23} \end{bmatrix}$$

This process starts by taking the first column of the second matrix and running it through each row of the first matrix. Removing all but the first M row and first N column, we would see only the following:

$$[m_{11} \quad m_{12}] \times \begin{bmatrix} n_{11} \\ n_{21} \end{bmatrix}$$

The first product would then be $m_{11}n_{11} + m_{12}n_{21}$. This process will be continued for each column of the N matrix to find the first full row of the product matrix, as shown below.

$$[m_{11} \quad m_{12}] \times \begin{bmatrix} n_{11} \\ n_{21} \end{bmatrix} = [m_{11}n_{11} + m_{12}n_{21} \quad m_{11}n_{12} + m_{12}n_{22} \quad m_{11}n_{13} + m_{12}n_{23}]$$

After completing the first row, the next step would be to simply move to the second row of the M matrix and repeat the process until all of the rows have been finished. The result is a 3×3 matrix.

$$\begin{bmatrix} m_{11} & m_{12} \\ m_{21} & m_{22} \\ m_{31} & m_{32} \end{bmatrix} \times \begin{bmatrix} n_{11} & n_{12} & n_{13} \\ n_{21} & n_{22} & n_{23} \end{bmatrix} = \begin{bmatrix} m_{11}n_{11} + m_{12}n_{21} & m_{11}n_{12} + m_{12}n_{22} & m_{11}n_{13} + m_{12}n_{23} \\ m_{21}n_{11} + m_{22}n_{21} & m_{21}n_{12} + m_{22}n_{22} & m_{21}n_{13} + m_{22}n_{23} \\ m_{31}n_{11} + m_{32}n_{21} & m_{31}n_{12} + m_{32}n_{22} & m_{31}n_{13} + m_{32}n_{23} \end{bmatrix}$$

If the operation were done in reverse $(N \times M)$, the result would be a 2×2 matrix.

$$\begin{bmatrix} n_{11} & n_{12} & n_{13} \\ n_{21} & n_{22} & n_{23} \end{bmatrix} \times \begin{bmatrix} m_{11} & m_{12} \\ m_{21} & m_{22} \\ m_{31} & m_{32} \end{bmatrix} = \begin{bmatrix} m_{11}n_{11} + m_{21}n_{12} + m_{31}n_{13} & m_{12}n_{11} + m_{22}n_{12} + m_{32}n_{13} \\ m_{11}n_{21} + m_{21}n_{22} + m_{31}n_{23} & m_{12}n_{21} + m_{22}n_{22} + m_{32}n_{23} \end{bmatrix}$$

EXAMPLE

A sporting-goods store sells baseballs, volleyballs, and basketballs.

Baseballs $3 each
Volleyballs $8 each
Basketballs $15 each

Here are the same store's sales numbers for one weekend:

	Baseballs	Volleyballs	Basketballs
Friday	5	4	4
Saturday	7	3	10
Sunday	4	3	6

Find the total sales for each day by multiplying matrices.

The first table can be represented by the following column-vector:

$$\begin{bmatrix} 3 \\ 8 \\ 15 \end{bmatrix}$$

And the second table can be represented by this matrix:

$$\begin{bmatrix} 5 & 4 & 4 \\ 7 & 3 & 10 \\ 4 & 3 & 6 \end{bmatrix}$$

Multiplying the second matrix by the first will result in a column vector showing the total sales for each day:

$$\begin{bmatrix} 5 & 4 & 4 \\ 7 & 3 & 10 \\ 4 & 3 & 6 \end{bmatrix} \times \begin{bmatrix} 3 \\ 8 \\ 15 \end{bmatrix} = \begin{bmatrix} 3 \times 5 + 8 \times 4 + 15 \times 4 \\ 3 \times 7 + 8 \times 3 + 15 \times 10 \\ 3 \times 4 + 8 \times 3 + 15 \times 6 \end{bmatrix} = \begin{bmatrix} 15 + 32 + 60 \\ 21 + 24 + 150 \\ 12 + 24 + 90 \end{bmatrix} = \begin{bmatrix} 107 \\ 195 \\ 126 \end{bmatrix}$$

From this, we can see that Friday's sales were \$107, Saturday's sales were \$195, and Sunday's sales were \$126.

SOLVING SYSTEMS OF EQUATIONS

Matrices can be used to represent the coefficients of a system of linear equations and can be very useful in solving those systems. Take for instance three equations with three variables:

$$a_1 x + b_1 y + c_1 z = d_1$$
$$a_2 x + b_2 y + c_2 z = d_2$$
$$a_3 x + b_3 y + c_3 z = d_3$$

where all a, b, c, and d are known constants.

To solve this system, define three matrices:

$$A = \begin{bmatrix} a_1 & b_1 & c_1 \\ a_2 & b_2 & c_2 \\ a_3 & b_3 & c_3 \end{bmatrix}; D = \begin{bmatrix} d_1 \\ d_2 \\ d_3 \end{bmatrix}; X = \begin{bmatrix} x \\ y \\ z \end{bmatrix}$$

The three equations in our system can be fully represented by a single matrix equation:

$$AX = D$$

We know that the identity matrix times X is equal to X, and we know that any matrix multiplied by its inverse is equal to the identity matrix.

$$A^{-1}AX = IX = X; \text{thus } X = A^{-1}D$$

Our goal then is to find the inverse of A, or A^{-1}. Once we have that, we can pre-multiply matrix D by A^{-1} (post-multiplying here is an undefined operation) to find matrix X.

Systems of equations can also be solved using the transformation of an augmented matrix in a process similar to that for finding a matrix inverse. Begin by arranging each equation of the system in the following format:

$$a_1x + b_1y + c_1z = d_1$$
$$a_2x + b_2y + c_2z = d_2$$
$$a_3x + b_3y + c_3z = d_3$$

Define matrices A and D and combine them into augmented matrix A_a:

$$A = \begin{bmatrix} a_1 & b_1 & c_1 \\ a_2 & b_2 & c_2 \\ a_3 & b_3 & c_3 \end{bmatrix}; \quad D = \begin{bmatrix} d_1 \\ d_2 \\ d_3 \end{bmatrix}; \quad A_a = \begin{bmatrix} a_1 & b_1 & c_1 & d_1 \\ a_2 & b_2 & c_2 & d_2 \\ a_3 & b_3 & c_3 & d_3 \end{bmatrix}$$

To solve the augmented matrix and the system of equations, use elementary row operations to form an identity matrix in the first 3×3 section. When this is complete, the values in the last column are the solutions to the system of equations:

$$\begin{bmatrix} 1 & 0 & 0 & x \\ 0 & 1 & 0 & y \\ 0 & 0 & 1 & z \end{bmatrix}$$

If an identity matrix is not possible, the system of equations has no unique solution. Sometimes only a partial solution will be possible. The following are partial solutions you may find:

$$\begin{bmatrix} 1 & 0 & k_1 & x_0 \\ 0 & 1 & k_2 & y_0 \\ 0 & 0 & 0 & 0 \end{bmatrix}$$ gives the non-unique solution $x = x_0 - k_1z$; $y = y_0 - k_2z$

$$\begin{bmatrix} 1 & j_1 & k_1 & x_0 \\ 0 & 0 & 0 & 0 \\ 0 & 0 & 0 & 0 \end{bmatrix}$$ gives the non-unique solution $x = x_0 - j_1y - k_1z$

This process can be used to solve systems of equations with any number of variables, but three is the upper limit for practical purposes. Anything more ought to be done with a graphing calculator.

GEOMETRIC TRANSFORMATIONS

The four *geometric transformations* are **translations**, **reflections**, **rotations**, and **dilations**. When geometric transformations are expressed as matrices, the process of performing the transformations is simplified. For calculations of the geometric transformations of a planar figure, make a $2 \times n$ matrix, where n is the number of vertices in the planar figure. Each column represents the rectangular coordinates of one vertex of the figure, with the top row containing the values of the x-coordinates and the bottom row containing the values of the y-coordinates. For example, given a planar triangular figure with coordinates (x_1, y_1), (x_2, y_2), and (x_3, y_3), the corresponding matrix is $\begin{bmatrix} x_1 & x_2 & x_3 \\ y_1 & y_2 & y_3 \end{bmatrix}$. You can then perform the necessary transformations on this matrix to determine the coordinates of the resulting figure.

TRANSLATION

A **translation** moves a figure along the x-axis, the y-axis, or both axes without changing the size or shape of the figure. To calculate the new coordinates of a planar figure following a translation, set up a matrix of the coordinates and a matrix of the translation values and add the two matrices.

$$\begin{bmatrix} h & h & h \\ v & v & v \end{bmatrix} + \begin{bmatrix} x_1 & x_2 & x_3 \\ y_1 & y_2 & y_3 \end{bmatrix} = \begin{bmatrix} h + x_1 & h + x_2 & h + x_3 \\ v + y_1 & v + y_2 & v + y_3 \end{bmatrix}$$

where h is the number of units the figure is moved along the x-axis (horizontally) and v is the number of units the figure is moved along the y-axis (vertically).

REFLECTION

To find the **reflection** of a planar figure over the x-axis, set up a matrix of the coordinates of the vertices and pre-multiply the matrix by the 2×2 matrix $\begin{bmatrix} 1 & 0 \\ 0 & -1 \end{bmatrix}$ so that $\begin{bmatrix} 1 & 0 \\ 0 & -1 \end{bmatrix}\begin{bmatrix} x_1 & x_2 & x_3 \\ y_1 & y_2 & y_3 \end{bmatrix} = \begin{bmatrix} x_1 & x_2 & x_3 \\ -y_1 & -y_2 & -y_3 \end{bmatrix}$. To find the reflection of a planar figure over the y-axis, set up a matrix of the coordinates of the vertices and pre-multiply the matrix by the 2×2 matrix $\begin{bmatrix} -1 & 0 \\ 0 & 1 \end{bmatrix}$ so that $\begin{bmatrix} -1 & 0 \\ 0 & 1 \end{bmatrix}\begin{bmatrix} x_1 & x_2 & x_3 \\ y_1 & y_2 & y_3 \end{bmatrix} = \begin{bmatrix} -x_1 & -x_2 & -x_3 \\ y_1 & y_2 & y_3 \end{bmatrix}$. To find the reflection of a planar figure over the line $y = x$, set up a matrix of the coordinates of the vertices and pre-multiply the matrix by the 2×2 matrix $\begin{bmatrix} 0 & 1 \\ 1 & 0 \end{bmatrix}$ so that $\begin{bmatrix} 0 & 1 \\ 1 & 0 \end{bmatrix}\begin{bmatrix} x_1 & x_2 & x_3 \\ y_1 & y_2 & y_3 \end{bmatrix} = \begin{bmatrix} y_1 & y_2 & y_3 \\ x_1 & x_2 & x_3 \end{bmatrix}$. Remember that the order of multiplication is important when multiplying matrices. The commutative property does not apply.

ROTATION

To find the coordinates of the figure formed by rotating a planar figure about the origin θ degrees in a counterclockwise direction, set up a matrix of the coordinates of the vertices and pre-multiply the matrix by the 2×2 matrix $\begin{bmatrix} \cos\theta & \sin\theta \\ -\sin\theta & \cos\theta \end{bmatrix}$. For example, if you want to rotate a figure 90° clockwise around the origin, you would have to convert the degree measure to 270° counterclockwise and solve the 2×2 matrix you have set as the pre-multiplier: $\begin{bmatrix} \cos 270° & \sin 270° \\ -\sin 270° & \cos 270° \end{bmatrix} = \begin{bmatrix} 0 & -1 \\ 1 & 0 \end{bmatrix}$. Use this as the pre-multiplier for the matrix $\begin{bmatrix} x_1 & x_2 & x_3 \\ y_1 & y_2 & y_3 \end{bmatrix}$ and solve to find the new coordinates.

DILATION

To find the **dilation** of a planar figure by a scale factor of k, set up a matrix of the coordinates of the vertices of the planar figure and pre-multiply the matrix by the 2×2 matrix $\begin{bmatrix} k & 0 \\ 0 & k \end{bmatrix}$ so that $\begin{bmatrix} k & 0 \\ 0 & k \end{bmatrix}\begin{bmatrix} x_1 & x_2 & x_3 \\ y_1 & y_2 & y_3 \end{bmatrix} = \begin{bmatrix} kx_1 & kx_2 & kx_3 \\ ky_1 & ky_2 & ky_3 \end{bmatrix}$. This is effectively the same as multiplying the matrix by the scalar k, but the matrix equation would still be necessary if the figure were being dilated by different factors in vertical and horizontal directions. The scale factor k will be greater than 1 if the figure is being enlarged, and between 0 and 1 if the figure is being shrunk. Again, remember that when multiplying matrices, the order of the matrices is important. The commutative property does not apply, and the matrix with the coordinates of the figure must be the second matrix.

REDUCED ROW-ECHELON FORMS

When a system of equations has a solution, finding the transformation of the augmented matrix will result in one of three reduced row-echelon forms. Only one of these forms will give a unique solution to the system of equations, however. The following examples show the solutions indicated by particular results:

$$\begin{bmatrix} 1 & 0 & 0 & x_0 \\ 0 & 1 & 0 & y_0 \\ 0 & 0 & 1 & z_0 \end{bmatrix}$$ gives the unique solution $x = x_0$; $y = y_0$; $z = z_0$

$$\begin{bmatrix} 1 & 0 & k_1 & x_0 \\ 0 & 1 & k_2 & y_0 \\ 0 & 0 & 0 & 0 \end{bmatrix}$$ gives a non-unique solution $x = x_0 - k_1z$; $y = y_0 - k_2z$

$$\begin{bmatrix} 1 & j_1 & k_1 & x_0 \\ 0 & 0 & 0 & 0 \\ 0 & 0 & 0 & 0 \end{bmatrix}$$ gives a non-unique solution $x = x_0 - j_1y - k_1z$

Measurement

COMMON METRIC MEASUREMENTS

FLUIDS

1 liter = 1000 milliliters
1 liter = 1000 cubic centimeters

Note: Do not confuse *cubic centimeters* with *centiliters*. 1 liter = 1000 cubic cent*imeters*, but 1 liter = 100 centi*liters*.

DISTANCE

1 meter = 1000 millimeters
1 meter = 100 centimeters

WEIGHT

1 gram = 1000 milligrams
1 kilogram = 1000 grams

MEASUREMENT PREFIXES

Kilo-: one thousand (1 *kilo*gram is one thousand grams.)
Centi-: one hundredth (1 *centi*meter is one hundredth of a meter.)
Milli-: one thousandth (1 *milli*liter is one thousandth of a liter.)

COMMON IMPERIAL MEASUREMENTS

VOLUME

1 cup = 8 fluid ounces

Note: This does NOT mean that one cup of something is the same as a half pound. Fluid ounces are measures of volume and have no correspondence with measures of weight.

1 pint = 2 cups
1 pint = 16 ounces

Again, the phrase, "A pint's a pound the world round," does not apply. A pint of something does not necessarily weigh one pound, since one fluid ounce is not the same as one ounce in weight. The expression is valid only for helping you remember the number 16, since most people can remember there are 16 ounces in a pound.

DISTANCE

1 yard = 3 feet
1 yard = 36 inches
1 mile = 5280 feet
1 mile = 1760 yards
1 acre = 43,560 square feet

VOLUME

1 quart = 2 pints
1 quart = 4 cups
1 gallon = 4 quarts
1 gallon = 8 pints
1 gallon = 16 cups

WEIGHT

1 pound = 16 ounces

Do not assume that because something weighs one pound that its volume is one pint. Ounces of weight are not equivalent to fluid ounces, which measure volume.

1 ton = 2000 pounds

In the United States, the word "ton" by itself refers to a short ton or a net ton. Do not confuse this with a long ton (also called a gross ton) or a metric ton (also spelled *tonne*), which have different measurement equivalents.

PRECISION, ACCURACY, AND ERROR

Precision: How reliable and repeatable a measurement is. The more consistent the data is with repeated testing, the more precise it is. For example, hitting a target consistently in the same spot, which may or may not be the center of the target, is precision.

Accuracy: How close the data is to the correct data. For example, hitting a target consistently in the center area of the target, whether or not the hits are all in the same spot, is accuracy.

Note: it is possible for data to be precise without being accurate. If a scale is off balance, the data will be precise, but will not be accurate. For data to have precision and accuracy, it must be repeatable and correct.

Approximate Error: The amount of error in a physical measurement. Approximate error is often reported as the measurement, followed by the ± symbol and the amount of the approximate error.

Maximum Possible Error: Half the magnitude of the smallest unit used in the measurement. For example, if the unit of measurement is 1 centimeter, the maximum possible error is $\frac{1}{2}$ cm, written as ± 0.5 cm following the measurement. It is important to apply significant figures in reporting maximum possible error. Do not make the answer appear more accurate than the least accurate of your measurements.

Geometry

LINES AND PLANES

A **point** is a fixed location in space; has no size or dimensions; commonly represented by a dot.

A **line** is a set of points that extends infinitely in two opposite directions. It has length, but no width or depth. A line can be defined by any two distinct points that it contains. A line segment is a portion of a line that has definite endpoints. A ray is a portion of a line that extends from a single point on that line in one direction along the line. It has a definite beginning, but no ending.

A **plane** is a two-dimensional flat surface defined by three non-collinear points. A plane extends an infinite distance in all directions in those two dimensions. It contains an infinite number of points, parallel lines and segments, intersecting lines and segments, as well as parallel or intersecting rays. A plane will never contain a three-dimensional figure or skew lines. Two given planes will either be parallel or they will intersect to form a line. A plane may intersect a circular conic surface, such as a cone, to form conic sections, such as the parabola, hyperbola, circle or ellipse.

Perpendicular lines are lines that intersect at right angles. They are represented by the symbol ⊥. The shortest distance from a line to a point not on the line is a perpendicular segment from the point to the line.

Parallel lines are lines in the same plane that have no points in common and never meet. It is possible for lines to be in different planes, have no points in common, and never meet, but they are not parallel because they are in different planes.

A **bisector** is a line or line segment that divides another line segment into two equal lengths. A perpendicular bisector of a line segment is composed of points that are equidistant from the endpoints of the segment it is dividing.

Intersecting lines are lines that have exactly one point in common. Concurrent lines are multiple lines that intersect at a single point.

A **transversal** is a line that intersects at least two other lines, which may or may not be parallel to one another. A transversal that intersects parallel lines is a common occurrence in geometry.

The **projection of a point on a line** is the point at which a perpendicular line drawn from the given point to the given line intersects the line. This is also the shortest distance from the given point to the line.

The **projection of a segment on a line** is a segment whose endpoints are the points formed when perpendicular lines are drawn from the endpoints of the given segment to the given line. This is similar to the length a diagonal line appears to be when viewed from above.

ANGLES

An **angle** is formed when two lines or line segments meet at a common point. It may be a common starting point for a pair of segments or rays, or it may be the intersection of lines. Angles are represented by the symbol ∠.

The **vertex** is the point at which two segments or rays meet to form an angle. If the angle is formed by intersecting rays, lines, and/or line segments, the vertex is the point at which four angles are formed. The pairs of angles opposite one another are called vertical angles, and their measures are equal.

- An *acute* angle is an angle with a degree measure less than 90°.
- A *right* angle is an angle with a degree measure of exactly 90°.
- An *obtuse* angle is an angle with a degree measure greater than 90° but less than 180°.
- A *straight angle* is an angle with a degree measure of exactly 180°. This is also a semicircle.
- A *reflex angle* is an angle with a degree measure greater than 180° but less than 360°.
- A *full angle* is an angle with a degree measure of exactly 360°.

Two angles whose sum is exactly 90° are said to be **complementary**. The two angles may or may not be adjacent. In a right triangle, the two acute angles are complementary.

Two angles whose sum is exactly 180° are said to be **supplementary**. The two angles may or may not be adjacent. Two intersecting lines always form two pairs of supplementary angles. Adjacent supplementary angles will always form a straight line.

Two angles that have the same vertex and share a side are said to be **adjacent**. Vertical angles are not adjacent because they share a vertex but no common side.

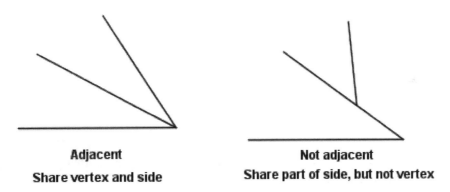

Adjacent
Share vertex and side

Not adjacent
Share part of side, but not vertex

When two parallel lines are cut by a transversal, the angles that are between the two parallel lines are **interior angles**. In the diagram below, angles 3, 4, 5, and 6 are interior angles.

When two parallel lines are cut by a transversal, the angles that are outside the parallel lines are **exterior angles**. In the diagram below, angles 1, 2, 7, and 8 are exterior angles.

When two parallel lines are cut by a transversal, the angles that are in the same position relative to the transversal and a parallel line are *corresponding angles*. The diagram below has four pairs of corresponding angles: angles 1 and 5; angles 2 and 6; angles 3 and 7; and angles 4 and 8. Corresponding angles formed by parallel lines are congruent.

When two parallel lines are cut by a transversal, the two interior angles that are on opposite sides of the transversal are called *alternate interior angles*. In the diagram below, there are two pairs of alternate interior angles: angles 3 and 6, and angles 4 and 5. Alternate interior angles formed by parallel lines are congruent.

When two parallel lines are cut by a transversal, the two exterior angles that are on opposite sides of the transversal are called *alternate exterior angles*.

In the diagram below, there are two pairs of alternate exterior angles: angles 1 and 8, and angles 2 and 7. Alternate exterior angles formed by parallel lines are congruent.

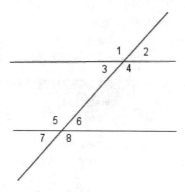

When two lines intersect, four angles are formed. The non-adjacent angles at this vertex are called vertical angles. Vertical angles are congruent. In the diagram, $\angle ABD \cong \angle CBE$ and $\angle ABC \cong \angle DBE$.

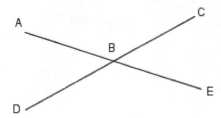

POLYGONS

Each straight line segment of a polygon is called a **side**.

The point at which two sides of a polygon intersect is called the **vertex**. In a polygon, the number of sides is always equal to the number of vertices.

A polygon with all sides congruent and all angles equal is called a **regular polygon**.

A line segment from the center of a polygon perpendicular to a side of the polygon is called the **apothem**. In a regular polygon, the apothem can be used to find the area of the polygon using the formula $A = \frac{1}{2}ap$, where a is the apothem and p is the perimeter.

A line segment from the center of a polygon to a vertex of the polygon is called a **radius**. The radius of a regular polygon is also the radius of a circle that can be circumscribed about the polygon.

- Triangle – 3 sides
- Quadrilateral – 4 sides
- Pentagon – 5 sides
- Hexagon – 6 sides
- Heptagon – 7 sides
- Octagon – 8 sides
- Nonagon – 9 sides

- Decagon – 10 sides
- Dodecagon – 12 sides

More generally, an *n*-gon is a polygon that has *n* angles and *n* sides.

The sum of the interior angles of an *n*-sided polygon is (n – 2)180°. For example, in a triangle $n = 3$, so the sum of the interior angles is $(3-2)180° = 180°$. In a quadrilateral, $n = 4$, and the sum of the angles is $(4-2)180° = 360°$. The sum of the interior angles of a polygon is equal to the sum of the interior angles of any other polygon with the same number of sides.

A **diagonal** is a line segment that joins two non-adjacent vertices of a polygon.

A **convex polygon** is a polygon whose diagonals all lie within the interior of the polygon.

A **concave polygon** is a polygon with a least one diagonal that lies outside the polygon. In the diagram below, quadrilateral *ABCD* is concave because diagonal $\overline{AC}$ lies outside the polygon.

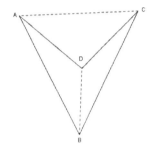

The number of diagonals a polygon has can be found by using the formula: number of diagonals $= \frac{n(n-3)}{2}$, where *n* is the number of sides in the polygon. This formula works for all polygons, not just regular polygons.

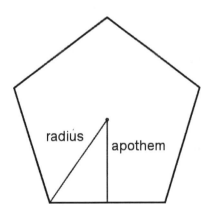

Congruent figures are geometric figures that have the same size and shape. All corresponding angles are equal, and all corresponding sides are equal. It is indicated by the symbol ≅.

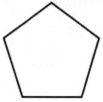 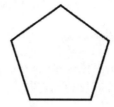

Congruent polygons

Similar figures are geometric figures that have the same shape, but do not necessarily have the same size. All corresponding angles are equal, and all corresponding sides are proportional, but they do not have to be equal. It is indicated by the symbol ~.

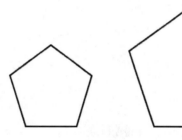

Similar polygons

Note that all congruent figures are also similar, but not all similar figures are congruent.

Review Video: Polygons, Similarity, and Congruence
Visit mometrix.com/academy and enter code: 686174

LINE OF SYMMETRY

A **line of symmetry** is a line that divides a figure or object into two symmetric parts. Each symmetric half is congruent to the other. An object may have no lines of symmetry, one line of symmetry, or more than one line of symmetry.

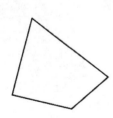 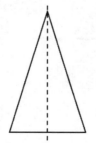 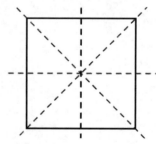

No lines of symmetry   One line of symmetry   Multiple lines of symmetry

Quadrilateral: A closed two-dimensional geometric figure composed of exactly four straight sides. The sum of the interior angles of any quadrilateral is 360°.

> **Review Video: Symmetry**
> Visit mometrix.com/academy and enter code: 528106

PARALLELOGRAM

A **parallelogram** is a quadrilateral that has exactly two pairs of opposite parallel sides. The sides that are parallel are also congruent. The opposite interior angles are always congruent, and the consecutive interior angles are supplementary. The diagonals of a parallelogram bisect each other. Each diagonal divides the parallelogram into two congruent triangles.

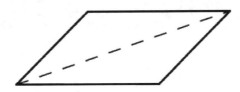

> **Review Video: Parallelogram**
> Visit mometrix.com/academy and enter code: 129981

TRAPEZOID

Traditionally, a **trapezoid** is a quadrilateral that has exactly one pair of parallel sides. Some math texts define trapezoid as a quadrilateral that has at least one pair of parallel sides. Because there are no rules governing the second pair of sides, there are no rules that apply to the properties of the diagonals of a trapezoid.

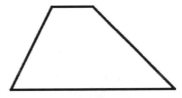

Rectangles, rhombuses, and squares are all special forms of parallelograms.

RECTANGLE

A **rectangle** is a parallelogram with four right angles. All rectangles are parallelograms, but not all parallelograms are rectangles. The diagonals of a rectangle are congruent.

RHOMBUS

A **rhombus** is a parallelogram with four congruent sides. All rhombuses are parallelograms, but not all parallelograms are rhombuses. The diagonals of a rhombus are perpendicular to each other.

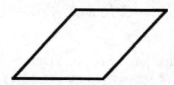

> **Review Video: Diagonals of Parallelograms, Rectangles, and Rhombi**
> Visit mometrix.com/academy and enter code: 320040

SQUARE

A **square** is a parallelogram with four right angles and four congruent sides. All squares are also parallelograms, rhombuses, and rectangles. The diagonals of a square are congruent and perpendicular to each other.

A quadrilateral whose diagonals bisect each other is a **parallelogram**. A quadrilateral whose opposite sides are parallel (2 pairs of parallel sides) is a parallelogram.

A quadrilateral whose diagonals are perpendicular bisectors of each other is a **rhombus**. A quadrilateral whose opposite sides (both pairs) are parallel and congruent is a rhombus.

A parallelogram that has a right angle is a **rectangle**. (Consecutive angles of a parallelogram are supplementary. Therefore if there is one right angle in a parallelogram, there are four right angles in that parallelogram.)

A rhombus with one right angle is a **square**. Because the rhombus is a special form of a parallelogram, the rules about the angles of a parallelogram also apply to the rhombus.

AREA AND PERIMETER FORMULAS

TRIANGLE

The *perimeter of any triangle* is found by summing the three side lengths; $P = a + b + c$. For an equilateral triangle, this is the same as $P = 3s$, where s is any side length, since all three sides are the same length.

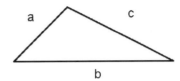

SQUARE

The *area of a square* is found by using the formula $A = s^2$, where and s is the length of one side.

The *perimeter of a square* is found by using the formula $P = 4s$, where s is the length of one side. Because all four sides are equal in a square, it is faster to multiply the length of one side by 4 than to add the same number four times. You could use the formulas for rectangles and get the same answer.

> **Review Video: Area and Perimeter of a Square**
> Visit mometrix.com/academy and enter code: 620902

RECTANGLE

The *area of a rectangle* is found by the formula $A = lw$, where A is the area of the rectangle, l is the length (usually considered to be the longer side) and w is the width (usually considered to be the shorter side). The numbers for l and w are interchangeable.

The *perimeter of a rectangle* is found by the formula $P = 2l + 2w$ or $P = 2(l + w)$, where l is the length, and w is the width. It may be easier to add the length and width first and then double the result, as in the second formula.

> **Review Video: Area and Perimeter of a Rectangle**
> Visit mometrix.com/academy and enter code: 933707

PARALLELOGRAM

The *area of a parallelogram* is found by the formula $A = bh$, where b is the length of the base, and h is the height. Note that the base and height correspond to the length and width in a rectangle, so this formula would apply to rectangles as well. Do not confuse the height of a parallelogram with the length of the second side. The two are only the same measure in the case of a rectangle.

The *perimeter of a parallelogram* is found by the formula $P = 2a + 2b$ or $P = 2(a + b)$, where a and b are the lengths of the two sides.

> **Review Video: Area and Perimeter of a Parallelogram**
> Visit mometrix.com/academy and enter code: 718313

TRAPEZOID

The *area of a trapezoid* is found by the formula $A = \frac{1}{2}h(b_1 + b_2)$, where h is the height (segment joining and perpendicular to the parallel bases), and b_1 and b_2 are the two parallel sides (bases). Do not use one of the other two sides as the height unless that side is also perpendicular to the parallel bases.

The *perimeter of a trapezoid* is found by the formula $P = a + b_1 + c + b_2$, where a, b_1, c, and b_2 are the four sides of the trapezoid.

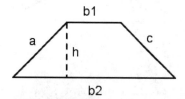

Review Video: <u>Area and Perimeter of a Trapezoid</u>
Visit mometrix.com/academy and enter code: 587523

TRIANGLES

An **equilateral triangle** is a triangle with three congruent sides. An equilateral triangle will also have three congruent angles, each 60°. All equilateral triangles are also acute triangles.

An **isosceles triangle** is a triangle with two congruent sides. An isosceles triangle will also have two congruent angles opposite the two congruent sides.

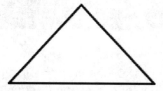

A **scalene triangle** is a triangle with no congruent sides. A scalene triangle will also have three angles of different measures. The angle with the largest measure is opposite the longest side, and the angle with the smallest measure is opposite the shortest side.

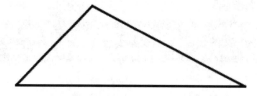

110

An **acute triangle** is a triangle whose three angles are all less than 90°. If two of the angles are equal, the acute triangle is also an isosceles triangle. If the three angles are all equal, the acute triangle is also an equilateral triangle.

A **right triangle** is a triangle with exactly one angle equal to 90°. All right triangles follow the Pythagorean theorem. A right triangle can never be acute or obtuse.

An **obtuse triangle** is a triangle with exactly one angle greater than 90°. The other two angles may or may not be equal. If the two remaining angles are equal, the obtuse triangle is also an isosceles triangle.

> **Review Video: Introduction to Types of Triangles**
> Visit mometrix.com/academy and enter code: 511711

TERMINOLOGY

ALTITUDE OF A TRIANGLE

A line segment drawn from one vertex perpendicular to the opposite side. In the diagram below, $\overline{BE}, \overline{AD}$, and $\overline{CF}$ are altitudes. The three altitudes in a triangle are always concurrent.

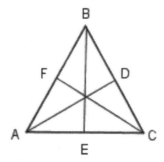

Height of a triangle

The length of the altitude, although the two terms are often used interchangeably.

Orthocenter of a triangle

The point of concurrency of the altitudes of a triangle. Note that in an obtuse triangle, the orthocenter will be outside the triangle, and in a right triangle, the orthocenter is the vertex of the right angle.

Median of a triangle

A line segment drawn from one vertex to the midpoint of the opposite side. This is not the same as the altitude, except the altitude to the base of an isosceles triangle and all three altitudes of an equilateral triangle.

Centroid of a triangle

The point of concurrency of the medians of a triangle. This is the same point as the orthocenter only in an equilateral triangle. Unlike the orthocenter, the centroid is always inside the triangle. The centroid can also be considered the exact center of the triangle. Any shape triangle can be perfectly balanced on a tip placed at the centroid. The centroid is also the point that is two-thirds the distance from the vertex to the opposite side.

PYTHAGOREAN THEOREM

The side of a triangle opposite the right angle is called the **hypotenuse**. The other two sides are called the legs. The Pythagorean theorem states a relationship among the legs and hypotenuse of a right triangle: $a^2 + b^2 = c^2$, where a and b are the lengths of the legs of a right triangle, and c is the length of the hypotenuse. Note that this formula will only work with right triangles.

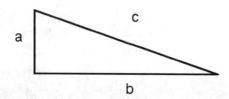

Review Video: Pythagorean Theorem
Visit mometrix.com/academy and enter code: 906576

GENERAL RULES

The *triangle inequality theorem* states that the sum of the measures of any two sides of a triangle is always greater than the measure of the third side. If the sum of the measures of two sides were equal to the third side, a triangle would be impossible because the two sides would lie flat across the third side and there would be no vertex. If the sum of the measures of two of the sides was less than the third side, a closed figure would be impossible because the two shortest sides would never meet.

The sum of the measures of the interior angles of a triangle is always 180°. Therefore, a triangle can never have more than one angle greater than or equal to 90°.

In any triangle, the angles opposite congruent sides are congruent, and the sides opposite congruent angles are congruent. The largest angle is always opposite the longest side, and the smallest angle is always opposite the shortest side.

The line segment that joins the midpoints of any two sides of a triangle is always parallel to the third side and exactly half the length of the third side.

SIMILARITY AND CONGRUENCE RULES

Similar triangles are triangles whose corresponding angles are equal and whose corresponding sides are proportional. Represented by AA. Similar triangles whose corresponding sides are congruent are also congruent triangles.

Review Video: Similar Triangles
Visit mometrix.com/academy and enter code: 398538

Three sides of one triangle are congruent to the three corresponding sides of the second triangle. Represented as SSS.

Two sides and the included angle (the angle formed by those two sides) of one triangle are congruent to the corresponding two sides and included angle of the second triangle. Represented by SAS.

Two angles and the included side (the side that joins the two angles) of one triangle are congruent to the corresponding two angles and included side of the second triangle. Represented by ASA.

Two angles and a non-included side of one triangle are congruent to the corresponding two angles and non-included side of the second triangle. Represented by AAS.

Note that AAA is not a form for congruent triangles. This would say that the three angles are congruent, but says nothing about the sides. This meets the requirements for similar triangles, but not congruent triangles.

AREA AND PERIMETER FORMULAS

The *perimeter of any triangle* is found by summing the three side lengths; $P = a + b + c$. For an equilateral triangle, this is the same as $P = 3s$, where s is any side length, since all three sides are the same length.

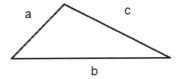

The area of any triangle can be found by taking half the product of one side length (base or b) and the perpendicular distance from that side to the opposite vertex (height or h). In equation form, $A = \frac{1}{2}bh$. For many triangles, it may be difficult to calculate h, so using one of the other formulas given here may be easier.

Another formula that works for any triangle is $A = \sqrt{s(s - a)(s - b)(s - c)}$, where A is the area, s is the semiperimeter $s = \frac{a+b+c}{2}$, and a, b, and c are the lengths of the three sides.

The area of an equilateral triangle can be found by the formula $A = \frac{\sqrt{3}}{4}s^2$, where A is the area and s is the length of a side. You could use the $30° - 60° - 90°$ ratios to find the height of the triangle and then use the standard triangle area formula, but this is faster.

The area of an isosceles triangle can be found by the formula, $A = \frac{1}{2}b\sqrt{a^2 - \frac{b^2}{4}}$, where A is the area, b is the base (the unique side), and a is the length of one of the two congruent sides. If you do not remember this formula, you can use the Pythagorean theorem to find the height so you can use the standard formula for the area of a triangle.

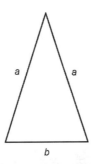

Review Video: Area and Perimeter of a Triangle
Visit mometrix.com/academy and enter code: 853779

ROTATION, CENTER OF ROTATION, AND ANGLE OF ROTATION

A *rotation* is a transformation that turns a figure around a point called the **center of rotation**, which can lie anywhere in the plane. If a line is drawn from a point on a figure to the center of rotation, and another line is drawn from the center to the rotated image of that point, the angle between the two lines is the **angle of rotation**. The vertex of the angle of rotation is the center of rotation.

> **Review Video: Rotation**
> Visit mometrix.com/academy and enter code: 602600

REFLECTION OVER A LINE AND REFLECTION IN A POINT

A reflection of a figure over a *line* (a "flip") creates a congruent image that is the same distance from the line as the original figure but on the opposite side. The **line of reflection** is the perpendicular bisector of any line segment drawn from a point on the original figure to its reflected image (unless the point and its reflected image happen to be the same point, which happens when a figure is reflected over one of its own sides).

A reflection of a figure in a *point* is the same as the rotation of the figure 180° about that point. The image of the figure is congruent to the original figure. The **point of reflection** is the midpoint of a line segment which connects a point in the figure to its image (unless the point and its reflected image happen to be the same point, which happens when a figure is reflected in one of its own points).

> **Review Video: Reflection**
> Visit mometrix.com/academy and enter code: 955068

EXAMPLE

Use the coordinate plane of the given image below to reflect the image across the *y*-axis.

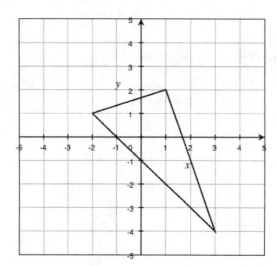

To reflect the image across the *y*-axis, replace each *x*-coordinate of the points that are the vertex of the triangle, *x*, with its negative, –*x*.

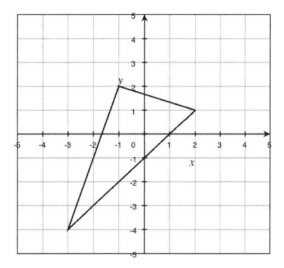

TRANSLATION

A *translation* is a transformation which slides a figure from one position in the plane to another position in the plane. The original figure and the translated figure have the same size, shape, and orientation.

Review Video: Translation
Visit mometrix.com/academy and enter code: 718628

TRANSFORMING A GIVEN FIGURE USING ROTATION, REFLECTION, AND TRANSLATION

To **rotate** a given figure: 1. Identify the point of rotation. 2. Using tracing paper, geometry software, or by approximation, recreate the figure at a new location around the point of rotation.

To **reflect** a given figure: 1. Identify the line of reflection. 2. By folding the paper, using geometry software, or by approximation, recreate the image at a new location on the other side of the line of reflection.

To **translate** a given figure: 1. Identify the new location. 2. Using graph paper, geometry software, or by approximation, recreate the figure in the new location. If using graph paper, make a chart of the x- and y-values to keep track of the coordinates of all critical points.

EVIDENCE OF TRANSFORMATION

To identify that a figure has been *rotated*, look for evidence that the figure is still face-up, but has changed its orientation.

To identify that a figure has been *reflected* across a line, look for evidence that the figure is now face-down.

To identify that a figure has been *translated*, look for evidence that a figure is still face-up and has not changed orientation; the only change is location.

To identify that a figure has been *dilated*, look for evidence that the figure has changed its size but not its orientation.

DILATION

A **dilation** is a transformation which proportionally stretches or shrinks a figure by a **scale factor**. The dilated image is the same shape and orientation as the original image but a different size. A polygon and its dilated image are similar.

EXAMPLE 1

Use the coordinate plane to create a dilation of the given image below, where the dilation is the enlargement of the original image.

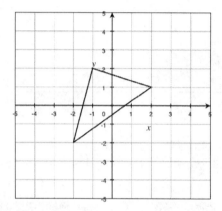

An enlargement can be found by multiplying each coordinate of the coordinate pairs located at the triangles vertices by a constant. If the figure is enlarged by a factor of 2, the new image would be:

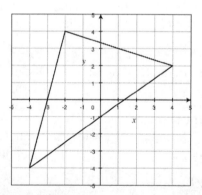

Review Video: Dilation
Visit mometrix.com/academy and enter code: 471630

TRIGONOMETRIC FORMULAS

In the diagram below, angle C is the **right angle**, and side c is the **hypotenuse**. Side a is the side adjacent to angle B and side b is the side adjacent to angle A. These formulas will work for any acute angle in a right triangle. They will *not* work for any triangle that is not a right triangle. Also, they will not work for the right angle in a right triangle, since there are not distinct adjacent and opposite sides to differentiate from the hypotenuse.

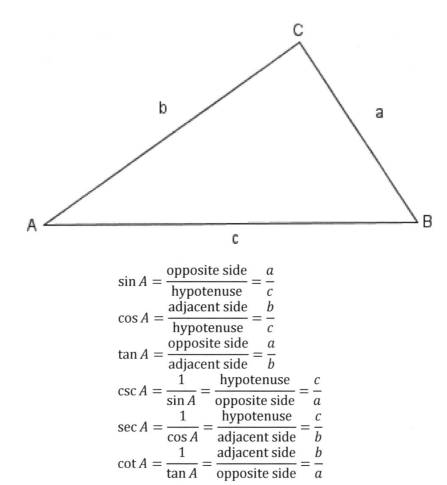

$$\sin A = \frac{\text{opposite side}}{\text{hypotenuse}} = \frac{a}{c}$$

$$\cos A = \frac{\text{adjacent side}}{\text{hypotenuse}} = \frac{b}{c}$$

$$\tan A = \frac{\text{opposite side}}{\text{adjacent side}} = \frac{a}{b}$$

$$\csc A = \frac{1}{\sin A} = \frac{\text{hypotenuse}}{\text{opposite side}} = \frac{c}{a}$$

$$\sec A = \frac{1}{\cos A} = \frac{\text{hypotenuse}}{\text{adjacent side}} = \frac{c}{b}$$

$$\cot A = \frac{1}{\tan A} = \frac{\text{adjacent side}}{\text{opposite side}} = \frac{b}{a}$$

LAWS OF SINES AND COSINES

The **law of sines** states that $\frac{\sin A}{a} = \frac{\sin B}{b} = \frac{\sin C}{c}$, where A, B, and C are the angles of a triangle, and a, b, and c are the sides opposite their respective angles. This formula will work with all triangles, not just right triangles.

The **law of cosines** is given by the formula $c^2 = a^2 + b^2 - 2ab(\cos C)$, where a, b, and c are the sides of a triangle, and C is the angle opposite side c. This formula is similar to the *pythagorean theorem*, but unlike the pythagorean theorem, it can be used on any triangle.

Review Video: <u>Cosine</u>
Visit mometrix.com/academy and enter code: 361120

CIRCLES

The **center** is the single point inside the circle that is **equidistant** from every point on the circle. (Point *O* in the diagram below.)

The **radius** is a line segment that joins the center of the circle and any one point on the circle. All radii of a circle are equal. (Segments *OX*, *OY*, and *OZ* in the diagram below.)

The **diameter** is a line segment that passes through the center of the circle and has both endpoints on the circle. The length of the diameter is exactly twice the length of the radius. (Segment *XZ* in the diagram below.)

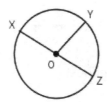

The **area of a circle** is found by the formula $A = \pi r^2$, where *r* is the length of the radius. If the diameter of the circle is given, remember to divide it in half to get the length of the radius before proceeding.

The **circumference** of a circle is found by the formula $C = 2\pi r$, where *r* is the radius. Again, remember to convert the diameter if you are given that measure rather than the radius.

Concentric circles are circles that have the same center, but not the same length of radii. A bulls-eye target is an example of concentric circles.

An **arc** is a portion of a circle. Specifically, an arc is the set of points between and including two points on a circle. An arc does not contain any points inside the circle. When a segment is drawn from the endpoints of an arc to the center of the circle, a sector is formed.

A **central angle** is an angle whose vertex is the center of a circle and whose legs intercept an arc of the circle. Angle *XOY* in the diagram above is a central angle. A minor arc is an arc that has a measure less than 180°. The measure of a central angle is equal to the measure of the minor arc it intercepts. A major arc is an arc having a measure of at least 180°. The measure of the major arc can be found by subtracting the measure of the central angle from 360°.

A **semicircle** is an arc whose endpoints are the endpoints of the diameter of a circle. A semicircle is exactly half of a circle.

An **inscribed angle** is an angle whose vertex lies on a circle and whose legs contain chords of that circle. The portion of the circle intercepted by the legs of the angle is called the intercepted arc. The measure of the intercepted arc is exactly twice the measure of the inscribed angle. In the following diagram, angle ABC is an inscribed angle. $\overset{\frown}{AC} = 2(m\angle ABC)$

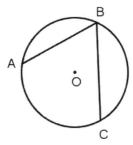

Any angle inscribed in a semicircle is a right angle. The intercepted arc is 180°, making the inscribed angle half that, or 90°. In the diagram below, angle ABC is inscribed in semicircle ABC, making angle ABC equal to 90°.

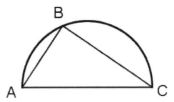

A **chord** is a line segment that has both endpoints on a circle. In the diagram below, $\overline{EB}$ is a chord.

Secant: A line that passes through a circle and contains a chord of that circle. In the diagram below, $\overleftrightarrow{EB}$ is a secant and contains chord $\overline{EB}$.

A **tangent** is a line in the same plane as a circle that touches the circle in exactly one point. While a line segment can be tangent to a circle as part of a line that is tangent, it is improper to say a tangent can be simply a line segment that touches the circle in exactly one point. In the diagram below, $\overleftrightarrow{CD}$ is tangent to circle A. Notice that $\overline{FB}$ is not tangent to the circle. $\overline{FB}$ is a line segment that touches the circle in exactly one point, but if the segment were extended, it would touch the circle in a second point. The point at which a tangent touches a circle is called the point of tangency. In the diagram below, point B is the point of tangency.

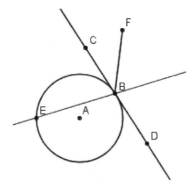

A **secant** is a line that intersects a circle in two points. Two secants may intersect inside the circle, on the circle, or outside the circle. When the two secants intersect on the circle, an inscribed angle is formed.

When two secants intersect inside a circle, the measure of each of two vertical angles is equal to half the sum of the two intercepted arcs. In the diagram below, $m\angle AEB = \frac{1}{2}(\widehat{AB} + \widehat{CD})$ and $m\angle BEC = \frac{1}{2}(\widehat{BC} + \widehat{AD})$.

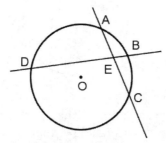

When two secants intersect outside a circle, the measure of the angle formed is equal to half the difference of the two arcs that lie between the two secants. In the diagram below, $m\angle AEB = \frac{1}{2}(\widehat{AB} - \widehat{CD})$.

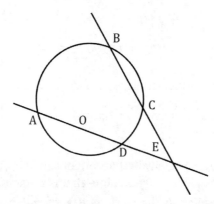

The **arc length** is the length of that portion of the circumference between two points on the circle. The formula for arc length is $s = \frac{\pi r\theta}{180°}$ where s is the arc length, r is the length of the radius, and θ is the angular measure of the arc in degrees, or $s = r\theta$, where θ is the angular measure of the arc in radians (2π radians = 360 degrees).

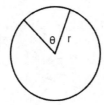

A **sector** is the portion of a circle formed by two radii and their intercepted arc. While the arc length is exclusively the points that are also on the circumference of the circle, the sector is the entire area bounded by the arc and the two radii.

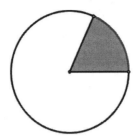

The **area of a sector** of a circle is found by the formula, $A = \frac{\theta r^2}{2}$, where A is the area, θ is the measure of the central angle in radians, and r is the radius. To find the area when the central angle is in degrees, use the formula, $A = \frac{\theta \pi r^2}{360}$, where θ is the measure of the central angle in degrees and r is the radius.

A circle is inscribed in a polygon if each of the sides of the polygon is tangent to the circle. A polygon is inscribed in a circle if each of the vertices of the polygon lies on the circle.

A circle is circumscribed about a polygon if each of the vertices of the polygon lies on the circle. A polygon is circumscribed about the circle if each of the sides of the polygon is tangent to the circle.

If one figure is inscribed in another, then the other figure is circumscribed about the first figure.

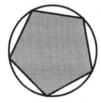

Circle circumscribed about a pentagon
Pentagon inscribed in a circle

OTHER CONIC SECTIONS

ELLIPSE

An **ellipse** is the set of all points in a plane, whose total distance from two fixed points called the foci (singular: focus) is constant, and whose center is the midpoint between the foci.

The standard equation of an ellipse that is taller than it is wide is $\frac{(y-k)^2}{a^2} + \frac{(x-h)^2}{b^2} = 1$, where a and b are coefficients. The center is the point (h, k) and the foci are the points $(h, k + c)$ and $(h, k - c)$, where $c^2 = a^2 - b^2$ and $a^2 > b^2$.

The major axis has length $2a$, and the minor axis has length $2b$.

Eccentricity (e) is a measure of how elongated an ellipse is, and is the ratio of the distance between the foci to the length of the major axis. Eccentricity will have a value between 0 and 1. The closer to 1 the eccentricity is, the closer the ellipse is to being a circle. The formula for eccentricity is $= \frac{c}{a}$.

PARABOLA

Parabola: The set of all points in a plane that are equidistant from a fixed line, called the **directrix**, and a fixed point not on the line, called the **focus**.

Axis: The line perpendicular to the directrix that passes through the focus.

For parabolas that open up or down, the standard equation is $(x - h)^2 = 4c(y - k)$, where h, c, and k are coefficients. If c is positive, the parabola opens up. If c is negative, the parabola opens down. The vertex is the point (h, k). The directrix is the line having the equation $y = -c + k$, and the focus is the point $(h, c + k)$.

For parabolas that open left or right, the standard equation is $(y - k)^2 = 4c(x - h)$, where k, c, and h are coefficients. If c is positive, the parabola opens to the right. If c is negative, the parabola opens to the left. The vertex is the point (h, k). The directrix is the line having the equation $x = -c + h$, and the focus is the point $(c + h, k)$.

HYPERBOLA

A **hyperbola** is the set of all points in a plane, whose distance from two fixed points, called foci, has a constant difference.

The standard equation of a horizontal hyperbola is $\frac{(x-h)^2}{a^2} - \frac{(y-k)^2}{b^2} = 1$, where a, b, h, and k are real numbers. The center is the point (h, k), the vertices are the points $(h + a, k)$ and $(h - a, k)$, and the foci are the points that every point on one of the parabolic curves is equidistant from and are found using the formulas $(h + c, k)$ and $(h - c, k)$, where $c^2 = a^2 + b^2$. The asymptotes are two lines the graph of the hyperbola approaches but never reaches, and are given by the equations $y = \left(\frac{b}{a}\right)(x - h) + k$ and $y = -\left(\frac{b}{a}\right)(x - h) + k$.

A **vertical hyperbola** is formed when a plane makes a vertical cut through two cones that are stacked vertex-to-vertex.

The standard equation of a vertical hyperbola is $\frac{(y-k)^2}{a^2} - \frac{(x-h)^2}{b^2} = 1$, where a, b, k, and h are real numbers. The center is the point (h, k), the vertices are the points $(h, k + a)$ and $(h, k - a)$, and the foci are the points that every point on one of the parabolic curves is equidistant from and are found using the formulas $(h, k + c)$ and $(h, k - c)$, where $c^2 = a^2 + b^2$. The asymptotes are two lines the graph of the hyperbola approaches but never reach, and are given by the equations $y = \left(\frac{a}{b}\right)(x - h) + k$ and $y = -\left(\frac{a}{b}\right)(x - h) + k$.

SOLIDS

The **surface area of a solid object** is the area of all sides or exterior surfaces. For objects such as prisms and pyramids, a further distinction is made between base surface area (B) and lateral surface area (LA). For a prism, the total surface area (SA) is $SA = LA + 2B$. For a pyramid or cone, the total surface area is $SA = LA + B$.

Review Video: <u>How to Calculate the Volume of 3D Objects</u>
Visit mometrix.com/academy and enter code: 163343

The **surface area of a sphere** can be found by the formula $A = 4\pi r^2$, where r is the radius. The volume is given by the formula $V = \frac{4}{3}\pi r^3$, where r is the radius. Both quantities are generally given in terms of π.

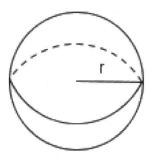

Review Video: <u>Volume and Surface Area of a Sphere</u>
Visit mometrix.com/academy and enter code: 786928

The **volume of any prism** is found by the formula $V = Bh$, where B is the area of the base, and h is the height (perpendicular distance between the bases). The surface area of any prism is the sum of the areas of both bases and all sides. It can be calculated as $SA = 2B + Ph$, where P is the perimeter of the base.

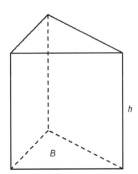

For a *rectangular prism*, the **volume** can be found by the formula $V = lwh$, where V is the volume, l is the length, w is the width, and h is the height. The surface area can be calculated as $SA = 2lw + 2hl + 2wh$ or $SA = 2(lw + hl + wh)$.

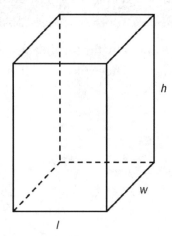

The **volume of a cube** can be found by the formula $V = s^3$, where s is the length of a side. The surface area of a cube is calculated as $SA = 6s^2$, where SA is the total surface area and s is the length of a side. These formulas are the same as the ones used for the volume and surface area of a rectangular prism, but simplified since all three quantities (length, width, and height) are the same.

Review Video: <u>Volume and Surface Area of a Cube</u>
Visit mometrix.com/academy and enter code: 664455

The **volume of a cylinder** can be calculated by the formula $V = \pi r^2 h$, where r is the radius, and h is the height. The surface area of a cylinder can be found by the formula $SA = 2\pi r^2 + 2\pi rh$. The first term is the base area multiplied by two, and the second term is the perimeter of the base multiplied by the height.

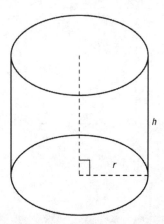

Review Video: <u>Volume and Surface Area of a Right Circular Cylinder</u>
Visit mometrix.com/academy and enter code: 226463

The **volume of a pyramid** is found by the formula $V = \frac{1}{3}Bh$, where B is the area of the base, and h is the height (perpendicular distance from the vertex to the base). Notice this formula is the same as $\frac{1}{3}$ times the volume of a prism. Like a prism, the base of a pyramid can be any shape.

Finding the **surface area of a pyramid** is not as simple as the other shapes we've looked at thus far. If the pyramid is a right pyramid, meaning the base is a regular polygon and the vertex is directly over the center of that polygon, the surface area can be calculated as $SA = B + \frac{1}{2}Ph_s$, where P is the perimeter of the base, and h_s is the slant height (distance from the vertex to the midpoint of one side of the base). If the pyramid is irregular, the area of each triangle side must be calculated individually and then summed, along with the base.

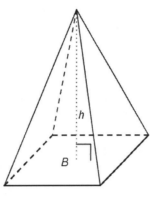

The **volume of a cone** is found by the formula $V = \frac{1}{3}\pi r^2 h$, where r is the radius, and h is the height. Notice this is the same as $\frac{1}{3}$ times the volume of a cylinder. The surface area can be calculated as $SA = \pi r^2 + \pi rs$, where s is the slant height. The slant height can be calculated using the Pythagorean Thereom to be $\sqrt{r^2 + h^2}$, so the surface area formula can also be written as $SA = \pi r^2 + \pi r\sqrt{r^2 + h^2}$.

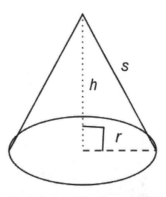

Probability

PROBABILITY TERMINOLOGY

Probability is a branch of statistics that deals with the likelihood of something taking place. One classic example is a coin toss. There are only two possible results: heads or tails. The likelihood, or probability, that the coin will land as heads is 1 out of 2 ($\frac{1}{2}$, 0.5, 50%). Tails has the same probability. Another common example is a 6-sided die roll. There are six possible results from rolling a single die, each with an equal chance of happening, so the probability of any given number coming up is 1 out of 6.

TERMS FREQUENTLY USED IN PROBABILITY

- **Event** – a situation that produces results of some sort (a coin toss)
- **Compound event** – event that involves two or more independent events (rolling a pair of dice; taking the sum)
- **Outcome** – a possible result in an experiment or event (heads, tails)
- **Desired outcome** (or success) – an outcome that meets a particular set of criteria (a roll of 1 or 2 if we are looking for numbers less than 3)
- **Independent events** – two or more events whose outcomes do not affect one another (two coins tossed at the same time)
- **Dependent events** – two or more events whose outcomes affect one another (two cards drawn consecutively from the same deck)
- **Certain outcome** – probability of outcome is 100% or 1
- **Impossible outcome** – probability of outcome is 0% or 0
- **Mutually exclusive outcomes** – two or more outcomes whose criteria cannot all be satisfied in a single event (a coin coming up heads and tails on the same toss)
- **Random variable** – refers to all possible outcomes of a single event which may be discrete or continuous.

> **Review Video: Intro to Probability**
> Visit mometrix.com/academy and enter code: 212374

CALCULATING PROBABILITY

Probability is the likelihood of a certain outcome occurring for a given event. The **theoretical probability** can usually be determined without actually performing the event. The likelihood of a outcome occurring, or the probability of an outcome occurring, is given by the formula

$$P(A) = \frac{\text{Number of acceptable outcomes}}{\text{Number of possible outcomes}}$$

where $P(A)$ is the probability of an outcome A occurring, and each outcome is just as likely to occur as any other outcome. If each outcome has the same probability of occurring as every other possible outcome, the outcomes are said to be equally likely to occur. The total number of acceptable outcomes must be less than or equal to the total number of possible outcomes. If the two are equal, then the outcome is certain to occur and the probability is 1. If the number of acceptable outcomes is zero, then the outcome is impossible and the probability is 0.

> **Review Video: Theoretical and Experimental Probability**
> Visit mometrix.com/academy and enter code: 444349

EXAMPLE:

There are 20 marbles in a bag and 5 are red. The theoretical probability of randomly selecting a red marble is 5 out of 20, ($\frac{5}{20} = \frac{1}{4}$, 0.25, or 25%).

PERMUTATIONS AND COMBINATIONS

When trying to calculate the probability of an event using the $\frac{\text{desired outcomes}}{\text{total outcomes}}$ formula, you may frequently find that there are too many outcomes to individually count them. **Permutation** and **combination formulas** offer a shortcut to counting outcomes. A permutation is an arrangement of a specific number of a set of objects in a specific order. The number of **permutations** of r items given a set of n items can be calculated as $_nP_r = \frac{n!}{(n-r)!}$. Combinations are similar to permutations, except there are no restrictions regarding the order of the elements. While ABC is considered a different permutation than BCA, ABC and BCA are considered the same combination. The number of **combinations** of r items given a set of n items can be calculated as $_nC_r = \frac{n!}{r!(n-r)!}$ or $_nC_r = \frac{_nP_r}{r!}$.

EXAMPLE:

Suppose you want to calculate how many different 5-card hands can be drawn from a deck of 52 cards. This is a combination since the order of the cards in a hand does not matter. There are 52 cards available, and 5 to be selected. Thus, the number of different hands is $_{52}C_5 = \frac{52!}{5! \times 47!} = 2,598,960$.

COMPLEMENT OF AN EVENT

Sometimes it may be easier to calculate the possibility of something not happening, or the **complement of an event**. Represented by the symbol $\bar{A}$, the complement of A is the probability that event A does not happen. When you know the probability of event A occurring, you can use the formula $P(\bar{A}) = 1 - P(A)$, where $P(\bar{A})$ is the probability of event A not occurring, and $P(A)$ is the probability of event A occurring.

ADDITION RULE

The **addition rule** for probability is used for finding the probability of a compound event. Use the formula $P(A \text{ or } B) = P(A) + P(B) - P(A \text{ and } B)$, where $P(A \text{ and } B)$ is the probability of both events occurring to find the probability of a compound event. The probability of both events occurring at the same time must be subtracted to eliminate any overlap in the first two probabilities.

CONDITIONAL PROBABILITY

Conditional probability is the probability of an event occurring once another event has already occurred. Given event A and dependent event B, the probability of event B occurring when event A has already occurred is represented by the notation $P(A|B)$. To find the probability of event B occurring, take into account the fact that event A has already occurred and adjust the total number of possible outcomes. For example, suppose you have ten balls numbered 1–10 and you want ball number 7 to be pulled in two pulls. On the first pull, the probability of getting the 7 is $\frac{1}{10}$ because there is one ball with a 7 on it and 10 balls to choose from. Assuming the first pull did not yield a 7, the probability of pulling a 7 on the second pull is now $\frac{1}{9}$ because there are only 9 balls remaining for the second pull.

MULTIPLICATION RULE

The **multiplication rule** can be used to find the probability of two independent events occurring using the formula $P(A \text{ and } B) = P(A) \times P(B)$, where $P(A \text{ and } B)$ is the probability of two independent events occurring, $P(A)$ is the probability of the first event occurring, and $P(B)$ is the probability of the second event occurring.

The multiplication rule can also be used to find the probability of two dependent events occurring using the formula $P(A \text{ and } B) = P(A) \times P(B|A)$, where $P(A \text{ and } B)$ is the probability of two dependent events occurring and $P(B|A)$ is the probability of the second event occurring after the first event has already occurred.

Before using the multiplication rule, you MUST first determine whether the two events are *dependent* or *independent*.

Use a **combination of the multiplication** rule and the rule of complements to find the probability that at least one outcome of the element will occur. This given by the general formula $P(\text{at least one event occurring}) = 1 - P(\text{no outcomes occurring})$. For example, to find the probability that at least one even number will show when a pair of dice is rolled, find the probability that two odd numbers will be rolled (no even numbers) and subtract from one. You can always use a tree diagram or make a chart to list the possible outcomes when the sample space is small, such as in the dice-rolling example, but in most cases it will be much faster to use the multiplication and complement formulas.

EXPECTED VALUE

Expected value is a method of determining expected outcome in a random situation. It is really a sum of the weighted probabilities of the possible outcomes. Multiply the probability of an event occurring by the weight assigned to that probability (such as the amount of money won or lost). A practical application of the expected value is to determine whether a game of chance is really fair. If the sum of the weighted probabilities is equal to zero, the game is generally considered fair because the player has a fair chance to at least to break even. If the expected value is less than zero, then players lose more than they win. For example, a lottery drawing might allow the player to choose any three-digit number, 000–999. The probability of choosing the winning number is 1:1000. If it costs \$1 to play, and a winning number receives \$500, the expected value is $\left(-\$1 \cdot \frac{999}{1,000}\right) +$ $\left(\$500 \cdot \frac{1}{1,000}\right) = -0.499$ or $-\$0.50$. You can expect to lose on average 50 cents for every dollar you spend.

EMPIRICAL PROBABILITY

Most of the time, when we talk about probability, we mean theoretical probability. **Empirical probability**, or experimental probability or relative frequency, is the number of times an outcome occurs in a particular experiment or a certain number of observed events. While theoretical probability is based on what *should* happen, experimental probability is based on what *has* happened. Experimental probability is calculated in the same way as theoretical, except that actual outcomes are used instead of possible outcomes.

Theoretical and experimental probability do not always line up with one another. Theoretical probability says that out of 20 coin-tosses, 10 should be heads. However, if we were actually to toss 20 coins, we might record just 5 heads. This doesn't mean that our theoretical probability is incorrect; it just means that this particular experiment had results that were different from what was predicted. A practical application of empirical probability is the insurance industry. There are no set functions that define lifespan, health, or safety. Insurance companies look at factors from hundreds of thousands of individuals to find patterns that they then use to set the formulas for insurance premiums.

OBJECTIVE PROBABILITY

Objective probability is based on mathematical formulas and documented evidence. Examples of objective probability include raffles or lottery drawings where there is a pre-determined number of possible outcomes and a predetermined number of outcomes that correspond to an event. Other cases of objective probability include probabilities of rolling dice, flipping coins, or drawing cards. Most gambling games are based on objective probability.

SUBJECTIVE PROBABILITY

Subjective probability is based on personal or professional feelings and judgments. Often, there is a lot of guesswork following extensive research. Areas where subjective probability is applicable include sales trends and business expenses. Attractions set admission prices based on subjective probabilities of attendance based on varying admission rates in an effort to maximize their profit.

SAMPLE SPACE

The total set of all possible results of a test or experiment is called a **sample space**, or sometimes a universal sample space. The sample space, represented by one of the variables S, Ω, or U (for universal sample space) has individual elements called outcomes. Other terms for outcome that may be used interchangeably include elementary outcome, simple event, or sample point. The number of outcomes in a given sample space could be infinite or finite, and some tests may yield multiple unique sample sets. For example, tests conducted by drawing playing cards from a standard deck would have one sample space of the card values, another sample space of the card suits, and a third sample space of suit-denomination combinations. For most tests, the sample spaces considered will be finite.

An **event**, represented by the variable E, is a portion of a sample space. It may be one outcome or a group of outcomes from the same sample space. If an event occurs, then the test or experiment will generate an outcome that satisfies the requirement of that event. For example, given a standard deck of 52 playing cards as the sample space, and defining the event as the collection of face cards, then the event will occur if the card drawn is a J, Q, or K. If any other card is drawn, the event is said to have not occurred.

For every sample space, each possible outcome has a specific likelihood, or probability, that it will occur. The probability measure, also called the **distribution**, is a function that assigns a real number probability, from zero to one, to each outcome. For a probability measure to be accurate, every outcome must have a real number probability measure that is greater than or equal to zero and less than or equal to one. Also, the probability measure of the sample space must equal one, and the probability measure of the union of multiple outcomes must equal the sum of the individual probability measures.

Probabilities of events are expressed as real numbers from zero to one. They give a numerical value to the chance that a particular event will occur. The probability of an event occurring is the sum of the probabilities of the individual elements of that event. For example, in a standard deck of 52 playing cards as the sample space and the collection of face cards as the event, the probability of drawing a specific face card is $\frac{1}{52} = 0.019$, but the probability of drawing any one of the twelve face cards is $12(0.019) = 0.228$. Note that rounding of numbers can generate different results. If you multiplied 12 by the fraction $\frac{1}{52}$ before converting to a decimal, you would get the answer $\frac{12}{52} =$ 0.231.

TREE DIAGRAM

For a simple sample space, possible outcomes may be determined by using a **tree diagram** or an organized chart. In either case, you can easily draw or list out the possible outcomes. For example, to determine all the possible ways three objects can be ordered, you can draw a tree diagram:

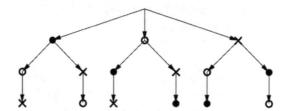

You can also make a chart to list all the possibilities:

First object	Second object	Third object
●	X	O
●	O	X
O	●	X
O	X	●
X	●	O
X	O	●

Either way, you can easily see there are six possible ways the three objects can be ordered.

If two events have no outcomes in common, they are said to be **mutually exclusive**. For example, in a standard deck of 52 playing cards, the event of all card suits is mutually exclusive to the event of all card values. If two events have no bearing on each other so that one event occurring has no influence on the probability of another event occurring, the two events are said to be independent. For example, rolling a standard six-sided die multiple times does not change that probability that a particular number will be rolled from one roll to the next. If the outcome of one event does affect the probability of the second event, the two events are said to be dependent. For example, if cards are drawn from a deck, the probability of drawing an ace after an ace has been drawn is different than the probability of drawing an ace if no ace (or no other card, for that matter) has been drawn.

In probability, the **odds in favor of an event** are the number of times the event will occur compared to the number of times the event will not occur. To calculate the odds in favor of an event, use the formula $\frac{P(A)}{1-P(A)}$, where $P(A)$ is the probability that the event will occur. Many times, odds in favor is given as a ratio in the form $\frac{a}{b}$ or $a{:}b$, where a is the probability of the event occurring and b is the complement of the event, the probability of the event not occurring. If the odds in favor are given as 2:5, that means that you can expect the event to occur two times for every 5 times that it does not occur. In other words, the probability that the event will occur is $\frac{2}{2+5} = \frac{2}{7}$.

In probability, the **odds against an event** are the number of times the event will not occur compared to the number of times the event will occur. To calculate the odds against an event, use the formula $\frac{1-P(A)}{P(A)}$, where $P(A)$ is the probability that the event will occur. Many times, odds against

130

is given as a ratio in the form $\frac{b}{a}$ or $b{:}a$, where b is the probability the event will not occur (the complement of the event) and a is the probability the event will occur. If the odds against an event are given as 3:1, that means that you can expect the event to not occur 3 times for every one time it does occur. In other words, 3 out of every 4 trials will fail.

EXPERIMENTAL AND THEORETICAL PROBABILITY

Probability, P(A), is the likelihood that event A will occur. Probability is often expressed as the ratio of ways an event can occur to the total number of **outcomes**, also called the **sample space**. For example, the probability of flipping heads on a two-sided coin can be written as $\frac{1}{2}$ since there is one side with heads and a total of two sides, which means that there are two possible outcomes. Probabilities can also be expressed as decimals or percentages.

Tree diagrams are used to list all possible outcomes. Suppose you are packing for vacation and have set aside 4 shirts, 3 pairs of pants, and 2 hats. How many possible outfits are there? To construct a tree diagram, start with the first group of events, the shirts. You can use letters to label each of the articles (SA refers to the first shirt, SB refers to the second shirt, and so on). Then, from each shirt draw branches to each pair of pants that it could be paired with. Next, from each pair of pants, draw a branch to each hat that it could be paired to and finally, repeat the process with the shoes. This method allows you to list all of the possible outcomes.

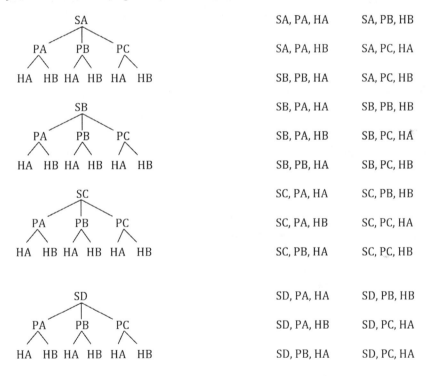

SA, PA, HA	SA, PB, HB
SA, PA, HB	SA, PC, HA
SB, PB, HA	SA, PC, HB
SB, PA, HA	SB, PB, HB
SB, PA, HB	SB, PC, HA
SB, PB, HA	SB, PC, HB
SC, PA, HA	SC, PB, HB
SC, PA, HB	SC, PC, HA
SC, PB, HA	SC, PC, HB
SD, PA, HA	SD, PB, HB
SD, PA, HB	SD, PC, HA
SD, PB, HA	SD, PC, HA

Altogether, there are 24 different combinations of shirts, pants, and hats.

ADDITION PRINCIPLE

The **addition principle** is used to determine the sample space of 2 or more events. The addition principle states that if two events, x and y, with a number of possible outcomes, n_x and n_y, have no shared outcomes, then the events are called **mutually exclusive** and the union of the events, or the total number of outcomes of the sample space, is: $x \cap y = n_x + n_y$.

For example: In a regular deck of 52 playing cards with events defined as $x =$ [drawing a jack] and $y =$ [drawing a king], there is no way for both of these to occur at the same time. Since there are 4 ways to get a jack and 4 ways to get a king the union of those events is: $x \cap y = 4 + 4 = 8$. There are 8 ways that one or the other event can occur.

If the two events share any outcomes then they are not mutually exclusive and the total number of possible outcomes for the two events is $x \cap y = n_x + n_y - (x \cup y)$. Where $(x \cup y)$ is the number of outcomes common to both events. An example of this with a regular deck of cards would be if event $x =$ [drawing a jack] and event $y =$ [drawing a spade]. Now, since there are 4 ways to draw a jack, 13 ways to draw a spade, and 1 way to draw the jack of spades, the union of the events would be $x \cap y = 4 + 13 - 1 = 16$. There are 16 ways that one or the other event can occur.

FUNDAMENTAL COUNTING PRINCIPLE

The **fundamental counting principle** deals specifically with situations in which the order that something happens affects the outcome. Specifically, the fundamental counting principle states that if one event can have x possible different outcomes, and after the first outcome has been established the event can then have y possible outcomes, then there are $x \times y$ possible different ways the outcomes can happen in that order. For example, if two dice are rolled, one at a time, there are 6 possible outcomes for the first die, and 6 possible outcomes for the second die, for a total of $6 \times 6 = 36$ total possible outcomes. Suppose you have a bag containing a penny, a nickel, a dime, a quarter, and a half dollar. There are 5 different possible outcomes the first time you pull a coin. Without replacing the first coin, there are 4 different possible outcomes for the second coin. This makes $5 \times 4 = 20$ different possible outcomes for the first two coins drawn when the order the coins are drawn makes a difference.

MULTIPLICATION COUNTING PRINCIPLE

A faster way to find the sample space without listing each individual outcome employs the **multiplication counting principle**. If one event can occur in a ways and a second event in b ways, then the two events can occur in $a \times b$ ways. In the previous example, there are 4 possible shirts, 3 possible pairs of pants, and 2 possible hats, so the possible number of combinations is $4 \times 3 \times 2$, or 24.

A similar principle is employed to determine the probability of two **independent events**. $P(A \text{ and } B) = P(A) \times P(B)$, where A is the first event and B is the second such that the outcome of B does not depend on the outcome of A. For instance, suppose you choose a marble from a bag of 2 red marbles, 7 blue marbles, and 4 green marbles. The probability that you would choose a red marble, replace it, and then choose a green marble is found by multiplying the probabilities of each independent event:

$$\frac{2}{13} \times \frac{4}{13} = \frac{8}{169}, \text{ or } 0.047, \text{ or } 4.7\%$$

This method can also be used when finding the probability of more than 2 independent events.

When two events are dependent on one another, the likelihood of the second event is affected by the outcome of the first event. This formula for finding the probability of **dependent events** is $P(A \text{ then } B) = P(A) \times P(B \text{ after } A)$. The probability that you choose a 2 and then choose a 5 from a deck of 52 cards without replacement is

$$\frac{4}{52} \times \frac{4}{51} = \frac{1}{13} \times \frac{4}{51} = \frac{4}{663} \text{ or } 0.0060, \text{ or } 0.60\%$$

Note that there are four of each number in a deck of cards, so the probability of choosing a 2 is $\frac{4}{52}$. Since you keep this card out of the deck, there are only 51 cards to choose from when selecting a 5.

Thus far, the discussion of probability has been limited to **theoretical probability, which is used to predict the likelihood of an event. Experimental probability** expresses the ratio of the number of times an event actually occurs to the number of **trials** performed in an experiment. Theoretically, the probability of rolling a one on an unloaded, six-sided die is $\frac{1}{6}$. Suppose you conduct an experiment to determine whether a dice is a fair one and obtain these results.

Trial #	1	2	3	4	5	6	7	8	9	10	11	12	13	14	15	16	17	18	19	20
Outcome	6	1	2	6	4	2	1	3	4	5	4	1	6	6	4	5	6	4	1	6

Out of the 20 trials, you rolled a 1 six times. $\frac{6}{20} = \frac{3}{10} = 0.30$, or 30%. This probability is different than the theoretical probability of $\frac{1}{6}$ or 16.6%. You might conclude that the die is loaded, but it would be advisable to conduct more trials to verify your conclusion: the larger the number of trials, the more accurate the experimental probability.

Statistics

STATISTICS TERMINOLOGY

Statistics is the branch of mathematics that deals with collecting, recording, interpreting, illustrating, and analyzing large amounts of **data**. The following terms are often used in the discussion of data and **statistics**:

- **Data** – the collective name for pieces of *information* (singular is datum).
- **Quantitative data** – measurements (such as length, mass, and speed) that provide information about *quantities* in numbers
- **Qualitative data** – information (such as colors, scents, tastes, and shapes) that *cannot be measured* using numbers
- **Discrete data** – information that can be expressed only by a *specific value*, such as whole or half numbers. For example, since people can be counted only in whole numbers, a population count would be discrete data.
- **Continuous data** – information (such as time and temperature) that can be expressed by *any value within a given range*
- **Primary data** – information that has been *collected* directly from a survey, investigation, or experiment, such as a questionnaire or the recording of daily temperatures. Primary data that has not yet been organized or analyzed is called raw data.
- **Secondary data** – information that has been collected, sorted, and *processed* by the researcher
- **Ordinal data** – information that *can be placed in numerical order*, such as age or weight
- **Nominal data** – information that *cannot be placed in numerical order*, such as names or places.

STATISTICS

POPULATION

In statistics, the **population** is the entire collection of people, plants, etc., that data can be collected from. For example, a study to determine how well students in the area schools perform on a standardized test would have a population of all the students enrolled in those schools, although a study may include just a small sample of students from each school. A **parameter** is a numerical value that gives information about the population, such as the mean, median, mode, or standard deviation. Remember that the symbol for the mean of a population is μ and the symbol for the standard deviation of a population is σ.

SAMPLE

A **sample** is a portion of the entire population. Whereas a parameter helped describe the population, a **statistic** is a numerical value that gives information about the sample, such as mean, median, mode, or standard deviation. Keep in mind that the symbols for mean and standard deviation are different when they are referring to a sample rather than the entire population. For a sample, the symbol for mean is $\bar{x}$ and the symbol for standard deviation is s. The mean and standard deviation of a sample may or may not be identical to that of the entire population due to a sample only being a subset of the population. However, if the sample is random and large enough, statistically significant values can be attained. Samples are generally used when the population is too large to justify including every element or when acquiring data for the entire population is impossible.

INFERENTIAL STATISTICS

Inferential statistics is the branch of statistics that uses samples to make predictions about an entire population. This type of statistics is often seen in political polls, where a sample of the population is questioned about a particular topic or politician to gain an understanding about the attitudes of the entire population of the country. Often, exit polls are conducted on election days using this method. Inferential statistics can have a large margin of error if you do not have a valid sample.

SAMPLING DISTRIBUTION

Statistical values calculated from various samples of the same size make up the **sampling distribution**. For example, if several samples of identical size are randomly selected from a large population and then the mean of each sample is calculated, the distribution of values of the means would be a sampling distribution.

The **sampling distribution of the mean** is the distribution of the sample mean, $\bar{x}$, derived from random samples of a given size. It has three important characteristics. First, the mean of the sampling distribution of the mean is equal to the mean of the population that was sampled. Second, assuming the standard deviation is non-zero, the standard deviation of the sampling distribution of the mean equals the standard deviation of the sampled population divided by the square root of the sample size. This is sometimes called the standard error. Finally, as the sample size gets larger, the sampling distribution of the mean gets closer to a normal distribution via the Central Limit Theorem.

SURVEY STUDY

A **survey study** is a method of gathering information from a small group in an attempt to gain enough information to make accurate general assumptions about the population. Once a survey study is completed, the results are then put into a summary report.

Survey studies are generally in the format of surveys, interviews, or questionnaires as part of an effort to find opinions of a particular group or to find facts about a group.

It is important to note that the findings from a survey study are only as accurate as the sample chosen from the population.

CORRELATIONAL STUDIES

Correlational studies seek to determine how much one variable is affected by changes in a second variable. For example, correlational studies may look for a relationship between the amount of time a student spends studying for a test and the grade that student earned on the test or between student scores on college admissions tests and student grades in college.

It is important to note that correlational studies cannot show a cause and effect, but rather can show only that two variables are or are not potentially correlated.

EXPERIMENTAL STUDIES

Experimental studies take correlational studies one step farther, in that they attempt to prove or disprove a cause-and-effect relationship. These studies are performed by conducting a series of experiments to test the hypothesis. For a study to be scientifically accurate, it must have both an experimental group that receives the specified treatment and a control group that does not get the treatment. This is the type of study pharmaceutical companies do as part of drug trials for new medications. Experimental studies are only valid when proper scientific method has been followed. In other words, the experiment must be well-planned and executed without bias in the testing process, all subjects must be selected at random, and the process of determining which subject is in which of the two groups must also be completely random.

OBSERVATIONAL STUDIES

Observational studies are the opposite of experimental studies. In observational studies, the tester cannot change or in any way control all of the variables in the test. For example, a study to determine which gender does better in math classes in school is strictly observational. You cannot change a person's gender, and you cannot change the subject being studied. The big downfall of observational studies is that you have no way of proving a cause-and-effect relationship because you cannot control outside influences. Events outside of school can influence a student's performance in school, and observational studies cannot take that into consideration.

RANDOM SAMPLES

For most studies, a **random sample** is necessary to produce valid results. Random samples should not have any particular influence to cause sampled subjects to behave one way or another. The goal is for the random sample to be a **representative sample**, or a sample whose characteristics give an accurate picture of the characteristics of the entire population. To accomplish this, you must make sure you have a proper **sample size**, or an appropriate number of elements in the sample.

BIASES

In statistical studies, biases must be avoided. **Bias** is an error that causes the study to favor one set of results over another. For example, if a survey to determine how the country views the president's job performance only speaks to registered voters in the president's party, the results will be skewed because a disproportionately large number of responders would tend to show approval, while a disproportionately large number of people in the opposite party would tend to express disapproval.

EXTRANEOUS VARIABLES

Extraneous variables are, as the name implies, outside influences that can affect the outcome of a study. They are not always avoidable, but could trigger bias in the result.

DATA ORGANIZATION

EXAMPLE

A nurse found the heart rates of ten different patients to be 76, 80, 90, 86, 70, 76, 72, 88, 88, and 68 beats per minute. Organize this information in a table.

There are several ways to organize data in a table. The table below is an example.

Patient Number	1	2	3	4	5	6	7	8	9	10
Heart Rate (bpm)	76	80	90	86	70	76	72	88	88	68

When making a table, be sure to label the columns and rows appropriately.

DATA ANALYSIS

MEASURES OF CENTRAL TENDENCY

The **measure of central tendency** is a statistical value that gives a general tendency for the center of a group of data. There are several different ways of describing the measure of central tendency. Each one has a unique way it is calculated, and each one gives a slightly different perspective on the data set. Whenever you give a measure of central tendency, always make sure the units are the same. If the data has different units, such as hours, minutes, and seconds, convert all the data to the same unit, and use the same unit in the measure of central tendency. If no units are given in the data, do not give units for the measure of central tendency.

MEAN

The **statistical mean** of a group of data is the same as the arithmetic average of that group. To find the mean of a set of data, first convert each value to the same units, if necessary. Then find the sum of all the values, and count the total number of data values, making sure you take into consideration each individual value. If a value appears more than once, count it more than once. Divide the sum of the values by the total number of values and apply the units, if any. Note that the mean does not have to be one of the data values in the set, and may not divide evenly.

$$\text{mean} = \frac{\text{sum of the data values}}{\text{quantity of data values}}$$

The mean of the data set {88, 72, 61, 90, 97, 68, 88, 79, 86, 93, 97, 71, 80, 84, 89, 72, 91, 95, 89, 83, 94, 90, 63, 69, 89} would be the sum of the twenty-five numbers divided by 25:

$$\frac{88 + 72 + 61 + 90 + 97 + \cdots + 94 + 90 + 63 + 69 + 89}{25}$$
$$= \frac{2078}{25}$$
$$= 83.12$$

While the mean is relatively easy to calculate and averages are understood by most people, the mean can be very misleading if used as the sole measure of central tendency. If the data set has outliers (data values that are unusually high or unusually low compared to the rest of the data values), the mean can be very distorted, especially if the data set has a small number of values. If unusually high values are countered with unusually low values, the mean is not affected as much. For example, if five of twenty students in a class get a 100 on a test, but the other 15 students have an average of 60 on the same test, the class average would appear as 70. Whenever the mean is

136

skewed by outliers, it is always a good idea to include the median as an alternate measure of central tendency.

MEDIAN

The **statistical median** is the value in the middle of the set of data. To find the median, list all data values in order from smallest to largest or from largest to smallest. Any value that is repeated in the set must be listed the number of times it appears. If there are an odd number of data values, the median is the value in the middle of the list. If there is an even number of data values, the median is the arithmetic mean of the two middle values.

MODE

The **statistical mode** is the data value that occurs the most number of times in the data set. It is possible to have exactly one mode, more than one mode, or no mode. To find the mode of a set of data, arrange the data like you do to find the median (all values in order, listing all multiples of data values). Count the number of times each value appears in the data set. If all values appear an equal number of times, there is no mode. If one value appears more than any other value, that value is the mode. If two or more values appear the same number of times, but there are other values that appear fewer times and no values that appear more times, all of those values are the modes.

The big disadvantage of using the median as a measure of central tendency is that is relies solely on a value's relative size as compared to the other values in the set. When the individual values in a set of data are evenly dispersed, the median can be an accurate tool. However, if there is a group of rather large values or a group of rather small values that are not offset by a different group of values, the information that can be inferred from the median may not be accurate because the distribution of values is skewed.

The main disadvantage of the mode is that the values of the other data in the set have no bearing on the mode. The mode may be the largest value, the smallest value, or a value anywhere in between in the set. The mode only tells which value or values, if any, occurred the most number of times. It does not give any suggestions about the remaining values in the set.

DISPERSION

The **measure of dispersion** is a single value that helps to "interpret" the measure of central tendency by providing more information about how the data values in the set are distributed about the measure of central tendency. The measure of dispersion helps to eliminate or reduce the disadvantages of using the mean, median, or mode as a single measure of central tendency, and give a more accurate picture of the dataset as a whole. To have a measure of dispersion, you must know or calculate the range, standard deviation, or variance of the data set.

RANGE

The **range** of a set of data is the difference between the greatest and lowest values of the data in the set. To calculate the range, you must first make sure the units for all data values are the same, and then identify the greatest and lowest values. Use the formula $range = highest\ value - lowest\ value$. If there are multiple data values that are equal for the highest or lowest, just use one of the values in the formula. Write the answer with the same units as the data values you used to do the calculations.

STANDARD DEVIATION

Standard deviation is a measure of dispersion that compares all the data values in the set to the mean of the set to give a more accurate picture. To find the standard deviation of a population, use the formula

$$\sigma = \sqrt{\frac{\sum_{i=1}^{n}(x_i - \bar{x})^2}{n}}$$

where σ is the standard deviation of a population, x represents the individual values in the data set, $\bar{x}$ is the mean of the data values in the set, and n is the number of data values in the set. The higher the value of the standard deviation is, the greater the variance of the data values from the mean. The units associated with the standard deviation are the same as the units of the data values.

VARIANCE

The **variance** of a population, or just variance, is the square of the standard deviation of that population. While the mean of a set of data gives the average of the set and gives information about where a specific data value lies in relation to the average, the variance of the population gives information about the degree to which the data values are spread out and tell you how close an individual value is to the average compared to the other values. The units associated with variance are the same as the units of the data values squared.

PERCENTILE

Percentiles and **quartiles** are other methods of describing data within a set. *Percentiles* tell what percentage of the data in the set fall below a specific point. For example, achievement test scores are often given in percentiles. A score at the 80th percentile is one which is equal to or higher than 80 percent of the scores in the set. In other words, 80 percent of the scores were lower than that score.

QUARTILE

Quartiles are percentile groups that make up quarter sections of the data set. The first quartile is the 25th percentile. The second quartile is the 50th percentile; this is also the median of the dataset. The third quartile is the 75th percentile.

SKEWNESS

Skewness is a way to describe the symmetry or asymmetry of the distribution of values in a dataset. If the distribution of values is symmetrical, there is no skew. In general the closer the mean of a data set is to the median of the data set, the less skew there is. Generally, if the mean is to the right of the median, the data set is *positively skewed*, or right-skewed, and if the mean is to the left of the median, the data set is *negatively skewed*, or left-skewed. However, this rule of thumb is not infallible. When the data values are graphed on a curve, a set with no skew will be a perfect bell curve. To estimate skew, use the formula

$$\text{skew} = \frac{\sqrt{n(n-1)}}{n-2}\left(\frac{\frac{1}{n}\sum_{i=1}^{n}(x_i - \bar{x})^3}{\left(\frac{1}{n}\sum_{i=1}^{n}(x_i - \bar{x})^2\right)^{\frac{3}{2}}}\right)$$

where n is the number of values is the set, x_i is the ith value in the set, and $\bar{x}$ is the mean of the set.

SIMPLE REGRESSION

In statistics, **simple regression** is using an equation to represent a relation between an independent and dependent variables. The independent variable is also referred to as the explanatory variable or the predictor, and is generally represented by the variable x in the equation. The dependent variable, usually represented by the variable y, is also referred to as the response variable. The equation may be any type of function – linear, quadratic, exponential, etc. The best way to handle this task is to use the regression feature of your graphing calculator. This will easily give you the curve of best fit and provide you with the coefficients and other information you need to derive an equation.

LINE OF BEST FIT

In a scatter plot, the **line of best fit** is the line that best shows the trends of the data. The line of best fit is given by the equation $\hat{y} = ax + b$, where a and b are the regression coefficients. The regression coefficient a is also the slope of the line of best fit, and b is also the y-coordinate of the point at which the line of best fit crosses the x-axis. Not every point on the scatter plot will be on the line of best fit. The differences between the y-values of the points in the scatter plot and the corresponding y-values according to the equation of the line of best fit are the residuals. The line of best fit is also called the least-squares regression line because it is also the line that has the lowest sum of the squares of the residuals.

CORRELATION COEFFICIENT

The **correlation coefficient** is the numerical value that indicates how strong the relationship is between the two variables of a linear regression equation. A correlation coefficient of –1 is a perfect negative correlation. A correlation coefficient of +1 is a perfect positive correlation. Correlation coefficients close to –1 or +1 are very strong correlations. A correlation coefficient equal to zero indicates there is no correlation between the two variables. This test is a good indicator of whether or not the equation for the line of best fit is accurate. The formula for the correlation coefficient is

$$r = \frac{\sum_{i=1}^{n}(x_i - \bar{x})(y_i - \bar{y})}{\sqrt{\sum_{i=1}^{n}(x_i - \bar{x})^2}\sqrt{\sum_{i=1}^{n}(y_i - \bar{y})^2}}$$

where r is the correlation coefficient, n is the number of data values in the set, (x_i, y_i) is a point in the set, and $\bar{x}$ and $\bar{y}$ are the means.

Z-SCORE

A **z-score** is an indication of how many standard deviations a given value falls from the mean. To calculate a z-score, use the formula $= \frac{x-\mu}{\sigma}$, where x is the data value, μ is the mean of the data set, and σ is the standard deviation of the population. If the z-score is positive, the data value lies above the mean. If the z-score is negative, the data value falls below the mean. These scores are useful in interpreting data such as standardized test scores, where every piece of data in the set has been counted, rather than just a small random sample. In cases where standard deviations are calculated from a random sample of the set, the z-scores will not be as accurate.

CENTRAL LIMIT THEOREM

According to the **central limit theorem**, regardless of what the original distribution of a sample is, the distribution of the means tends to get closer and closer to a normal distribution as the sample size gets larger and larger (this is necessary because the sample is becoming more all-encompassing of the elements of the population). As the sample size gets larger, the distribution of the sample mean will approach a normal distribution with a mean of the population mean and a variance of the population variance divided by the sample size.

SHAPE OF DATA DISTRIBUTION

SYMMETRY AND SKEWNESS

Symmetry is a characteristic of the shape of the plotted data. Specifically, it refers to how well the data on one side of the median *mirrors* the data on the other side.

A **skewed data** set is one that has a distinctly longer or fatter tail on one side of the peak or the other. A data set that is *skewed left* has more of its values to the left of the peak, while a set that is *skewed right* has more of its values to the right of the peak. When actually looking at the graph, these names may seem counterintuitive since, in a left-skewed data set, the bulk of the values seem to be on the right side of the graph, and vice versa. However, if the graph is viewed strictly in relation to the peak, the direction of skewness makes more sense.

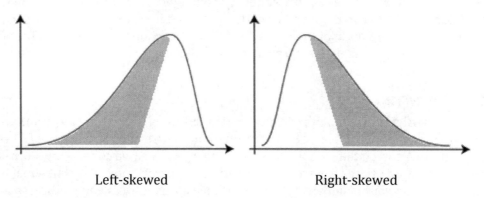

Left-skewed   Right-skewed

UNIMODAL VS. BIMODAL

If a distribution has a single peak, it would be considered **unimodal**. If it has two discernible peaks it would be considered **bimodal**. Bimodal distributions may be an indication that the set of data being considered is actually the combination of two sets of data with significant differences.

UNIFORMITY

A uniform distribution is a distribution in which there is *no distinct peak or variation* in the data. No values or ranges are particularly more common than any other values or ranges.

DISPLAYING INFORMATION

CHARTS AND TABLES

Charts and tables are ways of organizing information into separate rows and columns that are labeled to identify and explain the data contained in them. Some charts and tables are organized horizontally, with row lengths giving the details about the labeled information. Other charts and tables are organized vertically, with column heights giving the details about the labeled information.

FREQUENCY TABLES

Frequency tables show how frequently each unique value appears in the set. A *relative frequency table* is one that shows the proportions of each unique value compared to the entire set. Relative frequencies are given as percents; however, the total percent for a relative frequency table will not necessarily equal 100 percent due to rounding. An example of a frequency table with relative frequencies is below.

Favorite Color	Frequency	Relative Frequency
Blue	4	13%
Red	7	22%
Purple	3	9%
Green	6	19%
Cyan	12	38%

PICTOGRAPHS

A **pictograph** is a graph, generally in the horizontal orientation, that uses pictures or symbols to represent the data. Each pictograph must have a key that defines the picture or symbol and gives the quantity each picture or symbol represents. Pictures or symbols on a pictograph are not always shown as whole elements. In this case, the fraction of the picture or symbol shown represents the same fraction of the quantity a whole picture or symbol stands for. For example, a row with $3\frac{1}{2}$ ears of corn, where each ear of corn represents 100 stalks of corn in a field, would equal $3\frac{1}{2} \cdot 100 = 350$ stalks of corn in the field.

CIRCLE GRAPHS

Circle graphs, also known as *pie charts*, provide a visual depiction of the relationship of each type of data compared to the whole set of data. The circle graph is divided into sections by drawing radii to create central angles whose percentage of the circle is equal to the individual data's percentage of the whole set. Each 1% of data is equal to 3.6° in the circle graph. Therefore, data represented by a 90° section of the circle graph makes up 25% of the whole. When complete, a circle graph often looks like a pie cut into uneven wedges. The pie chart below shows the data from the frequency table referenced earlier where people were asked their favorite color.

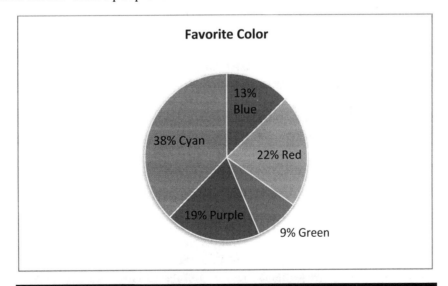

Review Video: <u>Pie Chart</u>
Visit mometrix.com/academy and enter code: 895285

LINE GRAPHS

Line graphs have one or more lines of varying styles (solid or broken) to show the different values for a set of data. The individual data are represented as ordered pairs, much like on a Cartesian plane. In this case, the *x*- and *y*-axes are defined in terms of their units, such as dollars or time. The individual plotted points are joined by line segments to show whether the value of the data is increasing (line sloping upward), decreasing (line sloping downward) or staying the same (horizontal line). Multiple sets of data can be graphed on the same line graph to give an easy visual comparison. An example of this would be graphing achievement test scores for different groups of students over the same time period to see which group had the greatest increase or decrease in performance from year-to-year (as shown below).

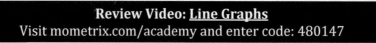

Review Video: <u>Line Graphs</u>
Visit mometrix.com/academy and enter code: 480147

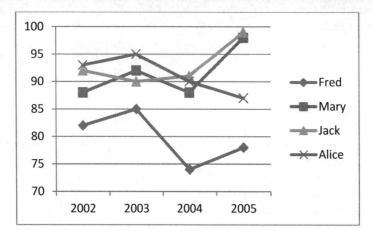

LINE PLOTS

A **line plot**, also known as a *dot plot*, has plotted points that are not connected by line segments. In this graph, the horizontal axis lists the different possible values for the data, and the vertical axis lists the number of times the individual value occurs. A single dot is graphed for each value to show the number of times it occurs. This graph is more closely related to a bar graph than a line graph. Do not connect the dots in a line plot or it will misrepresent the data.

Review Video: <u>Line Plot</u>
Visit mometrix.com/academy and enter code: 754610

STEM AND LEAF PLOTS

A **stem and leaf plot** is useful for depicting groups of data that fall into a range of values. Each piece of data is separated into two parts: the first, or left, part is called the stem; the second, or right, part is called the leaf. Each stem is listed in a column from smallest to largest. Each leaf that has the common stem is listed in that stem's row from smallest to largest. For example, in a set of two-digit numbers, the digit in the tens place is the stem, and the digit in the ones place is the leaf. With a stem and leaf plot, you can easily see which subset of numbers (10s, 20s, 30s, etc.) is the largest. This information is also readily available by looking at a histogram, but a stem and leaf plot also allows you to look closer and see exactly which values fall in that range. Using all of the test scores from above, we can assemble a stem and leaf plot like the one below.

Test Scores								
7	4	8						
8	2	5	7	8	8			
9	0	0	1	2	2	3	5	8	9

BAR GRAPHS

A **bar graph** is one of the few graphs that can be drawn correctly in two different configurations – both horizontally and vertically. A bar graph is similar to a line plot in the way the data is organized on the graph. Both axes must have their categories defined for the graph to be useful. Rather than placing a single dot to mark the point of the data's value, a bar, or thick line, is drawn from zero to the exact value of the data, whether it is a number, percentage, or other numerical value. Longer bar lengths correspond to greater data values. To read a bar graph, read the labels for the axes to find the units being reported. Then look where the bars end in relation to the scale given on the corresponding axis and determine the associated value.

The bar chart below represents the responses from our favorite color survey.

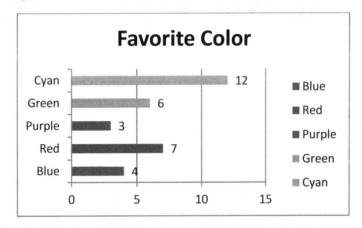

HISTOGRAMS

At first glance, a **histogram** looks like a vertical bar graph. The difference is that a bar graph has a separate bar for each piece of data and a histogram has one continuous bar for each *range* of data. For example, a histogram may have one bar for the range 0–9, one bar for 10–19, etc. While a bar graph has numerical values on one axis, a histogram has numerical values on both axes. Each range is of equal size, and they are ordered left to right from lowest to highest. The height of each column on a histogram represents the number of data values within that range. Like a stem and leaf plot, a histogram makes it easy to glance at the graph and quickly determine which range has the greatest quantity of values. A simple example of a histogram is below.

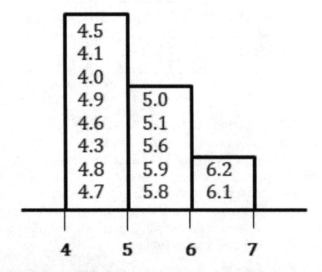

BIVARIATE DATA

Bivariate data is simply data from two different variables. (The prefix *bi-* means *two*.) In a *scatter plot*, each value in the set of data is plotted on a grid similar to a Cartesian plane, where each axis represents one of the two variables. By looking at the pattern formed by the points on the grid, you can often determine whether or not there is a relationship between the two variables, and what that relationship is, if it exists. The variables may be directly proportionate, inversely proportionate, or show no proportion at all. It may also be possible to determine if the data is linear, and if so, to find an equation to relate the two variables. The following scatter plot shows the relationship between preference for brand "A" and the age of the consumers surveyed.

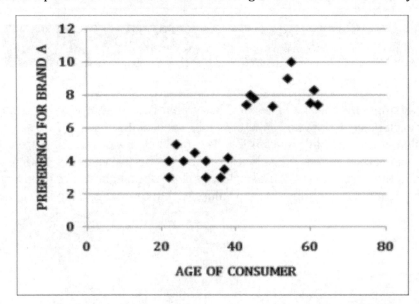

SCATTER PLOTS

Scatter plots are also useful in determining the type of function represented by the data and finding the simple regression. Linear scatter plots may be positive or negative. Nonlinear scatter plots are generally exponential or quadratic. Below are some common types of scatter plots:

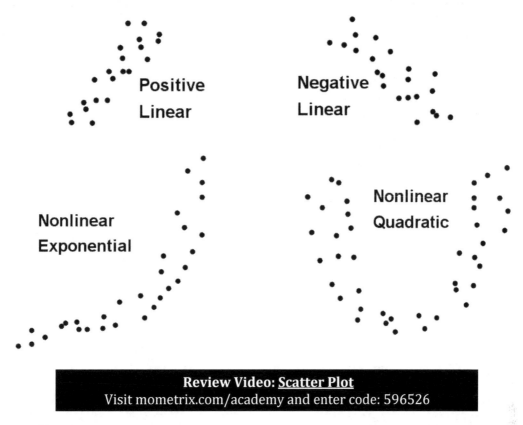

> **Review Video: Scatter Plot**
> Visit mometrix.com/academy and enter code: 596526

5-NUMBER SUMMARY

The **5-number summary** of a set of data gives a very informative picture of the set. The five numbers in the summary include the minimum value, maximum value, and the three quartiles. This information gives the reader the range and median of the set, as well as an indication of how the data is spread about the median.

BOX AND WHISKER PLOTS

A **box-and-whisker plot** is a graphical representation of the 5-number summary. To draw a box-and-whiskers plot, plot the points of the 5-number summary on a number line. Draw a box whose ends are through the points for the first and third quartiles. Draw a vertical line in the box through the median to divide the box in half. Draw a line segment from the first quartile point to the minimum value, and from the third quartile point to the maximum value.

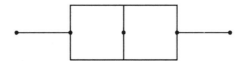

68-95-99.7 RULE

The **68–95–99.7 rule** describes how a normal distribution of data should appear when compared to the mean. This is also a description of a normal bell curve. According to this rule, 68 percent of the data values in a normally distributed set should fall within one standard deviation of the mean (34 percent above and 34 percent below the mean), 95 percent of the data values should fall within two standard deviations of the mean (47.5 percent above and 47.5 percent below the mean), and 99.7 percent of the data values should fall within three standard deviations of the mean, again, equally distributed on either side of the mean. This means that only 0.3 percent of all data values should fall more than three standard deviations from the mean. On the graph below, the normal curve is centered on the y-axis. The x-axis labels are how many standard deviations away from the center you are.

Therefore, it is easy to see how the 68-95-99.7 rule can apply.

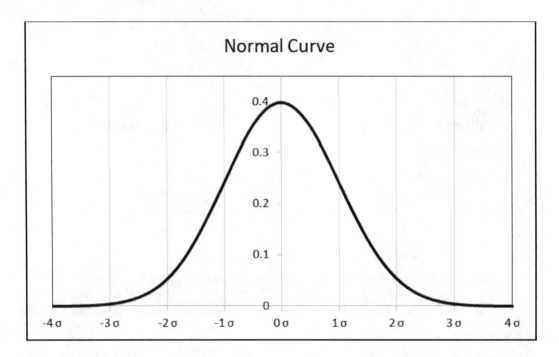

SHAPES OF FREQUENCY CURVES

The five general **shapes of frequency curves** are *symmetrical*, u-*shaped*, *skewed*, j-*shaped*, and *multimodal*. Symmetrical curves are also known as bell curves or normal curves. Values equidistant from the median have equal frequencies. U-shaped curves have two maxima – one at each end. Skewed curves have the maximum point off-center. Curves that are negative skewed, or left skewed, have the maximum on the right side of the graph so there is longer tail and lower slope on the left side. The opposite is true for curves that are positive-skewed, or right-skewed. J-shaped curves have a maximum at one end and a minimum at the other end. Multimodal curves have multiple maxima. For example, if the curve has exactly two maxima, it is called a bimodal curve.

INTERPRETATION OF GRAPHS

EXAMPLE

The following graph shows the ages of five patients being cared for in a hospital:

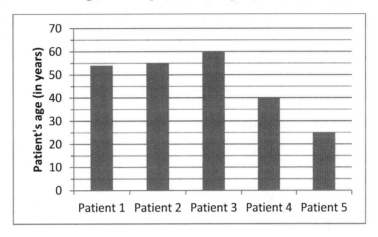

Determine the range of patient ages.

Patient 1 is 54 years old; Patient 2 is 55 years old; Patient 3 is 60 years old; Patient 4 is 40 years old; and Patient 5 is 25 years old. The range of patient ages is the age of the oldest patient minus the age of the youngest patient. In other words, $60 - 25 = 35$. The range of ages is 35 years.

CONSISTENCY BETWEEN STUDIES

EXAMPLE

In a drug study containing 100 patients, a new cholesterol drug was found to decrease low-density lipoprotein (LDL) levels in 25% of the patients. In a second study containing 50 patients, the same drug administered at the same dosage was found to decrease LDL levels in 50% of the patients. Are the results of these two studies **consistent** with one another?

Even though in both studies 25 people (25% of 100 is 25 and 50% of 50 is 25) showed improvements in their LDL levels, the results of the studies are inconsistent. The results of the second study indicate that the drug has a much higher efficacy (desired result) than the results of the first study. Because 50 out of 150 total patients showed improvement on the medication, one could argue that the drug is effective in one third (or approximately 33%) of patients. However, one should be wary of the reliability of results when they're not **reproducible** from one study to the next and when the **sample size** is fairly low.

Information Literacy and Research

CONNECTIONS AND DISTINCTIONS AMONG ELEMENTS IN TEXT

Students should be able to analyze how an informational text makes connections and distinctions among ideas, events, or individuals, such as by comparing them or contrasting them, making analogies between them, or dividing them into categories to show similarities and differences. For example, teachers can help eighth-graders analyze how to divide animals into categories of carnivores, which eat only meat; herbivores, which eat only plants; and omnivores, which eat both meat and plants. Teachers and students can identify the author's comparisons and contrasts of groups. Teachers can help students analyze these processes by supplying sentence frames. For example, "A _____ is a _____, so" and "A _____ is a _____ which means." The students fill these empty spaces in, such as, "A frog is a carnivore, so it eats only meat," and "A rabbit is an herbivore, which means it eats only plants."

TEXT FEATURES IN INFORMATIONAL TEXTS

The title of a text gives readers some idea of its content. The table of contents is a list near the beginning of a text, showing the book's sections and chapters and their coinciding page numbers. This gives readers an overview of the whole text, and helps them find specific chapters easily. An appendix, at the back of the book or document, adds important information not in the main text. Also at the back, an index lists the book's important topics alphabetically with their page numbers to help students find them easily. Glossaries, usually found at the backs of books, list technical terms alphabetically with their definitions to aid vocabulary learning and comprehension. Boldface print is used to emphasize certain words, often identifying words included in the text's glossary where readers can look up their definitions. Headings separate sections of text and show the topic of each. Subheadings divide subject headings into smaller, more specific categories to help readers organize information. Footnotes, at the bottom of the page, give readers more information, such as citations or links. Bullet points list items separately, making facts and ideas easier to see and understand. A sidebar is a box of information to one side of the main text giving additional information, often on a more focused or in-depth example of a topic.

Illustrations and photographs are pictures visually emphasizing important points in text. The captions below the illustrations explain what those images show. Charts and tables are visual forms of information that make something easier and faster to understand. Diagrams are drawings that show relationships or explain a process. Graphs visually show relationships of multiple sets of information plotted along vertical and horizontal axes. Maps show geographical information visually to help students understand the relative locations of places covered in the text. Timelines are visual graphics showing historical events in chronological order to help readers see their sequence.

> **Review Video: Informative Text**
> Visit mometrix.com/academy and enter code: 924964

TECHNICAL MATERIAL FOR NON-TECHNICAL READERS

Writing about technical subjects for non-technical readers differs from writing for colleagues in that authors begin with a different goal: it may be more important to deliver a critical message than to impart the maximum technical content possible. Technical authors also must assume that non-technical audiences do not have the expertise to comprehend extremely scientific or technical messages, concepts, and terminology. They must resist the temptation to impress audiences with their scientific knowledge and expertise, and remember that their primary purpose is to communicate a message that non-technical readers will understand, feel, and respond to. Non-technical and technical styles include similarities: both should formally cite references when used and acknowledge other authors' work utilized. Both must follow intellectual property and copyright regulations. This includes the author's protecting his/her own rights, or a public domain statement, as s/he chooses.

Writers of technical or scientific material may need to write for many non-technical audiences. Some readers have no technical or scientific background, and those who do may not be in the same field as the authors. Government and corporate policymakers and budget managers need technical information they can understand for decision-making. Citizens affected by technology and/or science are another audience. Non-governmental organizations can encompass many of the preceding groups. Elementary and secondary school programs also need non-technical language for presenting technical subject matter. Additionally, technical authors will need to use non-technical language collecting consumer responses to surveys, presenting scientific or para-scientific material to the public, writing about the history of science, and writing about science and technology in developing countries.

When authors of technical information must write about their subjects using non-technical language that readers outside their disciplinary fields can comprehend, they should not only use non-technical terms, they should also use normal, everyday language to accommodate non-native-language readers. For example, instead of writing that "eustatic changes" like "thermal expansion" causing "hazardous conditions" in the "littoral zone," an author would do better to write that a "rising sea level" is "threatening the coast." When technical terms cannot be avoided, authors should also define and/or explain them using non-technical language. Although authors must cite references and acknowledge others' work they use, they should avoid the kinds of references or citations that they would use in scientific journals—unless they reinforce author messages. They should not use endnotes, footnotes, or any other complicated referential techniques because non-technical journal publishers usually do not accept them. Including high-resolution illustrations, photos, maps, or satellite images and incorporating multimedia into digital publications will enhance public non-technical writing about technical subjects. Technical authors may publish using non-technical language in e-journals, trade journals, specialty newsletters, and daily newspapers.

EVALUATING ARGUMENTS MADE BY INFORMATIONAL TEXT WRITERS

When evaluating an informational text, the first step is to identify the argument's conclusion. Then identify the author's premises that support the conclusion. Try to paraphrase premises for clarification and make the conclusion and premises fit. List all premises first, sequentially numbered, then finish with the conclusion. Identify any premises or assumptions not stated by the author but required for the stated premises to support the conclusion. Read word assumptions sympathetically, as the author might. Evaluate whether premises reasonably support the conclusion: For inductive reasoning, the reader should ask if the premises are true, if the support the conclusion, and how strongly. For deductive reasoning, the reader should ask if the argument is valid or invalid. If all premises are true, the argument is valid unless the conclusion can be false. If it can, then the argument is invalid. Alter an invalid argument to become valid, adding any premises needed.

DETERMINING AN INFORMATIONAL AUTHOR'S PURPOSE

Informational authors' purposes are why they wrote texts. Readers must determine authors' motivations and goals. Readers gain greater insight into text by considering the author's motivation. This develops critical reading skills. Readers perceive writing as a person's voice, not simply printed words. Uncovering author motivations and purposes empowers readers to know what to expect from the text, read for relevant details, evaluate authors and their work critically, and respond effectively to the motivations and persuasions of the text. The main idea of a text is what the reader is supposed to understand from reading it; the purpose of the text is why the author has written it and what the author wants readers to do with its information. Authors state some purposes clearly, while others may be unstated but equally significant. When purposes stated contradict other parts of text, authors may have hidden agendas. Readers can better evaluate a text's effectiveness, whether they agree or disagree with it, and why they agree or disagree through identifying unstated author purposes.

IDENTIFYING AUTHOR'S POINT OF VIEW OR PURPOSE

In some informational texts, readers find it easy to identify the author's point of view and/or purpose, as when the author explicitly states his or her position and/or reason for writing. But other texts are more difficult, either because of the content or because the authors give neutral or balanced viewpoints. This is particularly true in scientific texts, in which authors may state the purpose of their research in the report, but never state their point of view except by interpreting evidence or data. To analyze text and identify point of view or purpose, readers should ask themselves the following four questions: (1) With what main point or idea does this author want to persuade readers to agree? (2) How do this author's choices of words affect the way that readers consider this subject? (3) How do this author's choices of examples and/or facts affect the way that readers consider this subject? And (4) What is it that this author wants to accomplish by writing this text?

USE OF RHETORIC

There are many ways authors can support their claims, arguments, beliefs, ideas, and reasons for writing informational texts. For example, authors can appeal to readers' sense of logic by communicating their reasoning through a carefully sequenced series of logical steps to help "prove" the points made. Authors can appeal to readers' emotions by using descriptions and words that evoke feelings of sympathy, sadness, anger, righteous indignation, hope, happiness, or any other emotion to reinforce what they express and share with their audience. Authors may appeal to the moral or ethical values of readers by using words and descriptions that can convince readers that something is right or wrong. By relating personal anecdotes, authors can supply readers with more accessible, realistic examples of points they make, as well as appealing to their emotions. They can provide supporting evidence by reporting case studies. They can also illustrate their points by making analogies to which readers can better relate.

RHETORICAL DEVICES

An anecdote is a brief story authors may relate, which can illustrate their point(s) in a more real and relatable way. Aphorisms concisely state common beliefs and may rhyme. For example, Benjamin Franklin's "Early to bed and early to rise / Make a man healthy, wealthy, and wise" is an aphorism. Allusions refer to literary or historical figures to impart symbolism to a thing or person, and/or create reader resonance. In John Steinbeck's *Of Mice and Men,* protagonist George's last name is Milton, alluding to John Milton who wrote *Paradise Lost,* to symbolize George's eventual loss of his dream. Satire ridicules or pokes fun at human foibles or ideas, as in the works of Jonathan Swift and Mark Twain. A parody is a form of satire that imitates another work to ridicule its topic and/or style. A paradox is a statement that is true despite appearing contradictory. Hyperbole is overstatement using exaggerated language. An oxymoron combines seeming contradictions, such as "deafening silence."

Analogies compare two things that share common elements. Similes (stated comparisons using the words "like" or "as") and metaphors (implied comparisons) are considered forms of analogy. When using logic to reason with audiences, syllogism refers either to deductive reasoning or a deceptive, very sophisticated, or subtle argument. Deductive reasoning moves from general to specific, inductive reasoning from specific to general. Diction is author word choice establishing tone and effect. Understatement achieves effects like contrast or irony by downplaying or describing something more subtly than warranted. Chiasmus uses parallel clauses, the second reversing the order of the first. Examples include T. S. Eliot's "Has the Church failed mankind, or has mankind failed the Church?" and John F. Kennedy's "Ask not what your country can do for you; ask what you can do for your country." Anaphora regularly repeats a word or phrase at the beginnings of consecutive clauses or phrases to add emphasis to an idea. A classic example of anaphora was Winston Churchill's emphasis of determination: "We shall fight in the trenches. We shall fight on the oceans. We shall fight in the sky."

EVALUATING MEDIA INFORMATION SOURCES

With the wealth of media in different formats available today, users are more likely to take media at face value. However, to understand the content of media, consumers must critically evaluate each source. Users should ask themselves about media sources: Who is delivering this message, and why? What methods do a media source's publishers employ to gain and maintain users' attention? Which points of view is the media source representing? What are the various ways a message could be interpreted? And what information is missing from the message? Is the source scholarly, i.e., peer-reviewed? Does it include author names and their credentials pertinent to the information? Who publishes it, and why? Who is the target audience? Is the language technically specific or non-technical/public? Are sources cited, research claims documented, conclusions based on furnished evidence, and references provided? Is the publication current? All of these questions and more can and should be asked of media sources.

For books, consider whether information is up-to-date and whether historical perspectives apply. Content is more likely to be scholarly if publishers are universities, government, or professional organizations. Book reviews can also provide useful information. For articles, identify the author, publisher, frequency of periodical publication, and what kind of advertising, if any, is included. Looking for book reviews also informs users. For articles, look for biographical author information; publisher name; frequency of periodical publication; and whether advertising is included and, if so, whether for certain occupations/disciplines. For web pages, check their domain names, identify publishers or sponsors (strip back URLs to uncover), look for author/publisher contact information, check dates of most recent page updates, and be alert to biases and verify information's validity. Quality and accuracy of web pages located through search engines rather than library databases ranges widely, requiring careful user inspection. Web page recommendations from reliable sources like university faculties can help indicate quality and accuracy. Citations of websites by credible or scholarly sources also show reliability. Authors' names, relevant credentials, affiliations, and contact information support their authority. Site functionality, such as ease of navigation, ability to search, site maps and/or indexes, are also criteria to consider.

PERSUASIVE MEDIA

Some media using persuasion are advertising, public relations, and advocacy. Advertisers use persuasion to sell goods and services. The public relations field uses persuasion to give good impressions of companies, governments, or organizations. Advocacy groups use persuasion to garner support or votes. Persuasion can come through commercials, public service announcements, speeches, websites, and newsletters, among others. Activists, lobbyists, government officials, and politicians use political rhetoric involving persuasive techniques. Basic techniques include using celebrity spokespersons, whom consumers admire or aspire to resemble; or, conversely, "everyday people" (albeit often portrayed by actors) with whom consumers identify. Using expert testimonials lends credibility. Explicit claims of content, effectiveness, quality, and reliability—which often cannot be proven or disproven—are used to persuade. While news and advocacy messages mostly eschew humor for credibility's sake (except in political satire), advertising often persuades via humor, which gets consumer attention and associates its pleasure with advertised products and services. "Weasel words," such as qualifiers, are often combined with exaggerated claims. Intensifiers—hyperbole, superlatives, and repetition—and sentimental appeals are also persuasive.

INTERMEDIATE TECHNIQUES

Dangerous propagandist Adolf Hitler said people suspect little lies more than big ones; hence the "Big Lie" is a persuasion method requiring consumers' keen critical thinking to identify. A related method is charisma, which can induce people to believe messages they would otherwise reject. Euphemism substitutes abstract, vague, or bland terms for more graphic, clear, and unpleasant ones. For example, the terms "layoffs" and "firing" are replaced by "downsizing," and "torture" is replaced with "intensive interrogation techniques." Extrapolation bases sweeping conclusions on small amounts of minor information to appeal to what consumers wish or hope. Flattery appeals to consumer self-esteem needs, such as L'Oreal's "You're worth it." Flattery is sometimes accomplished through contrast, like ads showing others' mistakes to make consumers feel superior and smarter. "Glittering generalities" are "virtue" concepts, such as beauty, love, health, democracy, freedom, and science. Persuaders hope these gain consumer acceptance without questioning what they mean. The opposite is name-calling to persuade consumers to reject someone or something.

American citizens love new ideas and technology. Persuaders exploit this by emphasizing the newness of products, services, and candidates. Conversely, they also use nostalgia to evoke consumers' happy memories, which they often remember more than unhappy ones. Citing "scientific evidence" is an intermediate version of the basic technique of expert testimonials. Consumers may accept this as proof, but some advertisers, politicians, and other persuaders may present inaccurate or misleading "evidence." Another intermediate technique is the "simple solution." Although the natures of people and life are complex, when consumers feel overwhelmed by complexity, persuaders exploit this by offering policies, products, or services they claim will solve complicated problems with simple means. Persuaders also use symbols—images, words, and names we associate with more general, emotional concepts like lifestyle, country, family, religion, and gender. While symbols have power, their significance also varies across individuals: for example, some consumers regard the Hummer SUV as a prestigious status symbol, while others regard it as environmentally harmful and irresponsible.

ADVANCED TECHNIQUES

Ad hominem, Latin for "against the man"—also called "shoot the messenger"—attacks someone delivering a message, not the message itself. It operates by association: problems with the messenger must indicate problems with the message. "Stacking the deck" misleads by presenting only selected information that supports one position. Denial evades responsibility, either directly or indirectly, for controversial or unpopular subjects: A politician saying, "I won't mention my opponent's tax evasion issues" manages to mention them while seeming less accusatory. Persuaders use majority belief, such as "Four out of five dentists recommend this brand" or the ubiquitous "[insert number] people can't be wrong." In an intensified version, persuaders exploit group dynamics at rallies, speeches, and other live-audience events where people are vulnerable to surrounding crowd influences. Scapegoating—blaming one person or group for complex problems, is a form of the intermediate "simple solution" technique, a practice common in politics. Timing also persuades, like advertising flowers and candy preceding Valentine's Day, ad campaigns preceding new technology rollouts, and politician speeches following big news events.

RESEARCH WRITING

A research question or problem is what a researcher wants to answer or resolve. In a research paper, the problem statement clearly identifies the issue, tells why the researcher cares about this issue, defines the scope of the research by focusing on specific variables, and shows why those variables matter. The problem statement follows the title and abstract in the research paper, supplying context for the rest and getting the reader's attention. Whether professionals or students, when researchers conduct academic research projects, their literature reviews, which thoroughly examine the extant body of literature on their chosen research topic, form a necessary component of the project by showing what work has already been done toward answering the research question that they have chosen to investigate.

ADDRESSING RESEARCH QUESTIONS

When asking a research question, the researcher may find through making a careful review of the existing literature that the question s/he has chosen have already been answered definitively. In this case, the researcher should modify the question or ask a different one. If the question has not been answered in the literature, researchers should consider the existing knowledge, the chronological sequence in which knowledge has been developed, whether there are any gaps in the knowledge, what needs and opportunities for additional research have been identified, and how one plans to fill in these gaps. Researchers should also consider whether consensus or controversy exists about pertinent matters and, with the latter, which positions exist. One should also consider research trajectories suggested by others' work and the most productive research direction indicated by the literature. Finally, researchers should realize there are no absolute answers: they must decide what is important in the context of their work.

LITERATURE REVIEW

One main part of a literature review is searching through existing literature. The other is actually writing the review. Researchers must take care not to get lost in the information without making any progress in their research goal. A good precaution is to write out the research question and keep it nearby. It is also wise to make a search plan and establish a time limit in advance. Finding a seemingly endless number of references indicates a need to revisit the research question because it is too broad. Finding too little material means that the research topic is too narrow. With cutting-edge research, one may find that nobody has investigated this particular question. This requires systematic searching, using abstracts in periodicals for an overview of available literature, research papers or other specific sources to explore its reference, and references in books and general sources.

When searching published literature on a research topic, one must take thorough notes. It is common to find a reference that could be useful later but is not needed now, so it is helpful to make a note of it so it will be easy to find later. These notes can be grouped in a word processing document, which also allows for easy compiling of links and quotes from Internet research. Researchers should connect to the Internet regularly, view resources for their research often, learn how to use resources correctly and efficiently, experiment with resources available within the discipline(s), open and examine databases, become familiar with reference desk materials, find publications with abstracts of articles and books on one's topic, use papers' references to locate the most utile journals and important authors, identify keywords for refining and narrowing database searches, and peruse library catalogues online for available sources—all while taking notes.

As one searches the available literature, one will gradually develop an overview of the body of literature for his or her subject. This signals the time to prepare for writing the literature review. The researcher should assemble his or her notes along with copies of all the journal articles and all the books acquired. Then one should again write the research question at the top of a page and list below it all of the author names and keywords discovered while searching. It is also helpful to observe whether any groups or pairs of these stand out. These activities are parts of structuring one's literature review—the first step for writing a thesis, dissertation, or research paper. Writers should rewrite as necessary rather than expecting to make only one draft. However, stopping to edit along the way can distract from the momentum of the first draft. It may be better to skip to a later portion of the paper and revisit the problem section at another time.

BODY AND CONCLUSION IN LITERATURE REVIEW

The first step of a literature review paper is to create a rough draft. The next step is to edit: rewrite for clarity, eliminate unnecessary verbiage, and change terminology that could confuse readers. After editing, a writer should ask others to read and give feedback. Additionally, the writer should read the paper aloud to hear how it sounds, editing as needed. Throughout a literature review, the writer should not only summarize and comment on each source reviewed, but should also relate these findings to the original research question. The writer should explicitly state in the conclusion how the research question and pertinent literature interaction is developed throughout the body, reflecting on insights gained through the process.

PRIMARY AND SECONDARY SOURCES

In literature review, one may examine both primary and secondary sources. Primary sources contain original information, like reports other researchers have made of their findings and other first-hand accounts written by experimenters or witnesses of discoveries or events. They may be found in academic books, journals and other periodicals, and authoritative databases. Secondary sources refer to information originally given by other people or found in other places. They may be cited, quoted, or described in books, magazines, newspapers, films, audio and video materials, databases, and websites. Accounts of research and its results are always informed and directed by reviews of the pertinent literature. These depict the present research as a cumulative process integral to the scientific method. Literature reviews also test the research question in relation to the existing knowledge about the topic.

> **Review Video: Validity, Reliability, and Relevance of Primary and Secondary Sources**
> Visit mometrix.com/academy and enter code: 716157

EDITING AND REVISING

After composing a rough draft of a research paper, the writer should edit it. The purpose of the paper is to communicate the answer to one's research question in an efficient and effective manner. This should be as concise and clear as possible, and the style should also be consistent. Editing is often easier to do after writing the first draft than during it, as distance allows writers to be more objective. If the paper includes an abstract and an introduction, the writer should compose these after writing the rest, when s/he will have a better grasp of the theme and arguments. Not all readers understand technical terminology or long words, so writers should use these sparingly. Finally, writers should keep a writing and style guide available to answer questions as they edit.

> **Review Video: Revising and Editing**
> Visit mometrix.com/academy and enter code: 674181

CITING SOURCES

Formal research writers must cite all sources used—books, articles, interviews, conversations, and anything else that contributed to the research. One reason is to avoid plagiarism and give others credit for their ideas. Another reason is to help readers find more information about the subject for further reading and research. Additionally, citing sources helps to make a paper academically authoritative. To prepare, research writers should keep a running list of sources consulted, in an electronic file or on file cards. For every source used, the writer needs specific information. For books, a writer needs to record the author and/or editor name, title, publication date, city, and publisher name. For articles, one needs the author name, title, journal (or magazine or newspaper) name, volume and issue number, publication date, and page numbers. For electronic resources, a writer will need the article information plus the URL, database name, name of the database's publisher, and the date of access.

Three common reference styles are MLA (Modern Language Association), APA (American Psychological Association), and Turabian (by expert author Kate Turabian). Each style formats citation information differently. Professors and instructors often specify that students use one of these. Generally, APA style is used in psychology and sociology papers, and MLA style is used in English literature papers and similar scholarly projects.

To refer to authoritative sources for citing more complicated or specialized resources, such as legislative publications, audiovisual resources, or manuscripts, see http://library.csudh.edu/cyberlib/research.htm, the section on Research and Writing Resources from the library website of California State University Dominguez Hills (CSUDH). The APA Manual is available in print: *Publication Manual of the American Psychological Association*, 6th ed., July 2009, and electronically in a Kindle edition. (The sixth is the latest edition as of February 2014.) APA has also adapted from this edition the *APA Style Guide to Electronic References*, and a pocket guide, *Concise Rules of APA Style*. Garner and Smith's *The Complete Guide to Citing Government Information Resources: A Manual for Writers and Librarians*, June 1993 (revised edition) is available in paperback on Amazon.com. *MLA Handbook for Writers of Research Papers* (7th edition, 2009) is available at MLA Bookstore's website. Turabian's *A Manual for Writers of Research Papers, Theses, and Dissertations* (8th edition, revised, 2013) is available from the University of Chicago Press website.

INTEGRATING REFERENCES AND QUOTATIONS

In research papers, one can include studies whose conclusions agree with one's position (Reed 284; Becker and Fagen 93), as well as studies that disagree (Limbaugh 442, Beck 69) by including parenthetical citations as demonstrated in this sentence. Quotations should be selective: writers should compose an original sentence and incorporate only a few words from a research source. If students cannot use more original words than quotation, they are likely padding their compositions.

When quoting sources, writers should work quotations and references seamlessly into their sentences instead of interrupting the flow of their own argument to summarize a source. Summarizing others' content is often a ploy to bolster word counts. Writing that analyzes the content, evaluates it, and synthesizes material from various sources demonstrates critical thinking skills and is thus more valuable.

> **Review Video: <u>Quotes</u>**
> Visit mometrix.com/academy and enter code: 191037

INCORPORATING OUTSIDE SOURCES

Writers do better to include short quotations rather than long. For example, six to eight long passages quoted in a 10-page paper are excessive. It is also better to avoid wording like "This quotation shows," "As you can see from this quotation," or "It talks about." These are amateurish, feeble efforts to interact with other authors' ideas. Also, writing about sources and quotations wastes words that should be used to develop one's own ideas. Quotations should be used to stimulate discussion rather than taking its place. Ending a paragraph, section, or paper with a quotation is not incorrect per se, but using it to prove a point, without anything more in one's own words regarding the point or subject, is avoiding thinking critically about the topic and considering multiple alternatives. It can also be a tactic to dissuade readers from challenging one's propositions. Writers should include references and quotations that disagree as well as agree with their thesis statements. Presenting evidence on both sides of an issue makes it easier for reasonably skeptical readers to agree with a writer's viewpoint.

Applied Writing Skills

PARTS OF SPEECH

Nouns are words for persons, places, or things. The words *girl, town*, and *house* are all nouns. Nouns are frequently the sentence subjects. Proper nouns are names. Pronouns replace nouns, including personal pronouns specifying person, number, gender, or case. Some common pronouns are *I, you, he, she, it, none,* and *which.* Personal pronouns may be subjective, such as sentence/clause subjects, or objective, like the objects of verbs or prepositions. Verbs are words for actions or states of being. Verbs are often sentence predicates. Adjectives are descriptive words modifying nouns, for example, *big* girl, *red* house, or other adjectives, such as *great* big house. Adverbs are descriptive words modifying verbs, adjectives, or other adverbs (including clauses), often ending in *–ly.* Examples include running *quickly* and *patiently* waiting. Conjunctive adverbs connect two clauses. The words *also, finally, however, furthermore, consequently, instead, meanwhile, next, still, then, therefore, indeed, incidentally,* and *likewise* are all conjunctive adverbs. Prepositions connect nouns/pronouns/phrases to other words in sentences, such as *on, in, behind, under, beside, against, beneath, over,* and *during.* Prepositional phrases include prepositions, their objects, and associated adjectives/adverbs. Conjunctions connect words/phrases/clauses. Common conjunctions include *and, when, but, or/nor, for, so,* and *yet.*

> **Review Video: <u>Nouns and Pronouns</u>**
> Visit mometrix.com/academy and enter code: 312073

FRAGMENTS AND RUN-ON SENTENCES

A sentence fragment is missing some essential component: a subject, predicate, or independent clause. An example of the latter is: "Although I knew that." This is incomplete because "although" makes it a dependent clause with no independent clause to complete the thought. By adding an independent clause, the sentence becomes complete: "Although I knew that, I forgot it." The statement "Going to dinner" has a subject (the gerund "going," a verbal functioning as a noun) and a prepositional phrase ("to dinner") but it does not have a proper subject. Again, adding a subject solves the problem: "We are going to dinner." To repair the statement "The friendly woman Mary," simply add a verb: "The friendly woman is Mary."

Run-on sentences lack necessary punctuation and/or connecting words: "We went to their party we had a very good time we plan to go again." This can be corrected several ways: "We went to their party. We had a very good time. We plan to go again." Or, less choppily: "We went to their party; we had a very good time, and we plan to go again."

> **Review Video: <u>Fragments and Run-On Sentences</u>**
> Visit mometrix.com/academy and enter code: 541989

COLONS VS. SEMICOLONS, ITS VS. IT'S, AND SAW VS. SEEN

Semicolons separate independent clauses, such as "She likes music; she likes to dance." Colons separate clauses when the second explains or illustrates the first: "She likes music: she likes to dance to it." People often misuse semicolons. For example, business letter salutations should use colons. "Dear Mr. Johnson:" is correct, while "Dear Mr. Johnson;" is not. Another common error is inserting an apostrophe into "its" to indicate possession. For example, the sentence, "The house is old; *its* paint is peeling" is correct. People often incorrectly spell this possessive personal pronoun as "it's." Their error is because some possessive nouns/pronouns use apostrophes, such as

157

"Barbara's idea" or "the man's hat." But "its," along with "yours," "hers," and "theirs" (without noun objects) do not. The only correct usage of "it's" is as a contraction of "it" and "is," as in "It's raining outside." "Saw" is the past tense of "to see." "Seen" is the perfect tense, used with auxiliary verbs to form present perfect "have seen," or past perfect, "had seen." This is why "I seen you" and "I have saw" are both incorrect.

> **Review Video: Colons**
> Visit mometrix.com/academy and enter code: 868673
>
> **Review Video: Semicolon Usage**
> Visit mometrix.com/academy and enter code: 370605
>
> **Review Video: Apostrophes**
> Visit mometrix.com/academy and enter code: 213068

PHRASES, CLAUSES, AND INDEPENDENT AND DEPENDENT CLAUSES

A clause has a subject and a predicate and the other elements of a sentence. An independent clause can stand on its own as a sentence. A dependent clause has a subject and a predicate, but it also has a subordinating conjunction, a relative pronoun, or some other connecting word or phrase that makes it unable to stand alone without an accompanying independent clause. For example, "I knew she was not at home" is an independent clause that can be a sentence on its own. But "because I saw her leave" is a dependent clause due to the subordinating conjunction "because," which makes it depend on the independent clause. The two clauses, joined together, form the complex sentence, "I knew she was not at home because I saw her leave." A phrase is neither a complete sentence nor a clause. It lacks a subject, or a predicate, or both. For example, "late at night" is an adverb phrase; "into the house" is a prepositional phrase. Phrases modify other sentence parts.

> **Review Video: Clauses**
> Visit mometrix.com/academy and enter code: 940170

INCONSISTENT VERB TENSES AND NON-PARALLEL STRUCTURE

While changing verb tenses in writing can indicate temporal relationships, switching tenses in a sentence if both or all verbs represent the same time frame is incorrect. For example, "The professor explained the theory to students who ask questions" uses inconsistent verb tenses. The verbs should be either "explained" and "asked" or "explains" and "asks." It is also incorrect to maintain the same verb tense when the time frame shifts among actions. The sentence, "Before they even saw the evidence, they decided" should actually read, "Before they even saw the evidence, they *had* decided" because "decided" occurred prior to "saw." "Susie loves the puppy she adopted" is correct: present-tense "loves" is true currently, while past-tense "adopted" is something Susie did previously and is not doing currently. An example of non-parallel structure is: "She enjoys skating, skiing, swimming, and to sail a boat." Because the first three objects are all gerunds ("-ing" participles used as nouns), the fourth should be "sailing" to be consistent, not the inconsistent infinitive "to sail."

> **Review Video: Verb Tenses**
> Visit mometrix.com/academy and enter code: 809578

SIMPLE, COMPOUND, AND COMPLEX SENTENCES

A simple sentence is an independent clause. It states a complete thought and includes a subject and predicate/verb. An example is, "Some students cram before tests." "Students" is the subject; "some"

158

is a modifying adjective. "Cram" is the verb; "before tests" is a modifying prepositional phrase. A compound sentence includes two independent clauses connected by a coordinator (*for, and, nor, but, or, yet, so*). For example, "Andrew likes history, but Cynthia prefers math" is a compound sentence. Independent clauses can also be joined by a semicolon instead of a coordinator: "Andrew likes history; Cynthia prefers math." A complex sentence has an independent clause and dependent clause, joined by a subordinator: "While Andrew likes history, Cynthia prefers math." The subordinating conjunction "while" makes the first clause dependent on the second. In the complex sentence, "Students are tired on exam day when they have crammed all night," the second clause, made subordinate by "when," depends on the independent clause that came first.

COMPOUND, COMPLEX, AND COMPOUND-COMPLEX SENTENCES

Compound sentences consist of two independent clauses, joined by a coordinating conjunction or punctuation like a semicolon, a colon, or sometimes a comma (for example, "He likes coffee, she likes tea"). Complex sentences consist of an independent clause and a dependent clause, connected by a subordinating word, making one clause subordinate to/dependent on the other. A compound-complex sentence includes two independent clauses, plus one or more dependent clauses. "Susan likes art, and Emily prefers science" is a compound sentence. "Although Susan likes art, Emily prefers science" is a complex sentence. An example of a compound-complex sentence is, "Susan, who draws well, likes art, but Emily, who is very methodical, prefers science." "Susan likes art" is an independent clause. "Who draws well" is a dependent clause with subordinator "who" modifying subject "Susan." "Emily prefers science" is another independent clause. "Who is very methodical" is another dependent clause with subordinator "who" modifying subject "Emily." "But" is the coordinating conjunction joining the two independent clauses.

> **Review Video: <u>Variation of Sentence Types</u>**
> Visit mometrix.com/academy and enter code: 845700

LIE VS. LAY

"To lie" is the infinitive form of the verb, as in "It is restful to lie down on a bed." Many people incorrectly use "lay down" instead. "To lay" is always a transitive verb, which means that it requires an object, and it means to make something lie down or to set something down, as in, "Lay that book on the table." The non-infinitive "lay" is the past tense of "to lie," e.g., "Yesterday I lay down." But the past tense of the transitive verb "to lay" is "laid," as in, "Yesterday I laid the book on the table." The present perfect and past perfect tenses of the intransitive verb "to lie" are both "lain," as in "I have lain here a long time" or "I had lain there all day before they came." However, the present and past perfect tenses of the transitive verb "to lay" are both "laid," as in "I have laid this book down for now" and "I had laid this book down last week."

COMPOUND WORDS

Compound words are words that consist of two single words that are used together to give a more specific meaning so commonly or often that they have been combined to form one word. These may be any part of speech, but are often nouns or adjectives. Some examples of nouns are *footsteps, heartbeat, countertop, gunshot, housewife, household, bookshelf, songbook, storybook, timetable, halfway, aftermath*, and *upkeep*. Some examples among adjectives include *paint-chipped, two-person, beat-up, pock-marked, war-torn, world-weary*, and *evidence-based*. Compound adjectives are often hyphenated, but not always, as in *bloodstained*. Also, authors may create compound adjectives when writing descriptively, as in *acne-scarred, hail-pitted*, and *flower-adorned*, to name a few.

DANGLING PARTICIPLES AND SQUINTING MODIFIERS

Dangling participles are common writing errors. They occur when someone writes a participial ("-ing") phrase followed by a clause, but the syntax makes the participle seemingly modify that clause when it really modifies something else that is unstated. Consider the following sentence, "Always getting into trouble, her life changes." The participle "getting" should modify an absent "she," but it incorrectly modifies "her life" instead. Her life is not always getting into trouble, she is. Or another example, "After eating his lunch, we left the restaurant." The dangling participle makes it sound as if we both ate his lunch. If the writer meant to indicate he ate, it should read, "After he ate his lunch, we left the restaurant." "Joanne's mother left when she was young" has a squinting modifier, making unclear who was young when the mother left—Joanne, her mother, or both. Possible corrections include: "When Joanne was young, her mother left," "Joanne's mother left as a young woman," or "Her young mother left when Joanne was a young child."

MISPLACED MODIFIERS

Misplaced modifiers are in the wrong part of a sentence, appearing to modify the wrong thing. For example, "This author creates a drama revolving around one character's journey in his new publication." This sounds like the new publication is a part of the character's journey. Correction involves moving the prepositional phrase: "In his new publication, this author creates a drama revolving around one character's journey."

Some other simple examples of how modifier placement affects meaning include: "She ate only fruit" versus "She only ate fruit." The first sentence means she ate nothing except fruit; the second means she did not plant, pick, wash, or cook fruit, but only ate it. Or, "He failed nearly every class he took" versus "He nearly failed every class he took." The former means he actually failed most of the classes he took, while the latter means he passed every class he took, but just barely. "Covered with flowers, she admired the field" means she was covered with flowers; "She admired the field covered with flowers" is correct.

> **Review Video: Misplaced Modifiers**
> Visit mometrix.com/academy and enter code: 312681

INCONSISTENT VERB TENSE

A narrative includes the following: "Anticipating the explosion, the insurgent watched the Humvees drive out of range. He frowned. Impatiently he jerks at the wire connected to the grenade's pin. But the handle was caught on something and had not detonated the grenade." This narrative switches tenses. To correct this, the verbs should be consistent in tense: "watched... frowned... jerked... was (caught)... had not detonated." Conversely, they could also be "watches... frowns... jerks... is (caught)... has not detonated." When the main narrative is in the past tense, the reference to something occurring earlier should be in the past perfect tense; when narrative is in the present tense, the reference should be in the present perfect tense.

PHRASES VS. CLAUSES AND TRANSITIVE VS. INTRANSITIVE VERBS

A clause makes a complete sentence, which can be just a subject and verb. However, the verb must be intransitive—one that does not require an object—for the sentence to be complete. For example, "I am," "I live," and "I love" are all complete sentences, but "I like" (or "I hate") is not because "like" needs an object—I like what? "I like it," "I like food," "I like to eat," and "I like eating" are all examples of complete sentences and independent clauses. A phrase lacks either a subject or a verb. For example, while "I like to go swimming" is a clause/sentence, "to go swimming" is a phrase: it

160

has a verb but no subject. The imperative "Go now" is a complete sentence wherein the subject "you" is understood; the meaning is "[You] go now."

PUNCTUATION ERRORS IN POSSESSIVE PRONOUNS

Many people make the error of misspelling the possessive pronoun "its" as "it's" when the apostrophe is only ever used in the contraction of "it is," and never in the possessive. Another common error is misspelling other possessive pronouns by using apostrophes, such as "your's" and "her's." These are always incorrect. A possessive pronoun taking a noun as its object, such as "his hat," "your hat," or "her hat" is not complicated by any –s ending. However, when the possessive pronoun does not have any noun object, the –s ending is added: "It is hers," "That hat is yours," or "She is a friend of theirs." Just like other possessive pronouns without –s endings (such as "mine"), the possessive pronouns ending with –s never include an apostrophe.

DRAWBACKS TO WORDPROCESSING SPELL CHECKERS

Microsoft Word is one of the most popular word processing programs. It has many excellent features facilitating composition. However, students and other writers must realize that its spell checkers, and those of similar programs, are far from perfect. One cannot rely on them without paying attention to what they do. For example, a college student writing a paper on Sophocles' *Oedipus Rex* correctly typed the name of key character Laius, king of Thebes and father of Oedipus, throughout his paper. However, his spell checker, not recognizing the name, "corrected" it to Louis. The student only realized this at the last minute while on his way to class, paper in hand, without a computer or printer nearby, and he had to rewrite every instance of the name by hand. Spell checkers commonly fail to recognize proper names and foreign language words. To eliminate the red zigzag underline that Word uses to indicate a misspelling, simply right-click and select "Add to dictionary" from the drop-down menu. Students and writers must consciously proofread everything they write, rather than assume spell checkers are always correct.

Microsoft Word's grammar check identifies many common errors, but is often incorrect. It does not recognize reflexive verbs, such as "assess themselves" or "do it for themselves," and suggests changing "themselves" to "them." Many writers and students get perplexed when writing a complete sentence to find Word underlining it with a green zigzag, labeling it a "fragment." Sometimes this reflects a true error, like leaving the verb out of a clause. But other times, it makes no sense by current writing standards. Right-clicking, selecting "Grammar" from the drop-down menu, and selecting "Ignore rule" eliminates such wrong "corrections." (Another option is to simply ignore the markups.) If they have questions, writers and students can consult reputable grammar experts' websites about suspect "corrections."

The grammar checkers in popular word processing software programs like Microsoft Word can catch many inadvertent errors often caused by hurried typing and/or careless writing. However, these programs are not always correct, and in fact are often incorrect. Not only will Word's grammar checker incorrectly label some constructions incorrect when they are not, but it will also fail to identify other errors. For example, Noam Chomsky's famous sample sentence, "Colorless green ideas sleep furiously" is grammatically, morphologically, and syntactically correct in its construction, but makes no sense semantically—which was Chomsky's point. Grammar checkers are not people who can think, reason, and understand; they are simply programmed to identify certain things categorized as errors. So the grammar checker has no problem with Chomsky's sentence and does not flag anything in it as wrong. This is an example of how grammar checkers not only over-correct by identifying correct usages as incorrect, but also under-correct by not identifying incorrect usages. Writers and students must use their own judgment and knowledge and consult grammatical experts and/or their websites when needed.

161

ESSAYS

The basic format of an essay can be said to have three major parts: the introduction, the body, and the conclusion. The body is further divided into the writer's main points. Short and simple essays may have three main points, while essays covering broader ranges and going into more depth can have almost any number of main points, depending on length.

An essay's introduction should answer three questions: (1) What is the subject of the essay? If a student writes an essay about a book, the answer would include the title and author of the book and any additional information needed—such as the subject or argument of the book. (2) How does the essay address the subject? To answer this, the writer identifies the essay's organization by briefly summarizing main points and/or evidence supporting them. (3) What will the essay prove? This is the thesis statement, usually the opening paragraph's last sentence, clearly stating the writer's message.

The body elaborates on all the main points related to the thesis and supporting evidence, introducing one main point at a time. Each body paragraph should state the point, explain its meaning, support it with quotations or other evidence, and then explain how this point and the evidence are related to the thesis. The writer should then repeat this procedure in a new paragraph for each additional main point. In addition to relating each point to the thesis, clearly restating the thesis in at least one sentence of each paragraph is also advisable.

The conclusion reiterates the content of the introduction, including the thesis, to review them for the reader. The essay writer may also summarize the highlights of the argument or description contained in the body of the essay, following the same sequence originally used in the body. For example, a conclusion might look like: Point 1 + Point 2 + Point 3 = Thesis, or Point 1 → Point 2 → Point 3 → Thesis Proof. Good organization makes essays easier for writers to compose and provides a guide for readers to follow. Well-organized essays hold attention better, and are more likely to get readers to accept their theses as valid.

> **Review Video: Reading Essays**
> Visit mometrix.com/academy and enter code: 169166

INFORMATIVE/EXPLANATORY VS. ARGUMENTATIVE WRITING

Informative/explanatory writing begins with the basis that something is true or factual, while argumentative writing strives to prove something that may or may not be true or factual. Whereas argument is intended to persuade readers to agree with the author's position, informative/explanatory text merely provides information and insight to readers. Informative/explanatory writing concentrates on informing readers about why or how something is as it is. This includes offering new information, explaining how a process works, and/or developing a concept for readers. In accomplishing these objectives, the writing may emphasize naming and differentiating various things within a category; providing definitions of things; providing details about the parts of something; explaining a particular function or behavior; and giving readers explanations for why a fact, object, event, or process exists or occurs.

NECESSARY SKILLS FOR INFORMATIVE/EXPLANATORY WRITING

For students to write in informative/explanatory mode, they must be able to locate and select pertinent information from primary and secondary sources. They must also combine their own experiences and existing knowledge with this new information they find. They must not only select facts, details, and examples relevant to their topics, but also learn to incorporate this information into their writing. Students need at the same time to develop their skills in various writing techniques, such as comparing and contrasting, making transitions between topics/points, and citing scenarios and anecdotes related to their topics. In teaching explanatory/informative writing, teachers must "read like writers" to use mentor texts to consider author craft and technique. They can find mentor texts in blogs, websites, newspapers, novels, plays, picture books, and many more. Teachers should know the grade-level writing standards for informative/explanatory writing to select classroom-specific, appropriate mentor texts.

> **Review Video: Informative Text**
> Visit mometrix.com/academy and enter code: 924964

NARRATIVE WRITING

Put simply, narrative writing tells a story. The most common examples of literary narratives are novels. Non-fictional biographies, autobiographies, memoirs, and histories also use narrative. Narratives should tell stories in such a way that the readers learn something, or gain insight or understanding. Students can write more interesting narratives by relating events or experiences that were meaningful to them. Narratives should not begin with long descriptions or introductions, but start with the actions or events. Students should ensure that there is a point to each story by describing what they learned from the experience they narrate. To write effective description, students should include sensory details, asking themselves what they saw, heard, felt/touched, smelled, and tasted during the experiences they describe. In narrative writing, the details should be concrete rather than abstract. Using concrete details enables readers to imagine everything that the writer describes.

> **Review Video: Narratives**
> Visit mometrix.com/academy and enter code: 280100

SENSORY DETAILS AND CONCRETE VS. ABSTRACT DESCRIPTIONS IN NARRATIVE

Students need vivid description to write descriptive essays. Narratives should also include description of characters, things, and events. Students should remember to describe not only the visual detail of what someone or something looks like, but details from other senses as well. For example, they can contrast the feelings of a sea breeze versus a mountain breeze, describe how they think something inedible would taste, and sounds they hear in the same location at different times of day and night. Readers have trouble visualizing images or imagining sensory impressions and feelings from abstract descriptions, so concrete descriptions make these more real.

Concrete language provides information that readers can grasp and may empathize with, while abstract language, which is more general, can leave readers feeling disconnected, empty, or even confused. "It was a lovely day" is abstract, but "The sun shone brightly, the sky was blue, the air felt warm, and a gentle breeze wafted across my skin" is concrete. "Ms. Couch was a good teacher" uses abstract language, giving only a general idea of the writer's opinion. But "Ms. Couch is excellent at helping us take our ideas and turn them into good essays and stories" uses concrete language, giving more specific examples of what makes Ms. Couch a good teacher. "I like writing poems but not essays" gives readers a general idea that the student prefers one genre over another, but not why. But by saying, "I like writing short poems with rhythm and rhyme, but I hate writing five-page essays that go on and on about the same ideas," readers understand that the student prefers the brevity, rhyme, and meter of short poetry over the length and redundancy of longer prose.

JOURNALS AND DIARIES

A journal is a personal account of events, experiences, feelings, and thoughts. Many people write journals to confide their feelings and thoughts or to help them process experiences they have had.

Since journals are private documents not meant for sharing with others, writers may not be concerned with grammar, spelling, or other mechanics. However, authors may write journals that they expect or hope to publish someday; in this case, they not only express their thoughts and feelings and process their experiences, but they additionally attend to their craft in writing them. Some authors compose journals to document particular time periods or series of related events, such as a cancer diagnosis, treatment, surviving the disease, and how these experiences have changed/affected them; experiences in recovering from addiction; journeys of spiritual exploration and discovery; trips to or time spent in another country; or anything else someone wants to personally document. Journaling can also be therapeutic: some people use them to work through feelings of grief over loss or to wrestle with big decisions.

The Diary of a Young Girl by Dutch Jew Anne Frank (1947) contains her life-affirming, nonfictional diary entries from 1942-1944 while her family hid in an attic from World War II's genocidal Nazis. *Go Ask Alice* (1971) by Beatrice Sparks is a cautionary, fictional novel in the form of diary entries by an unhappy, rebellious teen who takes LSD, runs away from home and lives with hippies, and eventually returns home. Frank's writing reveals an intelligent, sensitive, insightful girl, raised by intellectual European parents—a girl who believes in the goodness of human nature despite surrounding atrocities. Character Alice, influenced by early 1970s counterculture, becomes less optimistic. However, similarities can be found: Frank dies in a Nazi concentration camp while the fictitious Alice dies in a drug overdose; both are unable to escape their surroundings. Additionally, adolescent searches for personal identity are evident in both books.

LETTERS

Letters are messages written to other people. In addition to letters written between individuals, some writers compose letters to the editors of newspapers, magazines, and other publications; some write "Open Letters" to be published and read by the general public. Open letters, while intended for everyone to read, may also identify a group of people or a single person whom the letter directly addresses. In everyday use, the most-used forms are business letters and personal or friendly letters. Both kinds share common elements: business or personal letterhead stationery; the writer's return address at the top; the addressee's address next; a salutation, such as "Dear [name]" or some similar opening greeting, followed by a colon in business letters or a comma in personal letters; the body of the letter, with paragraphs as indicated; and a closing, like "Sincerely/Cordially/Best regards/etc." or "Love," in intimate personal letters.

The Greek word for "letter" is *epistolē*, which became the English word "epistle." The earliest letters were called epistles, including the New Testament's Epistles from the Apostles to the Christians. In ancient Egypt, the writing curriculum in scribal schools included the epistolary genre. Epistolary novels frame a story in the form of letters. For example, 18th-century English novelist Samuel Richardson wrote the popular epistolary novels *Pamela* (1740) and *Clarissa* (1749). Henry Fielding's satire of *Pamela,* entitled *Shamela* (1741) mocked epistolary writing. French author Montesquieu wrote *Lettres persanes* (1721); Jean-Jacques Rousseau wrote *Julie, ou la nouvelle Héloïse* (1761); and Pierre Choderlos de Laclos penned *Les Liaisons dangereuses* (1782), which was adapted into a screenplay for the multiple Oscar-winning 1988 English-language movie *Dangerous Liaisons*. German author Johann Wolfgang von Goethe wrote *The Sorrows of Young Werther* in epistolary form. Frances Brooke also wrote the first North American novel, *The History of Emily Montague* (1769) using epistolary form. In the 19th century, epistolary novels included Honoré de Balzac's *Letters of Two Brides* (1842) and Mary Shelley's *Frankenstein* (1818).

BLOGS

The word "blog" is derived from "web log" and refers to writing done exclusively on the Internet. Readers of reputable newspapers expect quality content and layouts that enable easy reading. These expectations also apply to blogs. For example, readers can easily move visually from line to line when columns are narrow; overly wide columns cause readers to lose their places. Blogs must also be posted with layouts enabling online readers to follow them easily. However, because the way people read on computer, tablet, and smartphone screens differs from how they read print on paper, formatting and writing blog content is more complex than writing newspaper articles. Two major principles are the bases for blog-writing rules: (1) While readers of print articles skim to estimate their length, online they must scroll down to scan; therefore, blog layouts need more subheadings, graphics, and other indications of what information follows. (2) Onscreen reading is harder than reading printed paper, so legibility is crucial in blogs.

RULES AND RATIONALES FOR WRITING BLOGS

Expert web designer, copywriter, and blogger Annabel Cady (http://www.successfulblogging.com/) shares the following blog-posting rules: Format all posts for smooth page layout and easy scanning. Column width should be a maximum of 80 characters, including spaces, for easier reading. Headings and subheadings separate text visually, enable scanning or skimming, and encourage continued reading. Bullet-pointed or numbered lists enable quick information location and scanning. Punctuation is critical, so beginners should use shorter sentences until confident. Blog paragraphs should be far shorter—two to six sentences each—than paragraphs written on paper to enable "chunking" because reading onscreen is more difficult. Sans serif fonts are usually clearer than serif fonts, and larger font sizes are better. Highlight important material and draw attention with **boldface**, but avoid overuse. Avoid hard-to-read *italics* and ALL CAPITALS. Include enough blank spaces: overly busy blogs tire eyes and brains. Images not only break up text, but also emphasize and enhance text, and can attract initial reader attention. Use background colors judiciously to avoid distracting the eye or making it difficult to read. Be consistent throughout posts, since people read them in different orders. Tell a story with a beginning, middle, and end.

CONSIDERATIONS TO TEACH STUDENTS ABOUT OCCASIONS, PURPOSES, AND AUDIENCES

Teachers can explain to students that organizing their ideas, providing evidence to support the points they make in their writing, and correcting their grammar and mechanics are not simply for following writing rules or correctness for its own sake, but rather for ensuring that specific reader audiences understand what they intend to communicate. For example, upper-elementary-grade students writing for lower-elementary-grade students should write in print rather than script, use simpler vocabulary, and avoid writing in long, complex, compound, or complex-compound sentences. The purpose for writing guides word choice, such as encouraging readers to question opposing viewpoints or stimulate empathy and/or sympathy. It also influences narrative, descriptive, expository, or persuasive/argumentative format. For instance, business letters require different form and language than parent thank-you notes. Persuasive techniques, like words that evoke certain reader emotions, description that appeals to reader beliefs, and supporting information can all affect reader opinions.

QUESTIONS TO DETERMINE CONTENT AND FORMAT

When student writers have chosen a viewpoint or idea about which to write, teachers can help them select content to include and the writing format(s) most appropriate to their subject. They should have students ask themselves what their readers need to know to enable them to agree with the viewpoint in the writing, or to believe what the writer is saying. Students can imagine another person hearing them say what they will write about, and responding, "Oh, yeah? Prove that!" Teachers should have students ask themselves what kinds of evidence they need to prove their positions/ideas to skeptical readers. They should have students consider what points might cause the reader to disagree. Students should consider what knowledge their reading audience shares in common with them. They should also consider what information they need to share with their readers. Teachers can have students adapt various writing formats, organizing techniques, and writing styles to different purposes and audiences to practice with choosing writing modes and language.

APPROPRIATE KINDS OF WRITING FOR DIFFERENT TASKS, PURPOSES, AND AUDIENCES

Students who are writing to persuade their parents to grant some additional privilege, such as permission for a more independent activity, should use more sophisticated vocabulary and diction that sounds more mature and serious to appeal to the parental audience. Students who are writing for younger children, however, should use simpler vocabulary and sentence structure, as well as choosing words that are more vivid and entertaining. They should treat their topics more lightly, and include humor as appropriate. Students who are writing for their classmates may use language that is more informal, as well as age-appropriate. Students wanting to convince others to agree with them should use persuasive/argumentative form. Those wanting to share an experience should use descriptive writing. Those wanting to relate a story and what can be learned from it should write narratives. Students can use speculative writing to invite others to join them in exploring ideas.

MAIN IDEAS, SUPPORTING DETAILS, AND OUTLINING A TOPIC

A writer often begins the first paragraph of a paper by stating the main idea or point, also known as the topic sentence. The rest of the paragraph supplies particular details that develop and support the main point. One way to visualize the relationship between the main point and supporting information is as a table: the tabletop is the main point, and each of the table's legs is a supporting detail or group of details. Both professional authors and students can benefit from planning their writing by first making an outline of the topic. Outlines facilitate quick identification of the main point and supporting details without having to wade through the additional language that will exist in the fully developed essay, article, or paper. Outlining can also help readers to analyze a piece of existing writing for the same reason. The outline first summarizes the main idea in one sentence. Then, below that, it summarizes the supporting details in a numbered list. Writing the paper then consists of filling in the outline with detail, writing a paragraph for each supporting point and adding an introduction and conclusion.

> **Review Video: Topics and Main Ideas**
> Visit mometrix.com/academy and enter code: 407801

WORDS THAT SIGNAL INTRODUCTION OF SUCCESSIVE DETAILS

When a paragraph opens with the topic sentence, the second sentence may begin with a phrase like "First of all," introducing the first supporting detail/example. The writer may introduce the second supporting item with words or phrases like "Also," "In addition," and "Besides." The writer might introduce succeeding pieces of support with wording like, "Another thing," "Moreover" "Furthermore," or "Not only that, but." The writer may introduce the last piece of support with "Lastly," "Finally," or "Last but not least." Writers get off the point by presenting "off-target" items not supporting the main point. For example, a main point "My dog is not smart" is supported by the statement, "He's six years old and still doesn't answer to his name." But "He cries when I leave for school" is not supportive, as it does not indicate lack of intelligence. Writers stay on point by presenting only supportive statements that are directly relevant to and illustrative of their main point.

PARAGRAPHS

A paragraph is a group of sentences that forms a unit separate from (but connected to) other paragraphs. Typically, all of one paragraph's sentences relate to one main idea or point. Two major properties that make paragraphs effective or ineffective are focus and development, or lack thereof. Paragraphs with poor focus impede comprehension because the sentences seem unrelated. When writers attempt to include too many ideas in a paragraph rather than focusing on the most important idea, or fail to supply transitions between ideas, they produce unfocused paragraphs. Undeveloped or inadequately-developed paragraphs may use good writing, but are still not effective. When a writer misunderstands the audience, depends overly on generalization, and fails to offer specific details, paragraph development will be poor. S/he may omit key term definitions, supporting evidence, setting description, context for others' ideas, background, and other important details, falsely assuming that readers already know these things.

WRITING EFFECTIVE PARAGRAPHS

The first thing a writer should do for a good paragraph is to focus on one main idea as the subject. A writer may introduce a paragraph by stating this main idea in a topic sentence. However, the main idea may be so obvious that writers can imply it rather than state it overtly and readers can easily infer it. Second, a writer should use specific details to develop the main idea. Details should capture readers' attention and also explain the author's ideas. Insufficient detail makes a paragraph too abstract, which readers find boring or confusing. Excessive detail makes a paragraph unfocused, which readers find overwhelming and also confusing. Third, a writer should develop paragraphs using structural patterns.

STRUCTURAL PATTERNS

Paragraphs have a nearly limitless range of structures, but certain patterns appear more often, including narration, description, definition, example and illustration, division and classification, comparison and contrast, analogy, cause and effect, and process.

NARRATION, DESCRIPTION, DEFINITION, EXAMPLE AND ILLUSTRATION, AND DIVISION AND CLASSIFICATION

In narration, a paragraph's main idea is developed with a story. Writers may use stories as anecdotal evidence to support the main point. In description, the writer constructs a clear image of a scene or event by including specific, sensory and other details that depict a person, thing, place, and/or time. Description shows readers instead of telling them. In definition, the writer provides a detailed explanation of a term that is central to the piece of writing. In example and illustration, the writer provides the readers with one or more examples that illustrate the point that the writer wants to make. Paragraphs using division divide a concept into its component parts—for example, body parts or experiment steps. Paragraphs using classification group separate things into categories by their similarities—such as mammals and insects, tragedies and comedies, and so on.

COMPARISON AND CONTRAST, ANALOGY, CAUSE AND EFFECT, AND PROCESS

Paragraphs that compare two or more things make note of their similarities. Paragraphs that contrast two or more things make note of how they differ. Another common paragraph technique is both comparing and contrasting two or more items within the same paragraph, showing both similarities and differences. Analogy compares two things in an unusual way, often things that belong to very different categories. This can afford new reader insight. Writers may use analogies to develop their ideas. Writers also develop their ideas in paragraphs through cause and effect, which either explains what caused some event or result, or shows the effects that something produced.

Paragraphs may start with causes and proceed to effects, or begin with effects and then give causes. Process paragraphs describe and/or explain some process. They often sequence the stages, phases, or steps of the process using chronological order.

COHERENCE

When a paragraph is coherent, the details fit together so that readers can clearly understand the main point, and its parts flow well. Writers produce more coherent paragraphs when they select structural patterns appropriate to the conceptual content. There are several techniques writers can use to make paragraphs more coherent. Repetition connects sentences by repeating key words or phrases. This not only helps sentences flow together, but it also signals to readers the significance of the ideas these words and phrases communicate. Parallelism uses parallel structure, within or between sentences. Humorist Bill Maher once said, "We're feeding animals too sick to stand to people too fat to walk." His parallelism emphasized and connected two issues: the practice of using downed cows as food and the obesity epidemic. Consistency keeps the viewpoint, tone, and linguistic register consistent within the paragraph or piece. Finally, transitions via connective words and phrases aid coherence immensely.

TRANSITIONS

Transitions between sentences and paragraphs guide readers from idea to idea. They also indicate relationships between sentences and paragraphs. Writers should be judicious in their use of transitions, inserting them sparingly. They should also be selected to fit the author's purpose—transitions can indicate time, comparison, and conclusion, among other purposes.

Review Video: Transitions in Writing
Visit mometrix.com/academy and enter code: 233246

TRANSITIONAL WORDS AND PHRASES

Transitional words and phrases indicating time include: afterward, immediately, earlier, meanwhile, recently, lately, now, since, soon, when, then, until, before, etc. Transitions indicating sequence include: too, first, second, further, moreover, also, again, and, next, still, too, besides, and finally. Transitions specifying comparison include: similarly, in the same way, likewise, also, again, and once more. Transitions that indicate contrast include: but, although, despite, however, instead, nevertheless, on the one hand... on the other hand, regardless, yet, and in contrast. Transitions indicating examples include: for example, for instance, such as, to illustrate, indeed, in fact, and specifically. Transitions indicating cause and effect include: because, consequently, thus, therefore, then, to this end, since, so, as a result, if... then, and accordingly.

Transitions indicating place include: near, far, here, there, to the left/right, next to, above, below, beyond, opposite, and beside. Transitions expressing concession include: granted that, naturally, of course, it may appear, and although it is true that. Transitions showing repetition, summary, or conclusion include: as mentioned earlier, as noted, in other words, in short, on the whole, to summarize, therefore, as a result, to conclude, and in conclusion. These tell readers how a sentence relates to the previous ones, and directs their thinking across ideas.

Review Video: Transitional Words and Phrases
Visit mometrix.com/academy and enter code: 197796

INTRODUCTION

Because readers encounter the introduction first, a writer should design the introductory paragraph to capture interest. Introductions should state the main point, thesis, or topic sentence soon and logically. Introductions should also prepare readers for the content of the body. To do this, the topic should first be narrowed to a main idea. The writer should then determine which main points support the main idea, and decide how to order those points. Supporting details can then be organized in sequential order. Some techniques for sequencing include strongest-to-weakest or weakest-to-strongest, logical progression, or sequencing by association. A writer should compose a thesis statement, which may contain the plan for the piece's structure and organization. Then it is time to write the first draft of the body of the document, including transitions between sentences and paragraphs. Finally, the writer creates the introduction, focusing on engaging the reader, integrating the thesis into the introduction, and maintaining the document's organization and structure.

> **Review Video: Introduction**
> Visit mometrix.com/academy and enter code: 961328

BODY

In an essay's introduction, the writer establishes the thesis and may indicate how the rest of the piece will be structured. In the body of the piece, the writer elaborates upon, illustrates, and explains the thesis statement. How writers sequence supporting details and their choices of paragraph types are development techniques. Writers may give examples of the concept introduced in the thesis statement. If the subject includes a cause-and-effect relationship, the author may explain its causality. A writer will explain and/or analyze the main idea of the piece throughout the body, often by presenting arguments for the veracity or credibility of the thesis statement. Writers may use development to define or clarify ambiguous terms. Paragraphs within the body may be organized with natural sequences, like space and time. Writers may employ inductive reasoning, using multiple details to establish a generalization or causal relationship, or deductive reasoning, proving a generalized hypothesis or proposition through a specific example/case.

> **Review Video: Drafting Body Paragraphs**
> Visit mometrix.com/academy and enter code: 724590

CONCLUSION

Two important principles to consider when writing a conclusion are strength and closure. A strong conclusion gives the reader a sense that the author's main points are meaningful and important, and that the supporting facts and arguments are convincing, solid, and well developed. When a conclusion achieves closure, it gives the impression that the writer has stated what needed stating and completed the work, rather than simply stopping after a specified length. Some things to avoid when writing concluding paragraphs include: introducing a completely new idea, beginning with obvious or unoriginal phrases like "In conclusion" or "To summarize," apologizing for one's opinions or writing, repeating the thesis word for word rather than rephrasing it, and believing that the conclusion must always summarize the piece.

> **Review Video: Drafting Conclusions**
> Visit mometrix.com/academy and enter code: 209408

COHERENCE VS. COHESION

Cohesive writing flows smoothly, helping readers move easily from sentence to sentence and holding all sentences together. Coherent writing contains sentences that are not only clear individually, but also combine into a unified paragraph or passage. While we are often warned against using passive voice, sometimes a paragraph or passage is more cohesive using a passive construction that allows sentences to flow together better. For example, "Scientists are studying black holes. A black hole is made when a dead star collapses." The passive voice allows repetition of "black hole" from the end of the first sentence to the beginning of the second, connecting this idea. Making one sentence follow from the previous one is the "old-to-new" technique. If the second sentence in active voice read, "When a dead star collapses, it becomes a black hole," the term "black hole" would be farther away from the first sentence and they would not connect or flow as well.

Writers can make text cohesive with the old-to-new principle: starting sentences with familiar information and ending them with new or unexpected information. A paragraph can be cohesive, with ideas flowing smoothly from one sentence to the next, but still not coherent. For example, a writer may connect words or ideas between sentences, but change the subject with each new sentence. When writing is coherent, readers can make sense of paragraphs or passages because sentence ideas integrate into a unified whole with interrelated concepts. Coherent writing enables readers to easily recognize individual sentence topics and understand how they combine into a group of connected ideas. Readers feel more comfortable when sentence topics appear earlier in sentences, and when a sequence of sentences indicates the import of the entire paragraph or passage.

Beginning sentences with familiar information in short and simple phrases, keeping topics consistent, and making obvious transitions between ideas will help produce cohesive and coherent writing.

> **Review Video: <u>Methods to Obtain Coherence in Writing</u>**
> Visit mometrix.com/academy and enter code: 831344

WRITING STYLE AND LINGUISTIC FORM

Linguistic form encodes the literal meanings of words and sentences. It comes from the phonological, morphological, syntactic, and semantic parts of a language. Writing style consists of different ways of encoding the meaning and indicating figurative and stylistic meanings. Writers' stylistic choices accomplish three basic effects on their audiences: (1) they communicate meanings beyond linguistically dictated meanings, (2) they communicate the author's attitude, such as persuasive/argumentative effects accomplished through style, and (3) they communicate or express feelings. Within style, component areas include: narrative structure; viewpoint; focus; sound patterns; meter and rhythm; lexical and syntactic repetition and parallelism; writing genre; representational, realistic, and mimetic effects; representation of thought and speech; meta-representation (representing representation); irony; metaphor and other indirect meanings; representation and use of historical and dialectal variations; gender-specific and other group-specific speech styles, both real and fictitious; and analysis of the processes for inferring meaning from writing.

OGET Practice Test

Reading and Written Communication

Directions: Use the following passage to answer questions 1-10.

"So that Nobody Has to Go to School if They Don't Want to"

An Excerpt by Roger Sipher

A decline in standardized test scores is but the most recent indicator that American education is in trouble. One reason for the crisis is that present mandatory-attendance laws force many to attend school that have no wish to be there. Such children have little desire to learn and are so antagonistic to school that neither they nor more highly motivated students receive the quality education that is the birthright of every American. The solution to this problem is simple: Abolish compulsory-attendance laws and allow only those who are committed to getting an education to attend.

Most parents want a high school education for their children. Unfortunately, compulsory attendance hampers the ability of public school officials to enforce legitimate educational and disciplinary policies and thereby make the education a good one. Private schools have no such problem. They can fail or dismiss students, knowing such students can attend public school. Without compulsory attendance, public schools would be freer to oust students whose academic or personal behavior undermines the educational mission of the institution.

Abolition of archaic attendance laws would produce enormous dividends:

- First, it would alert everyone that school is a serious place where one goes to learn. Schools are neither day-care centers nor indoor street corners. Young people who resist learning should stay away; indeed, an end to compulsory schooling would require them to stay away.
- Second, students opposed to learning would not be able to pollute the educational atmosphere for those who want to learn. Teachers could stop policing recalcitrant students and start educating.
- Third, grades would show what they are supposed to: how well a student is learning. Parents could again read report cards and know if their children were making progress.
- Fourth, public esteem for schools would increase. People would stop regarding them as way stations for adolescents and start thinking of them as institutions for educating America's youth.
- Fifth, elementary schools would change because students would find out early they had better learn something or risk flunking out later. Elementary teachers would no longer have to pass their failures on to junior high and high school.
- Sixth, the cost of enforcing compulsory education would be eliminated. Despite enforcement efforts, nearly 15 percent of the school-age children in our largest cities are almost permanently absent from school.

Communities could use these savings to support institutions to deal with young people not in school. If, in the long run, these institutions prove more costly, at least we would not confuse their mission with that of schools. Schools should be for

171

education. At present, they are only tangentially so. They have attempted to serve an all-encompassing social function, trying to be all things to all people. In the process they have failed miserably at what they were originally formed to accomplish.

1. Which of the following statements supports the conclusion that abolishing mandatory attendance laws would prove economical for school districts?

    a. It would eliminate the misconception that schools are day-care centers or indoor street corners.
    b. Public esteem for schools would increase.
    c. The cost of enforcing compulsory education would be eliminated.
    d. Report cards would reflect how well a student is learning.

2. Which of the following statements would the author most likely agree with?

    a. The longer students attend school, the more productive the community will be.
    b. Students should not be forced or entitled to an education.
    c. Truancy officers should be doubled in districts with low attendance rates.
    d. Report cards should reflect the effort of a student, rather than the ability of that student.

3. According to the author, abolishing attendance laws would allow school districts the freedom to _____.

    a. provide counseling to students with poor attendance.
    b. fail or dismiss students who have attendance or discipline issues, which disrupt the education of others.
    c. provide transportation to students unwilling to attend school.
    d. move students from elementary to middle school without proof that learning has occurred.

4. Which of the following is an assumption made by the author?

    a. Private schools can choose to fail or dismiss students.
    b. Nearly 15 percent of the school-age children in our largest cities are almost permanently absent from school.
    c. If we can improve student attendance, we can improve standardized test scores.
    d. Most parents want a high school education for their children.

5. Choose the option that best describes the central idea of the passage.

    a. Standardized test scores would increase if teachers could fail or dismiss students.
    b. Abolishing mandatory attendance laws would create better school environments for the students with a genuine desire to learn.
    c. Report cards should communicate with parents how well a student is learning.
    d. Private schools have an easier time with absenteeism than public schools.

6. Which of the following best summarizes the first paragraph?

    a. American education is in trouble.
    b. Students with little desire to learn are often absent.
    c. Abolishing the mandatory attendance laws would improve the quality of education in schools.
    d. Standardized test scores are the best indicator of student success.

7. Which of the following statements LEAST supports the main idea of the passage?

a. School is a serious place where one goes to learn.
b. Students opposed to learning would not be able to pollute the educational atmosphere for those who want to learn.
c. Grades would show what they are supposed to: how well a student is learning.
d. Public esteem for schools would increase.

8. According to the text, what effect do mandatory attendance laws have on the esteem of schools?

a. These laws prove that schools have the right to force education on all minors.
b. These laws undermine the integrity of schools.
c. These laws allow students to choose their own path of education.
d. These laws provide teachers with freedom to grade and dismiss as they see fit.

9. What can we infer from the text?

a. The author believes that school districts should reexamine their procedures for standardized testing.
b. The author believes that all students deserve an equal amount of attention from the teacher.
c. The author believes that stricter attendance laws would improve classroom dynamics.
d. The author believes that education is a privilege, not a right.

10. Which of the following is a synonym of the word, "recalcitrant," as used in Paragraph 3?

a. Absent
b. Organized
c. Disobedient
d. Responsible

Directions: Use the following passage to answer questions 11-20.

In 1603, Queen Elizabeth I of England died. She had never married and had no heir, so the throne passed to a distant relative: James Stuart, the son of Elizabeth's cousin and one-time rival for the throne, Mary, Queen of Scots. James was crowned King James I of England. At the time, he was also King James VI of Scotland, and the combination of roles would create a spirit of conflict that haunted the two nations for generations to come.

The conflict developed as a result of rising tensions among the people within the nations, as well as between them. Scholars in the 21st century are far too hasty in dismissing the role of religion in political disputes, but religion undoubtedly played a role in the problems that faced England and Scotland. By the time of James Stuart's succession to the English throne, the English people had firmly embraced the teachings of Protestant theology. Similarly, the Scottish Lowlands were decisively Protestant. In the Scottish Highlands, however, the clans retained their Catholic faith. James acknowledged the Church of England and sanctioned the largely Protestant translation of the Bible that still bears his name.

James's son King Charles I proved himself to be less committed to the Protestant Church of England. Charles married the Catholic Princess Henrietta Maria of France, and there were suspicions among the English and the Lowland Scots that Charles was quietly a Catholic. Charles's own political troubles extended beyond religion in

173

this case, and he was beheaded in 1649. Eventually, his son King Charles II would be crowned, and this Charles is believed to have converted secretly to the Catholic Church. Charles II died without a legitimate heir, and his brother James ascended to the throne as King James II.

James was recognized to be a practicing Catholic, and his commitment to Catholicism would prove to be his downfall. James's wife Mary Beatrice lost a number of children during their infancy, and when she became pregnant again in 1687 the public became concerned. If James had a son, that son would undoubtedly be raised a Catholic, and the English people would not stand for this. Mary gave birth to a son, but the story quickly circulated that the royal child had died, and the child named James's heir was a foundling smuggled in. James, his wife, and his infant son were forced to flee; and James's Protestant daughter Mary was crowned the queen.

In spite of a strong resemblance to the king, the young James was generally rejected among the English and the Lowland Scots, who referred to him as "the Pretender." But in the Highlands the Catholic princeling was welcomed. He inspired a group known as Jacobites, to reflect the Latin version of his name. His own son Charles, known affectionately as Bonnie Prince Charlie, would eventually raise an army and attempt to recapture what he believed to be his throne. The movement was soundly defeated at the Battle of Culloden in 1746, and England and Scotland have remained Protestant ever since.

11. According to the author, the tension between England and Scotland stemmed from what issue?

a. Politics
b. Rivalry within the Royal Families
c. Religion
d. Boundary disputes

12. According to the text, who was the successor of Queen Elizabeth I?

a. King Charles I
b. James Stuart
c. King James II
d. Queen Mary

13. Which of the following best summarizes paragraph 4?

a. The English were determined to convince the son of King James to bring Catholicism to England.
b. The son of King James died tragically as an infant, leaving no heir to the throne.
c. James and his wife had only one surviving child, a daughter named Mary.
d. The English feared that the son of King James would be raised Catholic, causing them to fabricate a story of his death and create a rumor of an illegitimate heir to the throne.

14. Which of the following best compares the religious beliefs of the Scottish Highlands and Lowlands?

    a. Scotland was devoutly Protestant in both the Highlands and Lowlands.

    b. The Highlands were devoutly Protestant, while the Lowlands embraced Catholicism.

    c. The Highlands were accepting of Catholicism, while the Lowlands were devoutly Protestant.

    d. Scotland embraced Catholicism in both the Highlands and the Lowlands.

15. Which of the following choices best describes the relationship between King James I of England and King James VI of Scotland?

    a. They were cousins.

    b. They were brothers.

    c. They were the same person.

    d. King James I was the father of King James VI.

16. Which of the following is a synonym for the term "foundling" as used in paragraph 4?

    a. Orphan

    b. Distant relative

    c. Son

    d. Foreigner

17. What can we infer from the text?

    a. Queen Elizabeth I died at a young age.

    b. King Charles I was not a devout Protestant.

    c. King James II was committed to his family.

    d. King James II was crowned King after his brother, King Charles II, died.

18. According to the text, which statement best supports the author's claim that the downfall of King James II was due to his belief in Catholicism?

    a. He was beheaded for forming the group known as the "Jacobites."

    b. The fear of a Catholic king caused the English to create rumors of an illegitimate son, forcing James to flee England.

    c. He was killed in the Battle of Culloden in 1746.

    d. His wife lost a number of infants, causing a strain in their relationship.

19. Which of the following best describes the term "Jacobites"?

    a. A group of Catholics inspired by the young son of King James II.

    b. A group of Protestants inspired by the young son of King James II.

    c. A group of Protestants inspired by the young Bonnie Prince Charlie.

    d. A group of Catholics inspired by the young son of King Charles II.

20. Choose the option that best describes the central idea of the passage.

    a. King James II tried to fool the English with an illegitimate son as heir to the throne.

    b. The troubles between England and Scotland were largely due to a clash in religious beliefs.

    c. Queen Elizabeth I was the head of a troubled royal family.

    d. James's wife, Mary Beatrice, suffered the loss of many infants.

21. Which of the following sentences has the modifier correctly placed?

    a. The ripped boy's jeans were muddy and wet.
    b. The hot mug was placed on the coffee table.
    c. The smashed girl's pumpkin lay at the bottom of the stairs.
    d. She only paid $45.00 for her concert ticket.

22. Which of the following sentences does <u>not</u> correctly place the modifier?

    a. I found a gold ring walking home.
    b. I slowly sipped the water.
    c. She returned the stained shirt to the store.
    d. Watching the fireworks, the child was mesmerized by the colors.

23. Choose the word that uses parallel structure to complete the sentence.

Chase watered the flowers, mowed the lawn, and _____ the pool.

    a. was vacuuming
    b. vacuumed
    c. he vacuumed
    d. vacuums

24. Choose the word that does <u>not</u> establish parallelism with the other answer choices.

    a. hiking
    b. swimming
    c. ran
    d. eating

25. Which of the following sentences does <u>not</u> use parallel sentence structure?

    a. Jose wants to return the item and spoke to a manager.
    b. The wall was spackled, sanded, and painted.
    c. She looked forward to picking, scooping, and carving the pumpkin.
    d. They visited the museum, the theater, and the Statue of Liberty.

26. Choose the option that contains a fragment.

    a. Thanksgiving always falls on a Thursday, which leads into Black Friday. Many people stay up all night.
    b. George practiced his multiplication facts every night for a week. Still, he failed the test.
    c. Jessie dreamed of owning a stable and raising horses. She knew exactly which horse would be her first purchase. The large horse with a beautiful mane.
    d. The castle was built on a hill to maintain privacy and intrigue.

27. Which of the following contains a comma splice?

    a. Many athletes have personal trainers, trainers help them stay fit in the off-season.
    b. The child didn't finish his dinner, so his mother would not allow him to have dessert.
    c. We were able to attend the dinner; however, we were not able to attend the after-party.
    d. Tom enjoys fiction, while Jack prefers autobiographies.

28. Identify the run-on sentence.

a. We loved climbing the mountain and enjoying the beautiful view.
b. Jonathan lived in Utah, but now he lives in Nebraska with his entire extended family.
c. I learned what marine biologists do I think I would like to pursue that career.
d. She is beautiful, but her manners are atrocious.

29. Which of the following contains an error in syntax?

a. Regardless, he purchased the wine.
b. Her foul mouth proved that she lacked manners.
c. She wanted to ensure a reservation at the restaurant.
d. For all intensive purposes, the book was discontinued.

30. "Do pigs fly?" is an example of which type of writing?

a. descriptive
b. rhetorical
c. sequential
d. expository

31. "The professor said on Monday she would return our papers" contains which of the following errors?

a. spelling
b. misplaced modifier
c. capitalization
d. comma splice

32. "The forecast called for rain, so James packed his umbrella" is an example of which type of organizational writing?

a. compare and contrast
b. sequential
c. spatial
d. problem and solution

33. "We adopted a dog. A giant Rhodesian Ridgeback." This contains _____.

a. a fragment
b. a capitalization error
c. an error in word usage
d. a spelling error

34. Determine the meaning of the underlined word.

The hikers immediately fed the emaciated dog.

a. vicious
b. abnormally thin
c. withdrawn
d. missing

35. Identify the synonym for the underlined word.

Stacey <u>abhorred</u> cooking, but loved to eat.

    a. enjoyed
    b. laborious
    c. cuisine
    d. detested

36. Identify the synonym for the underlined word.

Fiona's smirk showed her <u>content</u> with the outcome of the election.

    a. subject matter
    b. disapproval
    c. satisfaction
    d. condemnation

37. Identify the word that best completes the sentence.

The football player blasted _____ the defense and scored his first touchdown.

    a. threw
    b. through
    c. passed
    d. huddled

38. Choose the word that best completes the sentence.

Brody scored more baskets _____ Hank.

    a. then
    b. than
    c. thin
    d. above

Mathematics

1. Which of the following statements is true?

    a. -6 is to the right of -5 on the number line
    b. -7 is to the left of -2 on the number line
    c. 0 is to the left of -1 on the number line
    d. 7 is to the left of -2 on the number line

2. Giselle is selling notebooks at the school store. She earns $45.00 for selling 30 notebooks. How much is Giselle charging for each notebook?

    a. $135.00
    b. $3.00
    c. $1.50
    d. $1.25

3. The candy store charges $1.30 per pound. Artie's bag of candy weighs 2.1 pounds. How much will Artie have to pay for his candy?

    a. $2.73
    b. $3.40
    c. $27.30
    d. $0.80

4. Which of the following is equivalent to $5^3 + 18 \div 3$?

    a. 21
    b. 131
    c. $48\frac{2}{3}$
    d. 37

5. Find the value of $100 \div (9 + 1) \times 2$.

    a. 20
    b. 5
    c. 15
    d. 76

6. A triangle has angles measuring 40°, 100°, and 40°. Its sides measure 15 inches, 19 inches, and 15 inches. Which of the following choices accurately describes the triangle?

    a. It is an acute equilateral triangle
    b. It is an acute scalene triangle
    c. It is an obtuse isosceles triangle
    d. It is an acute isosceles triangle

7. Which of the following choices best describes a three-dimensional figure comprised of only one square base and four triangular sides?

    a. Square prism
    b. Triangular prism
    c. Triangular pyramid
    d. Square pyramid

8. A recipe calls for 2 cups of water for every 6 cups of flour. Josie wants to make a smaller batch using only two cups of flour. How much water should she use?

    a. $\frac{1}{2}$ cup

    b. 2 cups

    c. $\frac{2}{3}$ cup

    d. 12 cups

9. A scaled drawing for a new building has walls measuring 4 inches in height. The key indicates that each inch on the drawing represents 2 feet in real life. Based on the scaled drawing, how tall will the actual walls measure?

    a. 8 feet

    b. 4 feet

    c. 32 feet

    d. 12 feet

10. The ratio of boys to girls in a math class is 3 to 4. If there are 12 boys in the class, how many total students are in the class?

    a. 28 students

    b. 16 students

    c. 7 students

    d. 24 students

11. A Tyrannosaurus Rex is believed to have weighed 18,000 pounds. How can this weight be represented in scientific notation?

    a. 18×10^4 lb

    b. 1.8×10^{-4} lb

    c. 1.8×10^4 lb

    d. 18×10^{-4} lb

12. Andre is traveling at a speed of 65 miles per hour. At this rate, how long will it take Andre to travel 195 miles?

    a. 585 minutes

    b. 3.25 hours

    c. 3 hours

    d. 4.5 hours

13. Hector's car holds 12 gallons of gasoline. He filled his tank for $22.44. Assuming Hector's tank was completely empty when he filled up, how much money did Hector pay per gallon for gasoline?

    a. $1.87

    b. $269.28

    c. $18.70

    d. $2.05

14. Identify the property that has been applied to simplify the expression $4(5 + 8) = 20 + 32$.

    a. The commutative property
    b. The associative property
    c. The distributive property
    d. The multiplication property of zero

15. Jackie and Jessie collect 12 seashells each. They decide to paint and sell their shells to earn some extra spending money. Jackie sells her shells for $1.00 each, while Jessie charges $1.25 per shell. Which of the following expressions can be used to determine the total amount of money the girls will earn, assuming they each sell all of their shells?

    a. $(12 \times \$1.25) \times 2$
    b. $(12 \times \$1.00) + (12 \times \$1.25)$
    c. $(12 \times \$1.00) \times (12 \times \$1.25)$
    d. $(6 \times \$1.00) + (6 \times \$1.25)$

16. Connor and Pete have decided to split their tips equally. Connor earned $48.00 in tips, while Pete earned $62.00. Which of the following expressions can be used to find the amount of money each of them should receive if they are splitting their tips equally?

    a. $\$48.00 + \$62.00 \div 2$
    b. $(\$48.00 + \$62.00) \div 2$
    c. $(\$48.00 + \$62.00) \times 2$
    d. $\$62.00 - \$48.00 \div 2$

17. Solve for y when $\frac{y}{2} - 8 = 0$.

    a. $y = 4$
    b. $y = 8$
    c. $y = 2$
    d. $y = 16$

18. Consider the inequality $6x + 8 \leq 56$. Which of the following choices is a solution for the inequality?

    a. $x \geq 8$
    b. $x = 8$
    c. $x \leq 48$
    d. $x \leq 8$

19. The function $y = 5x + 10$ represents the amount of money Wilson will save after x weeks. Which of the following choices is a solution of the function?

    a. $(2, 10)$
    b. $(8, 50)$
    c. $(7, 22)$
    d. $(40, 6)$

20. Which of the following statements must be true in order for relations to satisfy the definition of a function?

    a. All of the *x*-coordinates are matched with only one *y*-coordinate

    b. An *x*-coordinate is matched with multiple *y*-coordinates

    c. There are at least six coordinates in the relation

    d. All coordinates in the relation are positive numbers

21. Which of the following statements best compares the slopes of the linear equations graphed below?

Graph 1   Graph 2

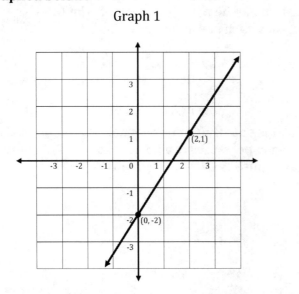 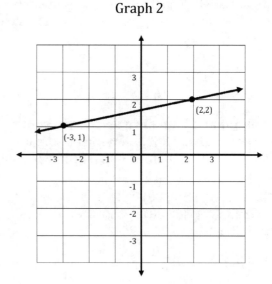

    a. Graph 2 has a greater slope because it has a negative *x*-coordinate.

    b. Graph 1 has a greater slope because $\frac{3}{2}$ is greater than $\frac{1}{5}$.

    c. Graph 1 has a greater slope because it has an *x*-coordinate of zero.

    d. Graph 2 has a greater slope because its line is less steep than that of Graph 1.

22. A teacher asked her students how many hours of television they watched over the weekend. The results are displayed below. How many students watched more than 8 hours of television over the weekend?

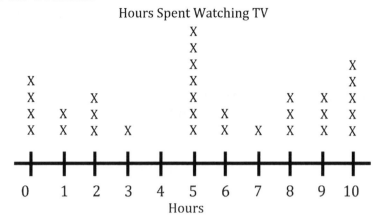

Hours Spent Watching TV

a. 3 students
b. 8 students
c. 11 students
d. 20 students

23. Which of the following choices could display data in a misleading way?

a. Starting the *y*-axis at zero, even when dealing with very large numbers
b. Listing categorical data in alphabetical order along the *x*-axis
c. Choosing very small intervals for the *y*-axis to exaggerate differences in data
d. Including all data collected, even if it is not consistent with the outcome you were hoping for

24. Find the mean of the data set {76, 193, 83, 43, 105}.

a. 500
b. 100
c. 83
d. 150

25. Consider the data set {196, 832, 736, 271, and 573}. Which of the following best describes the range of the data set?

a. 377
b. 636
c. 1,028
d. 573

26. Identify the median for the data set {53, 81, 85, 82, 91, 72}

a. 81.5
b. 81
c. 77
d. 83.5

27. **Joe plans to flip two coins. Which of the following choices demonstrates using the counting principle to determine the probability of both coins landing on tails?**

   a. $\frac{1}{2}$

   b. TT, TH, HT, HH

   c. 2×2

   d. $\frac{1}{2} \times \frac{1}{2}$

28. **Aniyah has two pairs of jeans and three shirts. How many different outfits can she create, assuming each outfit consists of one pair of jeans and a shirt?**

   a. 9 outfits

   b. 5 outfits

   c. 6 outfits

   d. 12 outfits

Information Literacy and Research

1. Of the following, which statement is correct regarding Standard English?

a. The formal Standard English applies to written language.
b. Standard English is universal in English-speaking nations.
c. Speech communities use the Standard English of writing.
d. The Standard English construct does not include dialects.

2. Which of the following is NOT typically categorized as a prewriting process?

a. Planning
b. Reflection
c. Visualization
d. Brainstorming

3. Which of the following correctly represents the sequence of stages or steps in the writing process?

a. Prewriting, drafting, revising, editing, publishing
b. Prewriting, drafting, editing, publishing, revising
c. Prewriting, editing, drafting, revising, publishing
d. Prewriting, drafting, editing, revising, publishing

4. Research has found that which of the following occur for students during revision and rewriting?

a. Students only correct their mechanical errors in revisions.
b. Students often incorporate new ideas when they rewrite.
c. Students retain their original writing goals during revision.
d. Students' planning in prewriting is unaffected in rewriting.

5. Arthur writes a paper. One classmate identifies ideas and words that resonated with her when she read it. Another describes how reading the paper changed his thinking. A third asks Arthur some questions about what he meant by certain statements in the paper. A fourth suggests that a portion of the paper needs more supporting information. This description is most typical of...

a. A portfolio assessment.
b. A holistic scoring.
c. A scoring rubric.
d. A peer review.

6. Which of the following is the best definition of Information Literacy?

a. It is the set of skills required for reading and comprehending different information.
b. It is the cognitive skill set necessary to amass a comprehensive base of knowledge.
c. It is the skill set required for the finding, retrieval, analysis, and use of information.
d. It is the set of skills necessary for effectively communicating information to others.

7. Of the following statements, which adheres to Information Literacy standards?

a. Students accessing information must critically evaluate it and its sources before using it.
b. Students accessing information can ascertain how much of it they need after they find it.
c. Students accessing information efficiently sacrifice broader scope and incidental learning.
d. Students accessing information ethically must eschew using it to attain specific purposes.

8. According to the MLA system for documenting sources in literature, which of the following typically combines signal phrases and parenthetical references?

    a. An MLA list of the works cited
    b. MLA in-text citations in a paper
    c. Adding MLA information notes
    d. All of the above

9. According to MLA guidelines for writing research papers, which of the following is correct regarding citations of web sources if you do not quickly see the author's name?

    a. Assume the author is not named, as this is a common occurrence on the Web.
    b. Do not name an agency or corporation as author if it is the sponsor of the source.
    c. Author names are often on websites, but need additional looking to discover.
    d. It is not permissible to cite the book or article title in lieu of an author's name.

10. When making in-text citations in a research paper, which of the following reflects MLA guidelines for citing Web sources with regard to page numbers?

    a. If a Web source does not include pagination, you are advised to avoid citing that source.
    b. If page numbers appear on a printout from a website, include these numbers in citations.
    c. In-text citations of online sources in research papers should never include page numbers.
    d. If the Web source is a PDF file, it is recommended to cite page numbers in your citations.

11. The MLA guidelines for citing multiple authors of the same source in the in-text citations of a research paper are to use the first author's name and "et al" for the other(s) in the case of...

    a. More than one author.
    b. Two or three authors.
    c. Three or more authors.
    d. Four or more authors.

12. A movie review is one example of what type and purpose of writing?

    a. Narration
    b. Description
    c. Persuasion
    d. Exposition

13. Of the following writing types and purposes, which can often be the hardest to write?

    a. Expository
    b. Persuasive
    c. Descriptive
    d. Narrative

14. When you have a writing assignment, which of the following is true about your audience?

    a. You need not identify the audience because it is the teacher who gave the assignment.
    b. You should consider how your readers are likely to use what you write.
    c. You should know your writing purpose more than a reader's purposes.
    d. You are overthinking to wonder about readers' likely attitude/reaction.

15. Which of the following statements is most accurate about writing the introduction to an essay?

   a. The introduction should use the technique of starting essays with dictionary definitions.
   b. The introduction should leave the most attention-getting material for later in the work.
   c. The introduction should move from the focused and specific to the broad and general.
   d. The introduction should move from the broad and general to the focused and specific.

16. When writing an essay, which part of the introduction should come first?

   a. Your thesis statement for the essay
   b Background on the essay's purpose
   c. Something original to engage reader attention
   d. A "road map" of how you will present the thesis

Essay Questions

1. In peaceful protest of what they believe to be oppression in America, many athletes of the National Football League have decided to kneel rather than standing for our National Anthem. Some viewers see this as a platform for public figures to bring awareness and change, while others view it as a disrespectful action towards our country, our flag, and those who serve and protect. Do athletes have the right to protest during the National Anthem? Does it disrespect our country, flag, and military?

2. The American Academy of Pediatrics recently announced that children as young as 18 months old can benefit from high-value, academic screen time, when supervised by an adult. Others argue that introducing electronics to children at such a young age will limit their ability to interact in the real world as they grow and mature. Do the advantages of educational programs outweigh the disadvantages?

Answer Key and Explanations

Reading and Written Communication

1. C: Although all four options are arguably benefits to eliminating mandatory attendance laws, the term "economical" tells us we're looking for a cost-effective advantage. According to the author, the cost of enforcing compulsory education is money ill-spent and could be better spent on students who *want* to be there.

2. B: According to the author, many problems that arise in schools are a direct result of students who are forced to be there. The author believes that attendance laws should be abolished in order to make education more valuable to students with a desire to learn.

3. B: The author believes that education is failing because teachers and schools spend far too much time disciplining behavior issues and mandating attendance. Teachers could better serve conscientious students if given the opportunity to fail or dismiss those who are disrupting the education of others.

4. D: An assumption is something we believe to be true because it is something we have been taught to believe and do not question. Here, the author is assuming that most parents want a high school education for their children. There is no evidence in the text supporting that claim, but the author believes it to be true based on his own experiences and beliefs.

5. B: Although all four options reflect the author's beliefs, only one of them describes the central idea, or main idea, of the writing. The author is trying to prove that abolishing mandatory attendance laws would create better school environments for the students with a genuine desire to learn. The other answer choices are used as supporting evidence to reinforce that claim.

6. C: A summary is a brief statement used to describe the main idea of writing, or a portion of that writing. The first paragraph of this article mentions all four choices, but the main idea is that abolishing mandatory attendance laws would improve the quality of education in schools. The other answer choices list ways in which the abolition of these laws could improve the climate of education or reasons why this abolition is necessary.

7. C: The author's main idea is that abolishing mandatory attendance laws would allow teachers the ability to dismiss disruptive students, preserving the sanctity of schools as a place for students to receive an esteemed education. Bullet three does not support that specific claim, but instead describes an issue with the grading of such students.

8. B: According to the text, mandatory attendance laws undermine the integrity of schools because teachers have no choice but to provide all students, regardless of behavior or attendance, the same educational opportunities. When there is no recourse for disrupting the learning environment, schools can be perceived as day cares or, as the author described, "indoor street corners."

9. D: An inference is defined as a conclusion reached on the basis of evidence and reasoning. Throughout the passage the author has provided several reasons why students with behavior and/or attendance concerns should not be afforded the opportunity to disrupt the education of others. From these claims we can infer that the author believes education is a privilege to those who want to put in the effort and not a birthright of every juvenile in a community.

189

10. C: Context clues are hints we can use within an author's writing to determine the meaning of an unknown word. The author writes, "Teachers could stop policing recalcitrant students and start educating." We can use context clues to determine that the term "recalcitrant" most similarly describes students who are disobedient, if they require the policing of teachers.

11. C: According to the author, the major clash between England and Scotland stemmed from religious differences. The countries clashed over Catholic and Protestant beliefs, causing tension among the citizens as well as members of the royal families.

12. B: According to the text, Queen Elizabeth I died in 1603. With no heir to her throne, the son of her cousin, James Stuart, was crowned King.

13. D: Paragraph 4 states that James and his wife lost many children during infancy. His son survived infancy, but the English feared that he would be raised Catholic and eventually become king, influencing Catholicism throughout England. To avoid this, they fabricated a story of his death and created a rumor that the king had replaced the young prince with an imposter, forcing James, his wife, and their young son to flee.

14. C: While England and the Scottish Lowlands were Protestant, the Highlands were accepting of Catholicism and even formed a group of Catholic followers known as "Jacobites."

15. C: When Queen Elizabeth I of England died, she had no heir. Therefore, her cousin's son, James, became King of England. He was named King James I of England, while already crowned King James VI of Scotland.

16. A: In paragraph 4, the author writes, "Mary gave birth to a son, but the story quickly circulated that the royal child had died, and the child named James's heir was a foundling smuggled in." We can use context clues to determine that the rumored child was illegitimate, and therefore most likely an orphan with no lawful rights to the throne.

17. C: An inference is a conclusion we make based on evidence and reasoning without the text explicitly giving us the information. The text states that King James II was being accused of having an illegitimate son as heir to the throne. The text also states that, rather than risk the safety of his family, James chose to flee with his wife and son, relinquishing his rightful seat as the King of England. From this, we can infer that King James II was committed to his family.

18. B: King James II was believed to be raising his son as a Catholic. The English were so fearful at the thought of a Catholic king that they created rumors of an illegitimate son, forcing James to flee England and abdicate his throne.

19. A: The term "Jacobites" refers to a group of Catholics inspired by the young son of King James II. The group was named to reflect the Latin version of James' name and gathered to practice Catholicism in the Highlands.

20. B: Although it is true that true that Mary Beatrice suffered the loss of many infants and Queen Elizabeth I was part of a troubled royal family, neither of these statements summarize the central idea of the passage. The author's main assertion is that the troubles between England and Scotland were largely due to a clash in religious beliefs.

21. B: A modifier is a word that can describe or change the meaning of another word or phrase in a sentence. A modifier should be placed next to the word or phrase it is describing. In choice B, the modifier (hot) is placed next to the mug it is describing, making B our correct answer.

22. A: When a modifier is misplaced, it gives an attribute to an unintended word or phrase. The sentence, "I found a gold ring walking home" uses the modifier "walking" to describe the ring. Instead, we should write the sentence as, "Walking home, I found a gold ring."

23. B: Parallel structure uses the same pattern of words when describing related events. Here, the words used to describe Chase's actions are "watered" and "mowed." The only choice that fits this pattern is choice B, "vacuumed," because it is written in past tense and does not have a pronoun preceding it.

24. C: Parallelism uses the same tense of words to create a pattern in writing structure. Here, three of the answer choices end in "–ing," insinuating present tense. Choice C, "ran" is written in past tense and therefore does not establish parallelism with the other choices.

25. A: Parallelism requires that verbs be written in the same form or tense. Choice A does not meet this criterion because Jose wants to return the item (which shows a desire for the future), yet states that he already spoke to a manager (insinuating past tense).

26. C: A complete sentence must contain a subject and a verb. A fragment may look like a sentence, but it is missing one of these components. Choice C contains the fragment, "The large horse with a beautiful mane," which is missing the verb.

27. A: A comma splice occurs when only a comma connects two independent clauses. Choice C can eliminate the comma splice by separating the thoughts into two complete sentences, by using a semicolon to separate the thoughts, or by rewriting the sentence as "Many athletes have personal trainers, because trainers help them stay fit in the off-season."

28. C: A run-on sentence contains two complete thoughts without appropriate punctuation separating them. Choice C contains two complete thoughts without any separation. We can rewrite it as, "I learned what marine biologists do, and I think I would like to pursue that career."

29. D: A syntax error is an error in the usage of language. Here, the phrase "intensive purposes" is mistaken for "intents and purposes."

30. B: The question, "Do pigs fly?" has an obvious answer, which does not require a response. It is often used to make a point that the answer to some other question is undoubtedly "no." This type of language is known as rhetorical.

31. B: The error is a misplaced modifier. Did the professor make this statement *on* Monday, or will the papers be *returned* on Monday? The sentence should be rewritten as, "On Monday, the professor said she would return our papers." Or, "The professor said she would return our papers on Monday."

32. D: The sentence explains that James packed an umbrella to solve the problem of getting wet in the rain. This type of organizational structure is known as problem and solution.

33. A: A sentence must contain a subject and a predicate (or verb). "A giant Rhodesian Ridgeback" is a fragment because it is missing a verb.

34. B: We can use context clues to determine that the hikers quickly fed the dog to satisfy his or her hunger. We can then conclude that "emaciated" must refer to the dog's physical condition, known by his or her thin appearance.

35. D: The conjunction, "but" is used to show a contrast in something that has already been stated. Here, we know that Stacey's feelings about eating differ from her feelings about cooking. If she enjoys eating, then she must detest cooking.

36. C: Fiona's smirk insinuates that she was pleased with the election results. This leads us to determine that the word "content," as used in this sentence, most closely illustrates Fiona's satisfaction.

37. B: Our answer has to be "through" as it is the only choice that provides the correct spelling and meaning for running past the defense.

38. B: "Than" is used to show a comparison, while "then" is used to show sequence or a moment in time and "thin" refers to a slim size. Here, we're comparing the number of baskets each player made, so "than" is the correct choice.

Mathematics

1. B: The number line orders numbers from least to greatest. When comparing any two numbers, the smaller value will always be to the left of the greater value. Because -7 is *less than* -2, -7 will always be to the *left* of -2 on the number line. All of the other options have greater values placed to the left of smaller values. This can never be true on any number line.

2. C: Each notebook costs $1.50. To find the cost of each notebook, we must divide the total amount of money earned, $45.00, by the number of notebooks sold, 30. When we divide 45 by 30, we know that 30 can "fit" into 45 one time, with a remainder of 15. We can turn our remainder into a fraction by making our remainder the numerator and our divisor the denominator, creating the fraction $\frac{15}{30}$, or $\frac{1}{2}$. When working with money, 1 whole and $\frac{1}{2}$ represents one and a half dollars, or $1.50. Giselle charged $1.50 for each notebook.

3. A: Artie will have to pay $2.73 for his candy. To find the answer, we must multiply the amount of candy Artie is purchasing, 2.1 pounds, by the price per pound, $1.30. When multiplying decimals, we can use the traditional algorithm, as if the decimal points weren't there. When we multiply 130 by 21, we get 2,730. To determine where to place the decimal point, we count the number of digits after each decimal point in each factor. Here, we have one digit after the decimal point in 2.1 and two digits after the decimal point in $1.30. That makes for a total of three digits after the decimal points in the factors. Because there are three digits to the right of the decimal points in the factors, we must have three digits after the decimal point in the product, turning 2,730 into 2.730, or $2.73.

4. B: Following the order of operations, we must start by finding the value of 5^3, which is equivalent to $5 \times 5 \times 5$, or 125. This simplifies our expression to $125 + 18 \div 3$. Next, we must solve the division of 18 and 3, which is 6, leaving us with a final expression of $125 + 6$. The sum of 125 and 6 is 131, making our solution 131.

5. A: Parentheses must be completed first. Here, $9 + 1 = 10$, so we can rewrite our expression as $100 \div 10 \times 2$. When dealing with multiplication and division, we must solve the operations in the order in which they appear, from left to right. Because division appears *before* multiplication, we must divide 100 by 10 before we multiply by 2. The quotient of 100 and 10 is 10, simplifying our expression to 10×2, or 20. Our final answer is 20.

6. C: Any triangle with an angle measuring over 90° is considered an obtuse triangle. Because this triangle has an angle measuring 100°, we must classify it as obtuse. To classify a triangle by its

sides, we must determine how many of the sides are equivalent. Here, we have two sides measuring 15 inches. A triangle with two equivalent sides is described as an isosceles triangle. This triangle must be described as an obtuse isosceles triangle.

7. D: The three-dimensional shape being described must be a pyramid because it only has one base and all triangular sides. We can envision the sides meeting at the top, forming the point of the pyramid. Furthermore, a pyramid is named for the shape of its base. Here, the pyramid has a square base so we must classify it as a square pyramid.

8. C: To start, we can write our ratio in fractional form as $\frac{2}{6}$. We know Josie wants to lessen the flour to only 2 cups, making our proportion $\frac{2}{6} = \frac{x}{2}$. To find the value of x, we can cross multiply the two diagonal values we know (2 and 2), and divide their product by the remaining value (6). The product of 2 and 2 is 4, and 4 divided by 6 is simply $\frac{4}{6}$, or $\frac{2}{3}$. This means Josie should use $\frac{2}{3}$ cup of water for every 2 cups of flour.

9. A: The picture is scaled so that each inch on the drawing represents two feet in real life. We can multiply 4 inches by 2 to find the actual height of the wall. Because the product of 4 and 2 is 8, we know the real wall must measure 8 feet.

10. A: We know the ratio of boys to girls is 3 to 4, which means there are 3 boys for every 7 students (because $3 + 4 = 7$). We can write the ratio of boys to total students as $\frac{3}{7}$. We also know that there are 12 boys in the class, so we can create the proportion $\frac{3}{7} = \frac{12}{x}$. To solve for x, we must determine how many times greater 12 is than 3. Because 12 is four times greater than 3, we need to multiply 7 by 4 to complete our proportion. The product of 7 and 4 is 28, so we know there are 28 total students in the class.

11. C: Scientific notation is a strategy for writing very large or very small numbers. To convert a number into scientific notation, we must first move the decimal point either left or right until we have a value that is between 1 and 10. For the number 18,000, we must move the decimal point four place values to the left, in order to create the value 1.8. Because we moved our decimal point four places to the left, our exponent will be positive 4. (Side note: If we had moved our decimal point 4 places to the right we would have expressed our exponent as -4.) Finally, we are able to write our value in scientific notation as 1.8×10^4.

12. C: We can express Andre's speed as the rate 65 miles to 1 hour, or $\frac{65}{1}$. Next, we can set up a proportion to determine how long it will take Andre to travel 195 miles. Our proportion should be $\frac{65}{1} = \frac{195}{x}$. To solve for x we must determine how much greater 195 is than 65. We can do this using division. The quotient of 195 and 65 is 3, which tells us that 195 is three times greater than 65. Now, we must multiply our denominator, 1, by 3 as well to keep our proportion balanced. The product of 1 and 3 is 3, making $x = 3$. It will take Andre 3 hours to travel 195 miles.

13. A: To find Hector's price per gallon we must divide the total amount of money Hector paid, $22.44, by the number of gallons he received, 12. We start by recognizing that our divisor, 12, is a whole number. That allows us to bring our decimal point straight up into our quotient and then divide following the traditional algorithm for long division. The quotient of $22.44 and 12 is $1.87, so Hector paid $1.87 per gallon for gasoline.

14. C: The distributive property is used to "distribute" a value outside of the parentheses to each of the numbers *inside* the parentheses. Here, we can simplify $4(5 + 8)$ by first multiplying 4 times 5, which gives us a product of 20. Next, we must multiply 4 by 8, which equals 32. The distributive property allows us to rewrite the expression as the sum of our products, 20 and 32, or $20 + 32$.

15. B: Jackie and Jessie are both selling 12 seashells, but for different prices, so we need to keep their calculations separate until we have the total amount of money each girl has earned. Jackie is selling her shells for $1.00 each, while Jessie is selling hers for $1.25 each. We can express the amount of money each girl earns as $12 \times \$1.00$ and $12 \times \$1.25$. Once we have the total amount of money each girl sells, we can add those totals together to find the total amount of money earned. We can calculate the total amount of money the girls earned using the following expression: $(12 \times \$1.00) + (12 \times \$1.25)$.

16. B: If Connor and Pete want to split their tips equally, we must first combine their tips to find the amount of money they earned together. Because Connor earned $48.00 and Pete earned $62.00, we can add $48.00 + $62.00. Next, we must divide the total by 2 to determine how much money each of them should receive. It is important that we have our addition problem in parentheses so that the total amount of money earned is calculated before the total is divided by two. The expression $(\$48.00 + \$62.00) \div 2$ can be used to find the amount of money each person should receive.

17. D: To solve for y, we must first complete the inverse of any addition or subtraction. Here, we need to add 8 to both sides of the equation. This simplifies our equation to $\frac{y}{2} = 8$. Next, we need to complete the inverse of division, which is multiplication. When we multiply both sides of the equation by 2, we find that $y = 16$. To check our answer, we can insert 16 into our original equation. Because $\frac{16}{2} - 8 = 0$, we know we have the correct value for y.

18. D: To find solutions for any inequality, we must isolate the variable by applying the inverse operations of those included in the problem. To start, we apply the inverse operation for any addition or subtraction. In this case, we need to subtract 8 from both sides of the inequality, simplifying our inequality to $6x \leq 48$. Next, we need to apply the inverse operation for any multiplication or division. Here, we'll have to divide both sides of the inequality by 6, which leaves us with $x \leq 8$. This tells us that any number less than or equal to 8 can be written in place of x. We can check our answer by rewriting our inequality with a number that fits those parameters to check that our inequality remains true. For example, because 5 is less than 8, we can write $6(5) + 8 \leq 56$. This simplifies to $38 \leq 56$. Because 38 *is* less than 56, we know we've identified the correct solution set for the inequality.

19. B: In any function, the x represents the independent variable, while the y represents the dependent variable. Here, our independent variable is the number of weeks that Wilson has been saving money. The amount of money Wilson has is the dependent variable because his total amount of money *depends* on the number of weeks he has been saving. We can think of the function $y = 5x + 10$ as "total money = 5 × (the number of weeks) + 10." When we look at our answer choices, the first value must always be substituted for x, while the second value is substituted for y. Through process of elimination, we can determine that the solution (8, 50) is the only choice that creates a true number sentence because $5 \times 8 + 10$ does, in fact, equal 50.

20. A: A relation is a set of input and output values, typically written as coordinates. In order for a relation to satisfy a function, each x-coordinate in the set must have only one corresponding y value. The number of coordinates in the relation is irrelevant, as are the inclusion of positive and negative values.

21. B: The slope of a line is *greater* than the slope of any other line when it rises more quickly, or is *steeper* in appearance. We can prove that a line is steeper by calculating and comparing the slopes of each line. To calculate slope, we must choose two points on the line and create the fraction $\frac{rise}{run}$. First, we determine the "rise" by finding the distance between the y-coordinates. Next, we determine the "run" by finding the distance between the x-coordinates. For graph A, the y-coordinates are 3 units apart, while the x-coordinates are 2 units apart. That makes the slope of Graph A $\frac{3}{2}$. Graph B has a slope of $\frac{1}{5}$ because the y-coordinates are 1 unit apart, while the x-coordinates 5 units apart. We can now determine that Graph A has a greater slope because $\frac{3}{2}$ is greater than $\frac{1}{5}$.

22. B: On a dot plot, each dot (or "x"), represents one response. Here, we're trying to determine how many students watched more than 8 hours of television over the weekend. "More than 8" tells us to only include students who responded with 9 or 10 hours because 9 and 10 are the only numbers on the graph that are greater than 8. We can't include the students who responded exactly 8 hours because 8 is not greater than 8 (8 is equal to 8). We can see that 3 students reported watching 9 hours of television, while 5 say they watched 10 hours of television. The sum of 3 and 5 is 8, which means 8 students watched more than 8 hours of television this weekend.

23. C: When displaying data collected in a survey, we must always choose intervals appropriate for the data collected. This includes starting our y-axis at zero, and choosing intervals that are appropriate for the data being collected. For example, imagine we are comparing the purchase prices of homes in an area. If the homes sold for $280,000, $282,000, and $284,000, most people would consider the homes to have sold for very similar prices, given that $2,000 increments are only marginally different when describing the cost of a house. If these prices were graphed with y-axis intervals of $10.00, the bar representing the $284,000 house would be much higher than the bar representing the house that sold for $282,000, even though the difference in price is only $2,000. That graph would mislead people into thinking the houses sold for prices that were considerably different from each other, which was not the case.

24. B: The mean of a data set is considered a measure of center. To calculate the mean (sometimes known as the "average"), we must first find the sum of all numbers included in the data set. Here, the sum of 76, 193, 83, 43, and 105 is 500. Next, we need to divide the sum of our data set by the number of values included in the set. This data set contains five values, so we'll divide our sum, 500, by 5. The quotient of 500 and 5 is 100, making our mean 100.

25. B: To calculate the range of any data set, we must find the difference between the largest value (known as the maximum) and the smallest value (known as the minimum). In this data set, our maximum is 832, while our minimum is 196. The difference of 832 and 196 is 636, so the range of the data set is also 636.

26. A: The median is the middle number of a data set when the set is listed from least to greatest. To find the median, we must first rewrite our set from least to greatest as: 53, 72, 81, 82, 85, 91. Because there are six data values, we have two numbers, 81 and 82, that can be described as the "middle numbers." To find the median of the set, we must find the mean of the two middle numbers. The mean of 81 and 82 is 81.5, so the median of our entire data set is also 81.5.

27. B: The counting principle is the strategy in which we list out all of the possible combinations that *could* occur in order to determine the probability of a specific event occurring. Here, Joe is flipping two coins and trying to find the probability of both coins landing on tails. When we write

out all of the possible flip combinations we get: TT, TH, HT, HH. Using this strategy, we would then circle the outcomes that meet our designated outcome (both coins landing on tails) and determine that the probability is 1 out of 4, or $\frac{1}{4}$. Although choice D would lead us to this answer, it is not an example of the counting principle being applied.

28. C: To find the number of options Aniyah can create, we can start by making an ordered list of the different options. To start, we can assign each piece of clothing an abbreviation, such as J1 for the first pair of jeans or S1 for shirt number 1. When we list all of the different options in an organized way, we find the following combinations: J1/S1, J1/S2, J1/S3, J2/S1, J2/S2, J2/S3. We can count the numbers of combinations created to conclude that Aniyah is able to create six different outfits from two pairs of jeans and three shirts. Another way to solve this problem is to simply multiply the number of options within each category. There are two options for jeans and three options for shirts. The product of 3 and 2 is 6, again confirming that Aniyah has six possible outfit combinations.

Information Literacy and Research

1. A: The formal version of Standard English is reflected in dictionaries and grammar books and applied in written language. In speech, Standard English is NOT universal (B): it differs in pronunciation between the regions of North America and between native English speakers in England, Ireland, Australia, India, and other English-speaking areas. Speech communities use a more flexible variety of *informal* Standard English rather than the Standard English of writing (C). The construct of Standard English actually includes a range of dialects (D) because formal Standard English is used in writing and not speech, which by nature dictates a less formal, more flexible version.

2. A: After prewriting (planning, visualizing, brainstorming), the correct sequence of steps in the writing process are drafting, in which the writer takes the material generated during prewriting work and makes it into sentences and paragraphs; revising, where the writer explores to improve the quality of the writing; editing, in which the writer examines his or her writing for factual and mechanical (grammar, spelling, punctuation) errors and correcting them; and publishing, when the writer finally shares what he or she has written with others who will read it and give feedback.

3. B: Researchers have found that the writing processes both form a hierarchy and are observably recursive in nature. Moreover, they find that when students continually revise their writing, they are able to consider new ideas and to incorporate these ideas into their work. Thus they do not merely correct mechanical errors when revising (A), they also add to the content and quality of their writing. Furthermore, research shows that writers, including students, not only revise their actual writing, during rewrites, they also reconsider their original writing goals rather than always retaining them (C), and they revisit their prewriting plans rather than leaving these unaffected (D).

4. D: This description is most typical of the process of peer review. Classmates read a peer's paper and then identify values in it, describe it, ask questions about it, and suggest points for revision. These are types of helpful feedback identified by experts on writing and collaborative writing. The other choices, however, are not typically collaborative. For a portfolio assessment (A), the teacher collects finished work products from a student over time, eventually assembling a portfolio of work. This affords a more authentic assessment using richer, more multidimensional, and more visual and tactile products for assessment instead of using only standardized test scores for assessment. Holistic scoring (B) is a method of scoring a piece of writing for overall quality (evaluating general elements such as focus, organization, support, and conventions) rather than being overly concerned

with any individual aspect of writing. A scoring rubric (C) is a guide that gives examples of the levels of typical characteristics in a piece of writing that correspond to each available score (for example, scores from 1-5).

5. C: According to the Association of College and Research Libraries, Information Literacy is the set of skills that an individual must have for finding, retrieving, analyzing, and using information. It is required not just for reading and understanding information (A). Information Literacy does not mean learning and retaining a lot of information (B), or only sharing it with others (D), but rather knowing how to find information one does not already have and how to evaluate that information critically for its quality and apply it judiciously to meet one's purposes.

6. A: It is a standard of Information Literacy (IL) that students must use their own critical thinking skills to evaluate the quality of the information and its sources before they use it. Another standard is that the student should ascertain how much information s/he needs for his/her purposes first, deciding this after uncovering excessive information is inefficient (B). An additional IL standard is to access necessary information in an efficient and effective way. However, none of these standards include the idea that students will lose incidental learning or broadness of scope by doing so (C). IL standards include the principle that students *should* use the information they find in ways that are effective for attaining their specific purposes (D).

7. B: The MLA (Modern Language Association) system for documenting literary sources defines in-line citations in a paper as combining signal phrases, which usually include the author's name and introduce information from a source via a fact, summary, paraphrase, or quotation; parenthetical references following the material cited, frequently at the end of the sentence; and, except for web sources that are unpaginated, page number(s). MLA defines a list of works cited (A) as an alphabetized list found at the end of a research paper that gives the information sources referenced in the paper, including each source's publication information, quotations, summaries, and paraphrases. Guidelines for preparing the list of works cited are provided in the *MLA Handbook*. MLA information notes (C) are an optional addition to the MLA parenthetical documentation system. These notes can be used to add important material without interrupting the paper's flow, and/or to supply comments about sources or make references to multiple sources. They may be endnotes or footnotes. Because only one of the answers is correct, Option D is not possible.

8. C: On the Internet, the name of an author is usually provided but may not be visible at first glance. Web sources frequently include the author's name on another page of the same site, such as the website's home page, or in a tiny font at the very end of the web page, rather than in a more conspicuous location. In such cases, students doing online research may have to search more thoroughly than usual to find the author's name. Therefore, they should not immediately assume the author is not named (A). Also, many Web sources are sponsored by government agencies or private corporations and do not give individual author names. In these cases, the research paper *should* cite the agency or corporation name as author (B). Finally, it is much more common for online sources to omit an author's name than it is in print sources. In these cases, it is both permitted and advised by the MLA to cite the article or book title instead (D).

9. D: When online sources you are citing in your research paper are in PDFs and other file formats that have stable pagination, the MLA advises including the page number in the research paper's in-text citation because these numbers are valid and do not change. If a Web source has no pagination, as often happens, the MLA does NOT advise avoiding the citation (A), it advises simply making the citation without a page number because there is not one available. Unlike in PDFs (above), when citing a source from a printout, the MLA advises NOT including page numbers even if you see them

because the same page numbers are not always found in all printouts (B). It is not true that in-text citations should never include page numbers (C).

10. D: The MLA guidelines for citing multiple authors of the same work in in-text citations (for both print and online sources) dictate using the first author's name plus "et al" for the other authors when there are four or more authors. If there are two (options A and B) or three (options B and C) authors, the guidelines say to name each author, either in a signal phrase [for example, "Smith and Jones note that... (45)" or "Smith, Jones, and Gray have noted... (45)"] or in a parenthetical reference ["(Smith, Jones, and Gray 45)."].

11. C: Persuasive writing has the purpose of expressing the writer's opinion and/or of convincing the reader of something. A movie review is one example of this writing purpose and type. Other examples include advertisements, editorials, book and music reviews, and literary essays. Narration (A) is a type of writing for telling stories. Description (B) is a type of writing for creating a picture using words that evoke imagery for the reader. Exposition (D) is a type of writing for informing and/or explaining.

12. B: Persuasive writing tries to convince readers to agree with the author's opinion or position regarding a topic. To convince others, writers must have sufficient knowledge about the topic, logical thinking skills, strong beliefs about the topic, and enough technical skill for making logical points, supporting one's opinions, and swaying the reader's emotions. Expository (A) writing aims to give information and/or explanations. It requires sufficient knowledge, practicality, and the technical skill for writing clarity, but it is not as hard as persuasion because it seeks not to convince the reader of anything, only to inform or explain. Descriptive (C) writing seeks to paint verbal pictures that make the described things real to readers through sensory details. This requires imagination and strong creative writing skills, but is not as difficult as persuading the reader to agree with the author's viewpoint. Narrative (D) writing tells a story and can be the easiest, as storytelling and enjoying stories are natural for most people.

13. A: *The Adventures of Huckleberry Finn* by Mark Twain is a fictional novel. *The Diary of a Young Girl* by Anne Frank is a non-fictional journal. "The Fall of the House of Usher" by Edgar Allan Poe is a fictional short story in the horror genre. Novels, personal narratives like diaries/journals, and short stories, as well as biographies and anecdotes are all types of narrative. Narration tells a story, often (but not always) advances chronologically, and has a beginning, middle, and end. Descriptive writing (B) paints a word picture using sensory imagery to make an event, scene, thing, or person more real to the imagination of the reader. Other than character sketches, picture captions, and some kinds of advertising, most writing is not completely descriptive: narrative works typically include descriptive parts. Exposition (C) is found in news stories, encyclopedias, research papers, informational essays, and instruction manuals rather than fiction or journals. Persuasion (D) is more characteristic of editorials, reviews, ads, and literary essays than novels, short stories or diaries.

14. B: For any writing assignment, you should first target an audience, perform an audience analysis, and develop an audience profile to determine what you should include in and omit from your writing. Even though the assigning teacher may be the only one to read your writing, you should not assume s/he is your main audience (A) because the teacher may expect you to write for other readers. In addition to first knowing your purpose for writing before beginning, you should also consider what purpose your writing will meet for your readers (C) and how they are likely to use it. Considering your audience's attitude toward what you will write and their likely reactions are also important to shaping your writing and is NOT overthinking (D).

15. D: It is best to begin an essay or paper with a broader, more general introduction to the topic, and move to a more focused and specific point regarding the topic—not vice versa (C)—by the end of the introduction. This point is your thesis statement. Writing experts advise *against* the technique of beginning an essay with a dictionary definition (A) because it has been so overused that it has become ineffective and uninteresting. To engage the reader's interest in your topic, it is best to begin with some very attention-getting material rather than leaving it for later (B).

16. C: The first part of the introduction to an essay or paper should be some original, fresh material that will engage the attention of readers enough so they are interested in continuing to read. Following this should be the transitional portion of the introduction, which gives some pertinent background information about the piece's particular purpose (B). This informs the reader of your reason for focusing on your paper or essay's specific topic. The transitional portion moves the piece to the third part of the introduction: the thesis statement (A), which is a clear expression of the main point you are trying to make in your essay or paper. An optional part of the introduction is an explanation of how you will defend your thesis, giving readers a general idea of how your essay or paper's various points will be organized. This is sometimes described as a "road map" (D).

Essay Sample Response #1

Many athletes of the National Football League have decided to kneel rather than standing for our national anthem. Most of these athletes are kneeling during the anthem in an effort to peacefully protest the unfair treatment and oppression of certain groups within our borders. While I agree with the need for change in America, I believe that kneeling during the national anthem is a disrespectful action toward our country, our flag, and those who serve and protect.

Historically, the national anthem is played as a sign of respect and gratitude for our Armed Forces. It is a way for America to stand at attention and show their appreciation for the men and women who have fought and continue to fight for our country. The anthem also shows the greatest respect toward those who have lost their lives protecting our freedoms. Kneeling during this time minimizes the sacrifices that these brave soldiers have made and continue to make for the citizens of the United States of America.

The athletes protesting the anthem have a right to show their discontent with oppression in America; however, they should do so using a different platform and in a way that does not disrespect those who have selflessly fought to protect our freedoms. Perhaps these athletes can volunteer their time in educating people on the unfair treatment of certain subgroups, or donate money to fund programs that are already making great strides towards equality in America. There are many avenues athletes can take in an effort to shine a light on these issues, but it seems that kneeling is their only action.

In conclusion, I support the athletes' right to bring awareness to causes that they feel strongly about and urge them to use their fame to improve cohesiveness and unite the citizens of our great country. However, during the national anthem is not the time or place to make a political statement. Kneeling does not solve the problem; it only adds more of a divide in a country that is already fractured.

Essay Sample Response #2

The American Academy of Pediatrics recently announced that children as young as 18 months old can benefit from high-value, academic screen time, when supervised by an adult. Though screen time may prove advantageous for curious minds, it also has the power to negatively affect the social development of very young children. In an ever-evolving world, parents often find themselves caught between wanting their children to succeed in a technology-rich environment without losing the ability to interact face-to-face. When used responsibly, the advantages of screen time definitely outweigh the disadvantages.

The biggest factor of the screen time debate lies in what people consider to be "screen time." Many critics depict screen time as non-educational videos or mindless games. These critics suggest the image of a child placed on a chair and given a tablet, for the sole purpose of keeping that child entertained and/or quiet for long periods of time. If this were the case, then screen time would absolutely be disadvantageous for developing minds. This depiction, however, is certainly not the type of activity that The American Academy of Pediatrics is endorsing.

For many parents, screen time consists of educational programs, most of which are interactive and involve young learners in a host of activities. In addition to videos, there are countless applications that are geared towards young learners that actually teach and practice concepts such as shape recognition, counting, phonics, and even reading. When used with parental supervision, these videos and applications can aid parents in creating educational environments at home, even if the parent has no experience "teaching" these skills.

Each year, the world depends on technology more and more. Young children should absolutely be exposed to this technology at a young age so that they are comfortable using the devices that they will eventually rely on for everyday tasks. In addition, educational screen time can provide parents and caretakers with endless opportunities to teach and engage in ways that might not be possible without the assistance of technology. When used appropriately, the advantages of electronic devices most certainly outweigh the disadvantages.

How to Overcome Test Anxiety

Just the thought of taking a test is enough to make most people a little nervous. A test is an important event that can have a long-term impact on your future, so it's important to take it seriously and it's natural to feel anxious about performing well. But just because anxiety is normal, that doesn't mean that it's helpful in test taking, or that you should simply accept it as part of your life. Anxiety can have a variety of effects. These effects can be mild, like making you feel slightly nervous, or severe, like blocking your ability to focus or remember even a simple detail.

If you experience test anxiety—whether severe or mild—it's important to know how to beat it. To discover this, first you need to understand what causes test anxiety.

Causes of Test Anxiety

While we often think of anxiety as an uncontrollable emotional state, it can actually be caused by simple, practical things. One of the most common causes of test anxiety is that a person does not feel adequately prepared for their test. This feeling can be the result of many different issues such as poor study habits or lack of organization, but the most common culprit is time management. Starting to study too late, failing to organize your study time to cover all of the material, or being distracted while you study will mean that you're not well prepared for the test. This may lead to cramming the night before, which will cause you to be physically and mentally exhausted for the test. Poor time management also contributes to feelings of stress, fear, and hopelessness as you realize you are not well prepared but don't know what to do about it.

Other times, test anxiety is not related to your preparation for the test but comes from unresolved fear. This may be a past failure on a test, or poor performance on tests in general. It may come from comparing yourself to others who seem to be performing better or from the stress of living up to expectations. Anxiety may be driven by fears of the future—how failure on this test would affect your educational and career goals. These fears are often completely irrational, but they can still negatively impact your test performance.

> **Review Video: <u>3 Reasons You Have Test Anxiety</u>**
> Visit mometrix.com/academy and enter code: 428468

Elements of Test Anxiety

As mentioned earlier, test anxiety is considered to be an emotional state, but it has physical and mental components as well. Sometimes you may not even realize that you are suffering from test anxiety until you notice the physical symptoms. These can include trembling hands, rapid heartbeat, sweating, nausea, and tense muscles. Extreme anxiety may lead to fainting or vomiting. Obviously, any of these symptoms can have a negative impact on testing. It is important to recognize them as soon as they begin to occur so that you can address the problem before it damages your performance.

> **Review Video: 3 Ways to Tell You Have Test Anxiety**
> Visit mometrix.com/academy and enter code: 927847

The mental components of test anxiety include trouble focusing and inability to remember learned information. During a test, your mind is on high alert, which can help you recall information and stay focused for an extended period of time. However, anxiety interferes with your mind's natural processes, causing you to blank out, even on the questions you know well. The strain of testing during anxiety makes it difficult to stay focused, especially on a test that may take several hours. Extreme anxiety can take a huge mental toll, making it difficult not only to recall test information but even to understand the test questions or pull your thoughts together.

> **Review Video: How Test Anxiety Affects Memory**
> Visit mometrix.com/academy and enter code: 609003

Effects of Test Anxiety

Test anxiety is like a disease—if left untreated, it will get progressively worse. Anxiety leads to poor performance, and this reinforces the feelings of fear and failure, which in turn lead to poor performances on subsequent tests. It can grow from a mild nervousness to a crippling condition. If allowed to progress, test anxiety can have a big impact on your schooling, and consequently on your future.

Test anxiety can spread to other parts of your life. Anxiety on tests can become anxiety in any stressful situation, and blanking on a test can turn into panicking in a job situation. But fortunately, you don't have to let anxiety rule your testing and determine your grades. There are a number of relatively simple steps you can take to move past anxiety and function normally on a test and in the rest of life.

> **Review Video: How Test Anxiety Impacts Your Grades**
> Visit mometrix.com/academy and enter code: 939819

Physical Steps for Beating Test Anxiety

While test anxiety is a serious problem, the good news is that it can be overcome. It doesn't have to control your ability to think and remember information. While it may take time, you can begin taking steps today to beat anxiety.

Just as your first hint that you may be struggling with anxiety comes from the physical symptoms, the first step to treating it is also physical. Rest is crucial for having a clear, strong mind. If you are tired, it is much easier to give in to anxiety. But if you establish good sleep habits, your body and mind will be ready to perform optimally, without the strain of exhaustion. Additionally, sleeping well helps you to retain information better, so you're more likely to recall the answers when you see the test questions.

Getting good sleep means more than going to bed on time. It's important to allow your brain time to relax. Take study breaks from time to time so it doesn't get overworked, and don't study right before bed. Take time to rest your mind before trying to rest your body, or you may find it difficult to fall asleep.

Review Video: <u>The Importance of Sleep for Your Brain</u>
Visit mometrix.com/academy and enter code: 319338

Along with sleep, other aspects of physical health are important in preparing for a test. Good nutrition is vital for good brain function. Sugary foods and drinks may give a burst of energy but this burst is followed by a crash, both physically and emotionally. Instead, fuel your body with protein and vitamin-rich foods.

Also, drink plenty of water. Dehydration can lead to headaches and exhaustion, especially if your brain is already under stress from the rigors of the test. Particularly if your test is a long one, drink water during the breaks. And if possible, take an energy-boosting snack to eat between sections.

Review Video: <u>How Diet Can Affect your Mood</u>
Visit mometrix.com/academy and enter code: 624317

Along with sleep and diet, a third important part of physical health is exercise. Maintaining a steady workout schedule is helpful, but even taking 5-minute study breaks to walk can help get your blood pumping faster and clear your head. Exercise also releases endorphins, which contribute to a positive feeling and can help combat test anxiety.

When you nurture your physical health, you are also contributing to your mental health. If your body is healthy, your mind is much more likely to be healthy as well. So take time to rest, nourish your body with healthy food and water, and get moving as much as possible. Taking these physical steps will make you stronger and more able to take the mental steps necessary to overcome test anxiety.

Review Video: <u>How to Stay Healthy and Prevent Test Anxiety</u>
Visit mometrix.com/academy and enter code: 877894

Mental Steps for Beating Test Anxiety

Working on the mental side of test anxiety can be more challenging, but as with the physical side, there are clear steps you can take to overcome it. As mentioned earlier, test anxiety often stems from lack of preparation, so the obvious solution is to prepare for the test. Effective studying may be the most important weapon you have for beating test anxiety, but you can and should employ several other mental tools to combat fear.

First, boost your confidence by reminding yourself of past success—tests or projects that you aced. If you're putting as much effort into preparing for this test as you did for those, there's no reason you should expect to fail here. Work hard to prepare; then trust your preparation.

Second, surround yourself with encouraging people. It can be helpful to find a study group, but be sure that the people you're around will encourage a positive attitude. If you spend time with others who are anxious or cynical, this will only contribute to your own anxiety. Look for others who are motivated to study hard from a desire to succeed, not from a fear of failure.

Third, reward yourself. A test is physically and mentally tiring, even without anxiety, and it can be helpful to have something to look forward to. Plan an activity following the test, regardless of the outcome, such as going to a movie or getting ice cream.

When you are taking the test, if you find yourself beginning to feel anxious, remind yourself that you know the material. Visualize successfully completing the test. Then take a few deep, relaxing breaths and return to it. Work through the questions carefully but with confidence, knowing that you are capable of succeeding.

Developing a healthy mental approach to test taking will also aid in other areas of life. Test anxiety affects more than just the actual test—it can be damaging to your mental health and even contribute to depression. It's important to beat test anxiety before it becomes a problem for more than testing.

Review Video: Test Anxiety and Depression
Visit mometrix.com/academy and enter code: 904704

Study Strategy

Being prepared for the test is necessary to combat anxiety, but what does being prepared look like? You may study for hours on end and still not feel prepared. What you need is a strategy for test prep. The next few pages outline our recommended steps to help you plan out and conquer the challenge of preparation.

STEP 1: SCOPE OUT THE TEST

Learn everything you can about the format (multiple choice, essay, etc.) and what will be on the test. Gather any study materials, course outlines, or sample exams that may be available. Not only will this help you to prepare, but knowing what to expect can help to alleviate test anxiety.

STEP 2: MAP OUT THE MATERIAL

Look through the textbook or study guide and make note of how many chapters or sections it has. Then divide these over the time you have. For example, if a book has 15 chapters and you have five days to study, you need to cover three chapters each day. Even better, if you have the time, leave an extra day at the end for overall review after you have gone through the material in depth.

If time is limited, you may need to prioritize the material. Look through it and make note of which sections you think you already have a good grasp on, and which need review. While you are studying, skim quickly through the familiar sections and take more time on the challenging parts. Write out your plan so you don't get lost as you go. Having a written plan also helps you feel more in control of the study, so anxiety is less likely to arise from feeling overwhelmed at the amount to cover. A sample plan may look like this:

- Day 1: Skim chapters 1–4, study chapter 5 (especially pages 31–33)
- Day 2: Study chapters 6–7, skim chapters 8–9
- Day 3: Skim chapter 10, study chapters 11–12 (especially pages 87–90)
- Day 4: Study chapters 13–15
- Day 5: Overall review (focus most on chapters 5, 6, and 12), take practice test

STEP 3: GATHER YOUR TOOLS

Decide what study method works best for you. Do you prefer to highlight in the book as you study and then go back over the highlighted portions? Or do you type out notes of the important information? Or is it helpful to make flashcards that you can carry with you? Assemble the pens, index cards, highlighters, post-it notes, and any other materials you may need so you won't be distracted by getting up to find things while you study.

If you're having a hard time retaining the information or organizing your notes, experiment with different methods. For example, try color-coding by subject with colored pens, highlighters, or post-it notes. If you learn better by hearing, try recording yourself reading your notes so you can listen while in the car, working out, or simply sitting at your desk. Ask a friend to quiz you from your flashcards, or try teaching someone the material to solidify it in your mind.

STEP 4: CREATE YOUR ENVIRONMENT

It's important to avoid distractions while you study. This includes both the obvious distractions like visitors and the subtle distractions like an uncomfortable chair (or a too-comfortable couch that makes you want to fall asleep). Set up the best study environment possible: good lighting and a comfortable work area. If background music helps you focus, you may want to turn it on, but otherwise keep the room quiet. If you are using a computer to take notes, be sure you don't have

timer. Pace yourself to make sure you finish the test with time to spare and go back to check your answers if you have time.

After each test, check your answers. On the questions you missed, be sure you understand why you missed them. Did you misread the question (tests can use tricky wording)? Did you forget the information? Or was it something you hadn't learned? Go back and study any shaky areas that the practice tests reveal.

Taking these tests not only helps with your grade, but also aids in combating test anxiety. If you're already used to the test conditions, you're less likely to worry about it, and working through tests until you're scoring well gives you a confidence boost. Go through the practice tests until you feel comfortable, and then you can go into the test knowing that you're ready for it.

Test Tips

On test day, you should be confident, knowing that you've prepared well and are ready to answer the questions. But aside from preparation, there are several test day strategies you can employ to maximize your performance.

First, as stated before, get a good night's sleep the night before the test (and for several nights before that, if possible). Go into the test with a fresh, alert mind rather than staying up late to study.

Try not to change too much about your normal routine on the day of the test. It's important to eat a nutritious breakfast, but if you normally don't eat breakfast at all, consider eating just a protein bar. If you're a coffee drinker, go ahead and have your normal coffee. Just make sure you time it so that the caffeine doesn't wear off right in the middle of your test. Avoid sugary beverages, and drink enough water to stay hydrated but not so much that you need a restroom break 10 minutes into the test. If your test isn't first thing in the morning, consider going for a walk or doing a light workout before the test to get your blood flowing.

Allow yourself enough time to get ready, and leave for the test with plenty of time to spare so you won't have the anxiety of scrambling to arrive in time. Another reason to be early is to select a good seat. It's helpful to sit away from doors and windows, which can be distracting. Find a good seat, get out your supplies, and settle your mind before the test begins.

When the test begins, start by going over the instructions carefully, even if you already know what to expect. Make sure you avoid any careless mistakes by following the directions.

Then begin working through the questions, pacing yourself as you've practiced. If you're not sure on an answer, don't spend too much time on it, and don't let it shake your confidence. Either skip it and come back later, or eliminate as many wrong answers as possible and guess among the remaining ones. Don't dwell on these questions as you continue—put them out of your mind and focus on what lies ahead.

Be sure to read all of the answer choices, even if you're sure the first one is the right answer. Sometimes you'll find a better one if you keep reading. But don't second-guess yourself if you do immediately know the answer. Your gut instinct is usually right. Don't let test anxiety rob you of the information you know.

If you have time at the end of the test (and if the test format allows), go back and review your answers. Be cautious about changing any, since your first instinct tends to be correct, but make sure you didn't misread any of the questions or accidentally mark the wrong answer choice. Look over any you skipped and make an educated guess.

At the end, leave the test feeling confident. You've done your best, so don't waste time worrying about your performance or wishing you could change anything. Instead, celebrate the successful completion of this test. And finally, use this test to learn how to deal with anxiety even better next time.

> **Review Video: 5 Tips to Beat Test Anxiety**
> Visit mometrix.com/academy and enter code: 570656

Important Qualification

Not all anxiety is created equal. If your test anxiety is causing major issues in your life beyond the classroom or testing center, or if you are experiencing troubling physical symptoms related to your anxiety, it may be a sign of a serious physiological or psychological condition. If this sounds like your situation, we strongly encourage you to seek professional help.

How to Overcome Your Fear of Math

The word *math* is enough to strike fear into most hearts. How many of us have memories of sitting through confusing lectures, wrestling over mind-numbing homework, or taking tests that still seem incomprehensible even after hours of study? Years after graduation, many still shudder at these memories.

The fact is, math is not just a classroom subject. It has real-world implications that you face every day, whether you realize it or not. This may be balancing your monthly budget, deciding how many supplies to buy for a project, or simply splitting a meal check with friends. The idea of daily confrontations with math can be so paralyzing that some develop a condition known as *math anxiety*.

But you do NOT need to be paralyzed by this anxiety! In fact, while you may have thought all your life that you're not good at math, or that your brain isn't wired to understand it, the truth is that you may have been conditioned to think this way. From your earliest school days, the way you were taught affected the way you viewed different subjects. And the way math has been taught has changed.

Several decades ago, there was a shift in American math classrooms. The focus changed from traditional problem-solving to a conceptual view of topics, de-emphasizing the importance of learning the basics and building on them. The solid foundation necessary for math progression and confidence was undermined. Math became more of a vague concept than a concrete idea. Today, it is common to think of math, not as a straightforward system, but as a mysterious, complicated method that can't be fully understood unless you're a genius.

This is why you may still have nightmares about being called on to answer a difficult problem in front of the class. Math anxiety is a very real, though unnecessary, fear.

Math anxiety may begin with a single class period. Let's say you missed a day in 6th grade math and never quite understood the concept that was taught while you were gone. Since math is cumulative, with each new concept building on past ones, this could very well affect the rest of your math career. Without that one day's knowledge, it will be difficult to understand any other concepts that link to it. Rather than realizing that you're just missing one key piece, you may begin to believe that you're simply not capable of understanding math.

This belief can change the way you approach other classes, career options, and everyday life experiences, if you become anxious at the thought that math might be required. A student who loves science may choose a different path of study upon realizing that multiple math classes will be required for a degree. An aspiring medical student may hesitate at the thought of going through the necessary math classes. For some this anxiety escalates into a more extreme state known as *math phobia*.

Math anxiety is challenging to address because it is rooted deeply and may come from a variety of causes: an embarrassing moment in class, a teacher who did not explain concepts well and contributed to a shaky foundation, or a failed test that contributed to the belief of math failure.

These causes add up over time, encouraged by society's popular view that math is hard and unpleasant. Eventually a person comes to firmly believe that he or she is simply bad at math. This belief makes it difficult to grasp new concepts or even remember old ones. Homework and test

209

grades begin to slip, which only confirms the belief. The poor performance is not due to lack of ability but is caused by math anxiety.

Math anxiety is an emotional issue, not a lack of intelligence. But when it becomes deeply rooted, it can become more than just an emotional problem. Physical symptoms appear. Blood pressure may rise and heartbeat may quicken at the sight of a math problem – or even the thought of math! This fear leads to a mental block. When someone with math anxiety is asked to perform a calculation, even a basic problem can seem overwhelming and impossible. The emotional and physical response to the thought of math prevents the brain from working through it logically.

The more this happens, the more a person's confidence drops, and the more math anxiety is generated. This vicious cycle must be broken!

The first step in breaking the cycle is to go back to very beginning and make sure you really understand the basics of how math works and why it works. It is not enough to memorize rules for multiplication and division. If you don't know WHY these rules work, your foundation will be shaky and you will be at risk of developing a phobia. Understanding mathematical concepts not only promotes confidence and security, but allows you to build on this understanding for new concepts. Additionally, you can solve unfamiliar problems using familiar concepts and processes.

Why is it that students in other countries regularly outperform American students in math? The answer likely boils down to a couple of things: the foundation of mathematical conceptual understanding and societal perception. While students in the US are not expected to *like* or *get* math, in many other nations, students are expected not only to understand math but also to excel at it.

Changing the American view of math that leads to math anxiety is a monumental task. It requires changing the training of teachers nationwide, from kindergarten through high school, so that they learn to teach the *why* behind math and to combat the wrong math views that students may develop. It also involves changing the stigma associated with math, so that it is no longer viewed as unpleasant and incomprehensible. While these are necessary changes, they are challenging and will take time. But in the meantime, math anxiety is not irreversible—it can be faced and defeated, one person at a time.

False Beliefs

One reason math anxiety has taken such hold is that several false beliefs have been created and shared until they became widely accepted. Some of these unhelpful beliefs include the following:

There is only one way to solve a math problem. In the same way that you can choose from different driving routes and still arrive at the same house, you can solve a math problem using different methods and still find the correct answer. A person who understands the reasoning behind math calculations may be able to look at an unfamiliar concept and find the right answer, just by applying logic to the knowledge they already have. This approach may be different than what is taught in the classroom, but it is still valid. Unfortunately, even many teachers view math as a subject where the best course of action is to memorize the rule or process for each problem rather than as a place for students to exercise logic and creativity in finding a solution.

Many people don't have a mind for math. A person who has struggled due to poor teaching or math anxiety may falsely believe that he or she doesn't have the mental capacity to grasp mathematical concepts. Most of the time, this is false. Many people find that when they are relieved of their math anxiety, they have more than enough brainpower to understand math.

Men are naturally better at math than women. Even though research has shown this to be false, many young women still avoid math careers and classes because of their belief that their math abilities are inferior. Many girls have come to believe that math is a male skill and have given up trying to understand or enjoy it.

Counting aids are bad. Something like counting on your fingers or drawing out a problem to visualize it may be frowned on as childish or a crutch, but these devices can help you get a tangible understanding of a problem or a concept.

Sadly, many students buy into these ideologies at an early age. A young girl who enjoys math class may be conditioned to think that she doesn't actually have the brain for it because math is for boys, and may turn her energies to other pursuits, permanently closing the door on a wide range of opportunities. A child who finds the right answer but doesn't follow the teacher's method may believe that he is doing it wrong and isn't good at math. A student who never had a problem with math before may have a poor teacher and become confused, yet believe that the problem is because she doesn't have a mathematical mind.

Students who have bought into these erroneous beliefs quickly begin to add their own anxieties, adapting them to their own personal situations:

I'll never use this in real life. A huge number of people wrongly believe that math is irrelevant outside the classroom. By adopting this mindset, they are handicapping themselves for a life in a mathematical world, as well as limiting their career choices. When they are inevitably faced with real-world math, they are conditioning themselves to respond with anxiety.

I'm not quick enough. While timed tests and quizzes, or even simply comparing yourself with other students in the class, can lead to this belief, speed is not an indicator of skill level. A person can work very slowly yet understand at a deep level.

If I can understand it, it's too easy. People with a low view of their own abilities tend to think that if they are able to grasp a concept, it must be simple. They cannot accept the idea that they are capable of understanding math. This belief will make it harder to learn, no matter how intelligent they are.

I just can't learn this. An overwhelming number of people think this, from young children to adults, and much of the time it is simply not true. But this mindset can turn into a self-fulfilling prophecy that keeps you from exercising and growing your math ability.

The good news is, each of these myths can be debunked. For most people, they are based on emotion and psychology, NOT on actual ability! It will take time, effort, and the desire to change, but change is possible. Even if you have spent years thinking that you don't have the capability to understand math, it is not too late to uncover your true ability and find relief from the anxiety that surrounds math.

Math Strategies

It is important to have a plan of attack to combat math anxiety. There are many useful strategies for pinpointing the fears or myths and eradicating them:

Go back to the basics. For most people, math anxiety stems from a poor foundation. You may think that you have a complete understanding of addition and subtraction, or even decimals and percentages, but make absolutely sure. Learning math is different from learning other subjects. For example, when you learn history, you study various time periods and places and events. It may be important to memorize dates or find out about the lives of famous people. When you move from US history to world history, there will be some overlap, but a large amount of the information will be new. Mathematical concepts, on the other hand, are very closely linked and highly dependent on each other. It's like climbing a ladder – if a rung is missing from your understanding, it may be difficult or impossible for you to climb any higher, no matter how hard you try. So go back and make sure your math foundation is strong. This may mean taking a remedial math course, going to a tutor to work through the shaky concepts, or just going through your old homework to make sure you really understand it.

Speak the language. Math has a large vocabulary of terms and phrases unique to working problems. Sometimes these are completely new terms, and sometimes they are common words, but are used differently in a math setting. If you can't speak the language, it will be very difficult to get a thorough understanding of the concepts. It's common for students to think that they don't understand math when they simply don't understand the vocabulary. The good news is that this is fairly easy to fix. Brushing up on any terms you aren't quite sure of can help bring the rest of the concepts into focus.

Check your anxiety level. When you think about math, do you feel nervous or uncomfortable? Do you struggle with feelings of inadequacy, even on concepts that you know you've already learned? It's important to understand your specific math anxieties, and what triggers them. When you catch yourself falling back on a false belief, mentally replace it with the truth. Don't let yourself believe that you can't learn, or that struggling with a concept means you'll never understand it. Instead, remind yourself of how much you've already learned and dwell on that past success. Visualize grasping the new concept, linking it to your old knowledge, and moving on to the next challenge. Also, learn how to manage anxiety when it arises. There are many techniques for coping with the irrational fears that rise to the surface when you enter the math classroom. This may include controlled breathing, replacing negative thoughts with positive ones, or visualizing success. Anxiety interferes with your ability to concentrate and absorb information, which in turn contributes to greater anxiety. If you can learn how to regain control of your thinking, you will be better able to pay attention, make progress, and succeed!

Don't go it alone. Like any deeply ingrained belief, math anxiety is not easy to eradicate. And there is no need for you to wrestle through it on your own. It will take time, and many people find that speaking with a counselor or psychiatrist helps. They can help you develop strategies for responding to anxiety and overcoming old ideas. Additionally, it can be very helpful to take a short course or seek out a math tutor to help you find and fix the missing rungs on your ladder and make sure that you're ready to progress to the next level. You can also find a number of math aids online: courses that will teach you mental devices for figuring out problems, how to get the most out of your math classes, etc.

Check your math attitude. No matter how much you want to learn and overcome your anxiety, you'll have trouble if you still have a negative attitude toward math. If you think it's too hard, or just have general feelings of dread about math, it will be hard to learn and to break through the anxiety. Work on cultivating a positive math attitude. Remind yourself that math is not just a hurdle to be cleared, but a valuable asset. When you view math with a positive attitude, you'll be much more likely to understand and even enjoy it. This is something you must do for yourself. You may find it helpful to visit with a counselor. Your tutor, friends, and family may cheer you on in your endeavors. But your greatest asset is yourself. You are inside your own mind – tell yourself what you need to hear. Relive past victories. Remind yourself that you are capable of understanding math. Root out any false beliefs that linger and replace them with positive truths. Even if it doesn't feel true at first, it will begin to affect your thinking and pave the way for a positive, anxiety-free mindset.

Aside from these general strategies, there are a number of specific practical things you can do to begin your journey toward overcoming math anxiety. Something as simple as learning a new note-taking strategy can change the way you approach math and give you more confidence and understanding. New study techniques can also make a huge difference.

Math anxiety leads to bad habits. If it causes you to be afraid of answering a question in class, you may gravitate toward the back row. You may be embarrassed to ask for help. And you may procrastinate on assignments, which leads to rushing through them at the last moment when it's too late to get a better understanding. It's important to identify your negative behaviors and replace them with positive ones:

Prepare ahead of time. Read the lesson before you go to class. Being exposed to the topics that will be covered in class ahead of time, even if you don't understand them perfectly, is extremely helpful in increasing what you retain from the lecture. Do your homework and, if you're still shaky, go over some extra problems. The key to a solid understanding of math is practice.

Sit front and center. When you can easily see and hear, you'll understand more, and you'll avoid the distractions of other students if no one is in front of you. Plus, you're more likely to be sitting with students who are positive and engaged, rather than others with math anxiety. Let their positive math attitude rub off on you.

Ask questions in class and out. If you don't understand something, just ask. If you need a more in-depth explanation, the teacher may need to work with you outside of class, but often it's a simple concept you don't quite understand, and a single question may clear it up. If you wait, you may not be able to follow the rest of the day's lesson. For extra help, most professors have office hours outside of class when you can go over concepts one-on-one to clear up any uncertainties. Additionally, there may be a *math lab* or study session you can attend for homework help. Take advantage of this.

Review. Even if you feel that you've fully mastered a concept, review it periodically to reinforce it. Going over an old lesson has several benefits: solidifying your understanding, giving you a confidence boost, and even giving some new insights into material that you're currently learning! Don't let yourself get rusty. That can lead to problems with learning later concepts.

Teaching Tips

While the math student's mindset is the most crucial to overcoming math anxiety, it is also important for others to adjust their math attitudes. Teachers and parents have an enormous influence on how students relate to math. They can either contribute to math confidence or math anxiety.

As a parent or teacher, it is very important to convey a positive math attitude. Retelling horror stories of your own bad experience with math will contribute to a new generation of math anxiety. Even if you don't share your experiences, others will be able to sense your fears and may begin to believe them.

Even a careless comment can have a big impact, so watch for phrases like *He's not good at math* or *I never liked math*. You are a crucial role model, and your children or students will unconsciously adopt your mindset. Give them a positive example to follow. Rather than teaching them to fear the math world before they even know it, teach them about all its potential and excitement.

Work to present math as an integral, beautiful, and understandable part of life. Encourage creativity in solving problems. Watch for false beliefs and dispel them. Cross the lines between subjects: integrate history, English, and music with math. Show students how math is used every day, and how the entire world is based on mathematical principles, from the pull of gravity to the shape of seashells. Instead of letting students see math as a necessary evil, direct them to view it as an imaginative, beautiful art form – an art form that they are capable of mastering and using.

Don't give too narrow a view of math. It is more than just numbers. Yes, working problems and learning formulas is a large part of classroom math. But don't let the teaching stop there. Teach students about the everyday implications of math. Show them how nature works according to the laws of mathematics, and take them outside to make discoveries of their own. Expose them to math-related careers by inviting visiting speakers, asking students to do research and presentations, and learning students' interests and aptitudes on a personal level.

Demonstrate the importance of math. Many people see math as nothing more than a required stepping stone to their degree, a nuisance with no real usefulness. Teach students that algebra is used every day in managing their bank accounts, in following recipes, and in scheduling the day's events. Show them how learning to do geometric proofs helps them to develop logical thinking, an invaluable life skill. Let them see that math surrounds them and is integrally linked to their daily lives: that weather predictions are based on math, that math was used to design cars and other machines, etc. Most of all, give them the tools to use math to enrich their lives.

Make math as tangible as possible. Use visual aids and objects that can be touched. It is much easier to grasp a concept when you can hold it in your hands and manipulate it, rather than just listening to the lecture. Encourage math outside of the classroom. The real world is full of measuring, counting, and calculating, so let students participate in this. Keep your eyes open for numbers and patterns to discuss. Talk about how scores are calculated in sports games and how far apart plants are placed in a garden row for maximum growth. Build the mindset that math is a normal and interesting part of daily life.

Finally, find math resources that help to build a positive math attitude. There are a number of books that show math as fascinating and exciting while teaching important concepts, for example: *The Math Curse; A Wrinkle in Time; The Phantom Tollbooth;* and *Fractals, Googols and Other Mathematical Tales*. You can also find a number of online resources: math puzzles and games, videos that show math in nature, and communities of math enthusiasts. On a local level, students can compete in a variety of math competitions with other schools or join a math club.

The student who experiences math as exciting and interesting is unlikely to suffer from math anxiety. Going through life without this handicap is an immense advantage and opens many doors that others have closed through their fear.

Self-Check

Whether you suffer from math anxiety or not, chances are that you have been exposed to some of the false beliefs mentioned above. Now is the time to check yourself for any errors you may have accepted. Do you think you're not wired for math? Or that you don't need to understand it since you're not planning on a math career? Do you think math is just too difficult for the average person?

Find the errors you've taken to heart and replace them with positive thinking. Are you capable of learning math? Yes! Can you control your anxiety? Yes! These errors will resurface from time to time, so be watchful. Don't let others with math anxiety influence you or sway your confidence. If you're having trouble with a concept, find help. Don't let it discourage you!

Create a plan of attack for defeating math anxiety and sharpening your skills. Do some research and decide if it would help you to take a class, get a tutor, or find some online resources to fine-tune your knowledge. Make the effort to get good nutrition, hydration, and sleep so that you are operating at full capacity. Remind yourself daily that you are skilled and that anxiety does not control you. Your mind is capable of so much more than you know. Give it the tools it needs to grow and thrive.

Thank You

We at Mometrix would like to extend our heartfelt thanks to you, our friend and patron, for allowing us to play a part in your journey. It is a privilege to serve people from all walks of life who are unified in their commitment to building the best future they can for themselves.

The preparation you devote to these important testing milestones may be the most valuable educational opportunity you have for making a real difference in your life. We encourage you to put your heart into it—that feeling of succeeding, overcoming, and yes, conquering will be well worth the hours you've invested.

We want to hear your story, your struggles and your successes, and if you see any opportunities for us to improve our materials so we can help others even more effectively in the future, please share that with us as well. **The team at Mometrix would be absolutely thrilled to hear from you!** So please, send us an email (support@mometrix.com) and let's stay in touch.

> **If you'd like some additional help, check out these other resources we offer for your exam:**
> **http://MometrixFlashcards.com/CEOE**

Additional Bonus Material

Due to our efforts to try to keep this book to a manageable length, we've created a link that will give you access to all of your additional bonus material.

Please visit http://www.mometrix.com/bonus948/oget to access the information.